D0915530

Pathways to Pacifism and Antiwar Activism among U.S. Veterans

Pathways to Pacifism and Antiwar Activism among U.S. Veterans

The Role of Moral Identity in Personal Transformation

Julie Putnam Hart
Anjel N. Stough-Hunter

LEXINGTON BOOKS
Lanham • Boulder • New York • London

Published by Lexington Books
An imprint of The Rowman & Littlefield Publishing Group, Inc.
4501 Forbes Boulevard, Suite 200, Lanham, Maryland 20706
www.rowman.com

Unit A, Whitacre Mews, 26-34 Stannary Street, London SE11 4AB

British Library Cataloguing in Publication Information Available

Library of Congress Cataloging-in-Publication Data Available

ISBN 9781498538633 (hardback : alk. paper) | ISBN 9781498538640 (electronic)

♾™ The paper used in this publication meets the minimum requirements of American
National Standard for Information Sciences Permanence of Paper for Printed Library
Materials, ANSI/NISO Z39.48-1992.

Printed in the United States of America

To all veterans who seek peace through their military service and beyond

Contents

Contents

Preface

It is fitting to start a book about stories with my own story about how this project began. In 1986, I was attending a peace lecture and was amazed by the speaker's story. Lieutenant Colonel Robert Bowman, was on a promotional tour for his book opposing a new military project proposed by President Ronald Reagan. Bowman had served 22 years in the U.S. Air Force. He held a PhD in Aeronautic and Nuclear Engineering from the California Institute of Technology and was the president of the Institute for Space and Security Studies. He was openly criticizing the Strategic Defense Initiative, also dubbed "Star Wars" advanced by a pro-military administration. I wondered, how could a man, who was so entrenched in the military, become such an outspoken critic of his former employer and commander in chief, the U.S. president?

This question led me to research the dramatic changes undergone by men and women in uniform who became antiwar activists. It took me several years, though, to develop this project. As a former nurse, I had returned to graduate school in 1990 to pursue a Master's degree in International Peace Studies and a PhD in sociology with a focus on two areas: peace and war and social psychology. My early research interests included understanding organizational and political transformation and now I was excited to explore individual transformation in attitudes and identity.

Besides my research, I actively participated in several peace-related organizations. From 1996 through 2015 I volunteered for a month each summer with Christian Peacemaker Teams doing human rights work in Haiti (1996), Israel/Palestine (1997–2000), and Colombia (2004–2015). I also lived and worked in Guatemala during a two-year sabbatical from 2001–2003 with the service arm of the Mennonite Church USA (Mennonite

Central Committee), doing peace and justice education among church and human rights leaders in Central America.

Not until 2005 did I return to the intriguing question of how and why a Lieutenant Colonel in the U.S. Air Force could become an antiwar activist. Although my father served in the Navy during the Korean War (stateside), at age 36, I joined the Mennonite Church USA, which holds a centuries-long tradition of advocating for peace and social justice. Mennonites are often pacifists (nonparticipants) during times of war. This required applying for Conscientious Objector status during times of universal conscription for men. I also taught at a Mennonite university in Kansas. In this setting, I met dozens of people who had experienced a significant attitude change about the appropriate use of war.

I began this research venture by asking for volunteers both within my church and within the university to share their pathway to pacifism. At first my research focused on any adults with a significant attitude change regarding war but I soon realized that the veterans' stories were especially dramatic. They had lived through combat experiences that remained deeply troubling. Some described painful episodes of feeling betrayed by their once-trusted leaders, while others had epiphanies about who God was and what God expected of them. In other cases, veterans attending college learned new information that challenged their thinking about U.S. history, policy or leadership.

This first set of veterans' stories made me eager to understand the process of change from a social psychological angle. What was the catalyst or trigger for change? Many of these veterans had journeyed down pathways that shifted their positions on war so dramatically that they felt compelled to become antiwar activists. They made major sacrifices as they moved toward a new way of thinking but they also found support along the way.

At first, I interpreted this qualitative data in the framework of cognitive dissonance, which stresses how people deal with the inner tension from acting outside of their beliefs. Then I realized that Identity Theory provided a fuller and deeper explanation of these veterans' experiences. As described in the Identity Theory chapter, veterans journeyed through multiple identity changes as a result of their beliefs about the appropriate use of war.

As I expanded my research to include veterans from outside the Mennonite Church USA, I developed a more comprehensive understanding of this complex topic. Three primary groups (Veterans for Peace, Iraq Veterans against the War, and Vietnam Veterans against the War) provided me access to veterans eager to share their stories.

I felt honored that they were willing to share their military experiences as well as the challenges of their post military lives. We discussed their family and military backgrounds, change processes, and pathways toward their new positions on war. Some veterans wept as they remembered the dark times. I listened to stories of job loss, broken marriages, alcohol addiction, and domestic violence. Some veterans had been homeless while others were estranged from their children. I was struck by the veterans' honesty and humility.

These interviews, then, are an additional gift from the veterans who had already given to their country. I hope that this book reinforces the idea that wars do not end with peace treaties but continue to impact the lives of all whom they touch. It took great courage for these veterans to serve their country and to share their stories and it takes great courage today for these veterans to work for peace.

SECOND AUTHOR'S STORY

The first author had already spent years on this research before I joined the project in 2012. I was fresh out of graduate school and interested in opportunities to publish, develop my research agenda, and build professional relationships. Trained as both a medical anthropologist and rural sociologist, I was able to add a fresh perspective to the data. My roles in the project included transcription, coding, and data analysis. During my graduate work, I had studied gender issues. The opportunity to study masculinity in a gendered institution (military) was impossible to resist.

On a personal note, I have had limited experience and interaction with the military. My father was in the Air Force during the Vietnam War, while one of my grandfathers served in both World War II and the Korean War. However, our family rarely talked about the military. My only childhood memories were of my dad sharing stories of the rigorous discipline of the Air Force. Like many American civilians, I knew little about the military but had a high regard for "servicemen"—a term I deliberately use here because my image of the military was always a "masculine" image.

At the time I started working on this project, I had a number of students that were former military personnel. Most of these students were in their early 20s and were attending college using funds from the GI bill. These students provided insight into the military culture, as well as opening my eyes to aspects of military service such as the practical challenges of being stationed in a foreign country. These students, both male and female, were usually polite, respectful and disciplined. Their presence in my classroom increased my respect and appreciation for the military.

Unlike the first author, I was never a pacifist. I would consider myself as a moderate regarding the use of war. While the first author and I share a faith foundation, we approach issues of war and violence from differing perspectives. As a non-pacifist, I was able to challenge the first author as we analyzed the data. I served the function of the "outsider" (also called "peer debriefer" as defined by Lienberg, 2013, 50).

Acknowledgments

Writing this book has been a 12-year journey and many people have joined me along the way. Without these people, the book would not have been written. My constant companion has been my husband of 43 years, Phil Hart. He has always believed in me as a scholar and doer who could accomplish just about anything I set my mind to. This gave me the courage and confidence to persist despite multiple setbacks. Following the first 50 interviews, as I began to analyze patterns in the transcripts, his questions and insights were invaluable.

I am deeply grateful to the 114 veterans themselves who volunteered for the study. Through their stories from childhood, to the military and post military, they revealed deep wounds, joys and sorrows that I feel honored to hold and to share in these pages.

Early in the process, Duane Friesen, emeritus professor of bible and religion at Bethel College (Kansas) and Christian ethicist advised me on the structure of the militarism to pacifism scale. This scale was used in the study to determine each veteran's moral identity standards regarding issues of war at age 18 and in adulthood.

In 2008, my dear friend Connie Clarke joined me in the journey. She assisted with reading and coding the transcripts but more than that, she provided encouragement and insights on the transcripts from the perspective of a practicing therapist.

In 2010, Todd Callais, a professor of criminology and criminal justice at Ohio Dominican University, joined me in the journey for a few years. He provided both encouragement to persist in publishing in academic journals and invaluable insights on the transcripts themselves.

In 2012, fellow sociologist at Ohio Dominican University, Anjel Stough-Hunter joined me in the journey. She was interested in the analysis of masculine identity for the veterans and joined me in analyzing, coding and publishing an article on this topic. It was the presentation and publication of this research that led to an invitation from Rowman & Littlefield to write this book. Anjel has been a constant companion on this journey since 2012 and I am certain that without her encouragement and scholarly insight, this book would never have been written. She has been there with much needed feedback, patience and kindness since 2012.

In 2013, I was granted a six-month sabbatical from my teaching at Ohio Dominican University. This gift of time allowed me to engage in phase II of the interviews and delve more deeply into the identity change process and the role of religion and masculinity in the veteran's transformations.

Several scholars in the field of masculinity, namely Susan Alexandar and Matt Filteau, read earlier versions of the masculinity chapter and provided important feedback. In addition, during the spring of 2016, we enlisted a colleague to help us with the editing process. Gail Ukockis PhD social work joined us in refining the book and preparing it for publication. We value her insights, expertise, and additions.

Our editor Sarah Craig has been most helpful in providing answers to a multitude of questions in this our first attempt to write a book for the academic press. There is nothing better than an editor who responds immediately to questions, offers clear feedback, and kind suggestions for improvement.

Finally, the foundation of my life is a belief in the presence of Divine Love or God in each person. I believe this presence inspires each of us to seek truth and we are guided in this journey by a moral conscience. I am grateful to my family, my church and my friends who have continually affirmed and modeled being present to the Divine in themselves and in each person they meet. My hope is that both our research question: what causes significant identity change regarding issues of war and the answers to that question found in this book have been led by that divine spirit.

Julie Putnam Hart

It was my privilege to join Julie on this journey in 2012. This book is an outflowing of the passion for peace and justice she lives every day. I gained much more than I gave in sharing this pursuit with her. It is nearly impossible to share the rich life stories of the veterans in this book without being challenged to reflect on your own identity. For that gift I thank both Julie and the veterans that were willing to share.

I am so grateful for my family and friends in supporting me with words of encouragement and always being willing to listen. Many people were there to listen when I needed to talk out an idea or vent a frustration, but perhaps none as patient with my rants as my husband, Leland Hunter, and my mother, Kathy Stough. However, I am most thankful for my family's sacrifice of time. An endeavor such as this takes a great deal of time. This meant late

Friday evenings in the office, early Saturday mornings at Panera, and holiday weekends at the computer. My young daughter quickly learned the phrase "mommy work." My sincere hope is that this work will bring her pride and joy.

Finally, I thank Jesus, the author and finisher of my faith. To Him I attribute the most important identity change in my life and the foundation of my moral identity.

Anjel Stough-Hunter

Introduction

This book seeks to answer the question, how and why do some military personnel become antiwar activists? In exploring this question, we examine the stories of 114 veterans' pathways from a militaristic perspective to either a Just War or pacifist perspective. We find that the vast majority of these veterans did not merely change their attitudes about war but they transformed their entire identities from being pro-war to antiwar. We argue that this post-service process of identity change was not pathological but healthy as it offered healing and integration of multiple roles and social aspects of the veterans' lives. After living through a disruption and transformation of one of their core identities (moral), these veterans report feeling authentic and whole again.

We use Identity Theory as a lens for exploring the identity change process of the veterans' in our study. Identity Theory is a theory rooted in Structural Symbolic Interactionism that explains the formation of one's self via a continuous self-regulating cycle of identity verification. According to Identity Theory, one's identity is formed, maintained and changed via a self-regulating feedback loop through which one receives input about his or her behaviors related to an identity, compares this input to his or her identity standards and then must choose how to respond to identity standards being either verified or unverified. Identity Theory emphasizes the importance of social interaction in the formation of the identities that make up one's self (Burke & Stets, 2009).

We are certainly not the first scholars to be interested in studying military personnel. In fact, military sociology is a well-established area within the discipline of sociology. However, much of this work focuses on the military as an institution and the individual's relationship to that institution (see, for example, Cockerham, 1978a, 1978b; Higate, 2003; Kummel et al., 2009).

Within the military sociology literature masculinity is a key area of focus (see, for example, Belkin, 2012; Higate, 2003; Kilshaw, 2009). We are also not the only scholars interested in the relationship between the military and antiwar activism (see, for example, Franke 1999; Leitz 2014). This seemingly contradictory relationship provides fertile ground for understanding identity formation and conflict within social movements. We especially build on the work of Lisa Leitz. Her book *Fighting for Peace: Veterans and Military Family in the Anti-Iraq War Movement*, published in 2014, examines the participation of veterans, soldiers and military families in the antiwar/peace movement occurring during the Iraq and Afghanistan wars between 2006 and 2012. Through participant observation, her detailed and compelling ethnography provides great insight into the recent military peace movement and the way in which identities (namely the military identity) played a key role in that movement. In her conclusion, Leitz points out the role antiwar movements play in the healing process for some individuals returning from war with feelings of guilt and shame. This point is a major focus of our research.

We extend Leitz's work by examining military identities, not just at one point in time, but rather the identity change process over time. We focus not on one movement, but rather on the role of movement participation in the identity change process. Additionally, we move beyond the exploration of identity conflicts at one point in time to an attempt to understand both the hierarchy of identities and the processing of identity conflict over time. In doing so, we make several unique contributions to the literature on military sociology including our understanding of identity change through the Identity Theory framework and the relationship between higher level identities such as moral identities and masculinity. We also integrate concepts of moral injury, from psychology, and collective identity into Identity Theory.

We treat identity change as a holistic process beginning when higher level identities such as the moral identity are disrupted. We do this by following the identity change process from pro-war to an antiwar identity through the narratives of the veterans in our study. These narratives offer a complex and compelling description of the process of identity transformation using veterans own voices as they renegotiated their past to form authentic and congruent new identities. We describe the role of combat, religion, education and betrayal in identity disruption. Additionally, we examine the importance of social status and group affiliation in the ability to embrace particular minority identities such as pacifism and antiwar activist. We also find that identity conflicts for the veterans in our study, rather than being pathological, are inherent in exiting that military and adjusting to civilian life.

By capturing actual stories of the identity change process over time, we extend literature on Identity Theory. Burke and Stets (2006) note that there is a need to explore the identity change process in real versus laboratory contexts. Most of the work on Identity Theory has involved quantitative research often in a laboratory setting or through the use of questionnaires. As such, the thick description and deeper understanding of context and input mechanisms involved in identity shifts in real individuals are often missing. Additionally, we integrate research on moral identity disruption from sociology with the role of collective identity and the newer concept of moral injury from psychology. Again through rich interview data, relationships between moral identity disruption, moral injury, collective identity and the identity change process are uncovered.

SOCIAL MOVEMENT ORGANIZATIONS AND FAITH TRADITIONS INVOLVED IN THIS STUDY

While some may regard the concept of "antiwar veterans" as a contradiction, the veterans in this study saw no contradiction in their identities or in their sense of self. Instead, many became involved in organizations that supported their cause. Three military peace organizations provided access to their members for this study and make up 85 percent of the interviewees. The other fifteen percent came from the Mennonite Church USA and a convenience sample of veterans attending or surrounding a small Midwestern university. The military peace movement organizations, Veterans for Peace, Iraq Veterans against the War and Vietnam Veterans against the War, played a key role in the process of identity consolidation, where two very different identities (military and antiwar) are combined in the collective identity of the group (Leitz, 2014, 79).

Veterans for Peace (VFP)

Veterans for Peace was founded in 1985 by Jerry Genesio, a Marine whose brother died in Vietnam and whose sons were in the military. During the 1980s, Jerry and his wife traveled to Central America and became disturbed by U.S. military intervention there. In response, the Genesio's spoke out against U.S. involvement and sought veterans who could speak directly of the horrors of war. This activism culminated in the first meeting of VFP in April of 1985.

The meeting drew veterans and active duty military personnel from World War II to Vietnam, still the bulk of its membership today. By the Iraq War in 2003, VFP was a recognized United Nations nongovernmental organization with 144 chapters in the U.S. Membership grew ten-fold from 2001 to 2007 to seven thousand paid members. Their mission statement claims they are an "educational and humanitarian organization dedicated to the abolishment of war" (Leitz, 2014, 38).

Although a peace organization, VFP is not necessarily a pacifist or totally antiwar group. VFP might support a truly defensive war. During and prior to the interviews for this book (2005–2013), VFP members were heavily involved in protests, vigils, and marches against the Iraq War. In 2008, VFP members voted to add their opposition to the U.S. occupation in Afghanistan (Leitz, 2014, 39).

Besides protests against unjust wars, VFP also does humanitarian work around the world in areas where the U.S. has been at war. Members also speak in high schools to counter military recruitment and promote alternatives to military service. Most of the study's veterans mentioned VFP as a primary support system in their antiwar activism work today.

Iraq Veterans against the War (IVAW)

In March of 2004, former Air Force technician Tim Goodrich met Marine Lance Corporal Mike Hoffman at a protest against the Iraq War. They discussed the need for an organization for Iraq War Veterans. By July of 2004, six Iraq War veterans took the stage at the annual VFP convention to announce the formation of Iraq Veterans against the War. The six had initially supported the war on terror, but concluded after serving in the Middle East that the Iraq invasion was wrong (Leitz, 2014, 43). One of these six founding members is part of this study.

Still recovering from their war time experiences, the six original founders were glad to be mentored by older members of VFP, Military Families Speak Out, and members of Vietnam Veterans against the War. By the fall of 2008, IVAW had 1,300 members who met the criteria of serving in the U.S. Armed Services (including National Guard and Reserves) since September 11, 2001. IVAW became an international organization in 2006 to incorporate service members who resisted war deployments and fled to Canada or were on active duty in Iraq, Afghanistan and Germany. This study includes one of those active duty veterans. By 2009, members voted to add a resolution opposing the Afghanistan War.

The members of IVAW began with three common goals:

* The U.S. and its allies should immediately withdraw from Iraq;
* American governmental and corporate control of Iraq's resources should end, and America should provide reparations for the human and other damages caused by the war; and
* Returning American service members should receive full benefits, including both mental and physical health care (Leitz, 2014, 44).

Vietnam Veterans against the War (VVAW)

Vietnam Veterans against the War, Inc. is a national veterans' organization founded in New York City in 1967 after six Vietnam veterans marched together in a peace demonstration. These men organized VVAW to give voice to the growing opposition among returning veterans to the still-raging war in southeast Asia. VVAW grew rapidly to over 30,000 members in the United States as well as active duty soldiers stationed in Vietnam. Through ongoing actions and grassroots organizations, VVAW exposed the reality of U.S. involvement in Southeast Asia hoping that their stories would educate "other Americans to see the unjust nature of that war" (www.vvaw.org/about).

VVAW members not only opposed the war, but also advocated for the rights and needs of veterans. In 1970, they began rap discussion groups to deal with the traumatic after-effects of war. The group exposed "the neglect of many disabled vets in VA Hospitals and helped draft legislation to improve educational benefits and create job programs." They supported amnesty for war resisters and publicized the negative health effects of exposure to chemical defoliants such as Agent Orange (www.vvaw.org/about).

Although an aging population, they remain active today and base their work on opposition to unjust wars as well as support of veterans. Below is a quote about their mission:

> We believe that service to our country and communities did not end when we were discharged. We remain committed to the struggle for peace and for social and economic justice for all people. We will continue to oppose senseless military adventures and to teach the real lessons of the Vietnam War. We will do all we can to prevent another generation from being put through a similar tragedy and we will continue to demand dignity and respect for veterans of all eras. This is real patriotism and we remain true to our mission. (www.vvaw.org/about)

The Mennonite Church USA

Mennonites are a Christian group formed in Europe in the 1500s. Today they are a group of 80,000 adult members in the U.S. and 1.6 million in 57 countries around the world. They believe that "God calls us to be followers of Jesus Christ and, by the power of the Holy Spirit, to grow as communities of grace, joy and peace, so that God's healing and hope flow through us to the world" (www.mennoniteusa.org).

One distinct trait of the Mennonites is their peace church tradition. They attempt to follow Jesus in daily life, put following Jesus as a peacemaker above nationalism and materialism, and live simply and in service to others in witnessing to God's love for the world (www.mennoniteusa.org/confession-of-faith). The majority of Mennonites would self-identify as pacifists, which means not participating in war or responding with violence to defend themselves against others.

Because they do not support war, Mennonites have developed an active conflict resolution, social justice and reconciliation ministry both in the United States and abroad. Mennonites believe that the good news of the Bible contains powerful alternatives to violence and war. The church also engages in counter recruiting, thus promoting alternatives to military service among their members and beyond. In addition, the Strategies for Trauma Awareness and Resilience (STAR) program originated at the Eastern Mennonite University to provide healing and hope for veterans and others with Post-Traumatic Stress Disorder. Hart, the main researcher, is an active member of the Mennonite Church USA.

Structure of the Book

The book's structure emphasizes the pathways to the sense of peace (that we call identity verification) that the veterans found and followed in their lives. Chapter 1 outlines the major theoretical perspective, Identity Theory, which offers an explanatory model for the veterans' decisions to become antiwar. The chapter also explains moral identity, moral injury and collective identity, three key concepts to understanding the veterans' identity changes. Chapter 2, which explicates the methodology used in this study, stresses the value of qualitative research.

The next four chapters include the stories of veterans in the context of catalysts that we believe motivated the identity changes. Chapter 3 discusses how combat experiences disrupted the moral identity and served as the catalyst for change for many veterans. Chapter 4 describes how a sense of betrayal by political and military leadership disrupted the moral identity for other veterans. The catalyst in chapter 5 identifies how religious conviction motivates some veterans to reconcile their experiences of war with their faith commitments. The fourth catalyst, education for critical thinking, appears in chapter 6.

Not all veterans became antiwar activists, of course. Chapter 7 shares insights about a comparison group that adopted the Just War criteria but did not become antiwar activists. It also includes explanations by the study's antiwar activist veterans for why they believe many fellow veterans still support the Iraq or other wars. Because most of the veterans were male, chapter 8 discusses the impact of antiwar activism on the masculine identity. Chapter 9 uses the research findings to suggest additional factors or periods in the Identity Change process that may add to our theoretical understanding of the theory. We also attempt to integrate concepts of Moral Injury and Collective Identity into the Identity Change Process. We conclude by discussing directions for future research, as well as implications for institutions such as the military, the Veteran's Administration and faith-based communities to better serve the needs of both soldiers and veterans.

We hope that this book contributes new understandings both to the academic community and the non-academic community. First, we seek to enhance understanding of Identity Theory and particularly the moral identity change process for the academic community. Second, we hope our analysis aids the non-academic reader in understanding the depths of the military and post-military experience from the Identity Theory perspective and builds understanding for veterans who have chosen to oppose the Iraq War in particular or all wars in general. Because the journey to pacifism and antiwar activism has been quite painful and protracted for some veterans, we hope that the reader will consider the suggestions offered by both the veterans and the authors as we all seek a more peaceful world.

Chapter One

Identity Theory

How did antiwar veterans experience their transitions from pro-war soldier to antiwar activist? Identity Theory provides a lens to analyze these experiences, especially since it leads to a more holistic understanding of change. This theory provides the Identity Control System Model, which best explains how these veterans found their way from a pro-war perspective to either a Just War perspective (i.e., a war should be morally justified) or pacifism (i.e., opposing all wars). The veteran's experiences, starting with a disruption of an existing identity, followed by a period of reflection and identity reconstruction led to a cascade of religious, career, political and lifestyle changes over years or decades. Veterans used similar expressions to describe their feelings about their new antiwar activist identity:

- Peace of mind
- Being true to myself
- Feeling blessed
- Having a sense of integrity
- I have a clean conscience
- I'm no longer ashamed of what I did

These feelings and beliefs, then, reflect a state of identity verification that Identity Theory names as the goal for all social interactions. By using Identity Theory, we can explore the process which created these positive outcomes.

IDENTITY THEORY AND THE IDENTITY CONTROL SYSTEM

Identity Theory focuses on the importance of social interaction in the formation of one's self. Based on Symbolic Interactionism, Burke's (1991) Identity
Theory finds that individuals engage in a continuous self-regulating cycle of
identity verification. This cycle includes four components:

- One's self identity standards
- One's choice of output behaviors to verify identity standards
- One's perceptions of inputs from the self and the social environment in
response to one's behaviors
- An internal "comparator" to evaluate the differences between one's iden-
tity standards and one's perceptions of the inputs (Burke & Stets, 2009).

One's self *identity standards* contain the meanings and criteria an individual
associates with each of his or her identities. Identities and their associated
identity standards are divided into three categories: person, role, and group.
Person identities contain the unique attributes an individual holds of him or
herself such as being intelligent, organized and caring. In contrast to person
identities, role identities include positions one holds such as being a male, a
parent, a teacher, or a soldier. The group identity includes important groups
one identifies with such as Christian, U.S. Marine, and Republican (Burke &
Stets, 2009).

Each person, role or group identity holds specific criteria or standards one
must meet in each setting and group that they encounter. In our study, 89
percent of our veterans identified as being a male. Common standards for
them as 18 year old males included: to be strong, brave, athletic, attractive to
females and a hard worker. These males faced pressure to meet these standards for their masculine identity because identity verification is the goal of
the identity control process.

Inputs include perceptions of one's own and other's behavior within a
particular environment. Individuals receive a constant flow of sights and
sounds from the environment that feed the part of one's mind that holds the
identity standards. Thus, individuals have constant feedback on their behaviors related to gender identity and other identities. Inputs include three areas:
self perceptions of our own behavior, our perceptions of others responses or
feedback to our behavior and our perceptions of how our behaviors meet the
particular situational meanings and demands.

Perceptions of others may include compliments or rejections. For instance, a soldier may receive positive evaluations from her superiors—or a
reprimand from a supervisor who disapproved of her behavior. Situational
meanings are an individual's interpretation of a setting as having expectations for interaction, goals to be achieved, roles to be played, identities to be

verified, behaviors to be enacted and feelings to be expressed. This situational information both determines the identity that is stimulated and guides the behavioral responses. In the case of the soldier receiving evaluations, she may decide that she is an incompetent soldier and that she should change her behavior in order to receive more positive evaluations. Self perceptions arise from a reflected self-appraisal process that compares how one sees oneself in relation to one's standards or expectations of a particular identity standard that is salient or important in a particular situation (Burke & Stets, 2009).

One's perceptions of the multiple inputs from self and others, rather than the reality of the situation, determine what is perceived and processed in the comparator. Thus two people can perceive the same situation very differently and have two very different responses to it based on different perceptions and expectations, for example a soldier in combat.

The comparator takes one's perceptions or input from the environment and compares them to the stored identity standard meanings. The result is either identity standard verification or an error signal that represents the difference between the input and the identity standard meanings. When these are not equal, there is non-verification while the goal is always identity verification (Stets & Carter, 2012).

The outputs from the comparator process may lead to positive emotions from identity verification or negative emotions from non-verification. Negative emotions such as shame or guilt motivate the identity control system to reduce the inconsistency by behaving differently in order to change the next set of inputs from the environment. The identity control process is continually receiving inputs and creating outputs to the environment in order to achieve identity verification. For example, a man receives input from the environment that his masculinity is at a level four and he compares this to his identity standard for the situation which is a level six. He will probably choose to behave more "manly" to appear stronger, more athletic, or as a harder worker. However, he may choose to lessen the perception of masculine strength if the inputs from self or others suggest that his masculinity is higher than it should be for the situation.

Negative emotions result from a mismatch between inputs and expected identity standard levels. Shame, for example, may occur if the individual evaluates one's male performance as bad or worthless. One response or output option to shame is to escape the situation. Guilt may occur when the individual evaluates the self as doing a bad behavior that is out of bounds for being a good male. The resulting output may be remorse and a need to confess, apologize or repair (Stets & Carter, 2012). Men attempting to prove their masculinity may need to alter their behaviors in different situations (combat or college) to receive positive inputs for being masculine.

Identity Theory and the Moral Identity

An identity hierarchy ranks one's identities based on importance. The position of a particular identity in the hierarchy is determined by its prominence and salience. For example, an infantryman may consider his camaraderie to be more prominent or important to the self than his intelligence during active duty. Salience refers to one's commitment to and likelihood of an identity being invoked in a particular situation. This infantryman, then, probably spends more time socializing with fellow soldiers than reading. This commitment is measured by what a person might lose, in terms of relationships and access to resources if they fail to maintain an identity (Burke & Stets, 2009). Camaraderie makes socializing with unit friends on weekends more important than keeping up with the latest news.

The cost for failing to maintain an identity is determined in part by the number of persons one is related to through that identity. For example, there

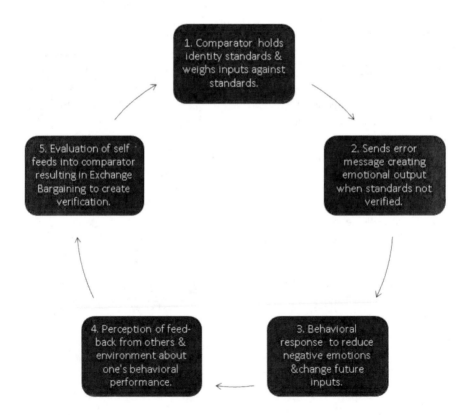

Figure 1.1.   Identity verification process modified based on Identity Theory Model (Burke & Stets, 2009).

will be a greater cost for not demonstrating obedience to authority while holding the soldier identity in combat than for an ex- soldier who is now a pastor or student. As an individual's commitment to an identity increases, the higher the identity becomes in salience in the identity hierarchy (Stryker, 1968, [1980] 2002; Wells & Stryker, 1988). The higher an identity is in the hierarchy, the more influence it holds over other identities lower in the hierarchy.

One example for an identity hierarchy would be a college student who is also a boyfriend, roommate, son, soccer player, church member, and education major. If asked to prioritize his identities in terms of how much time he committed to each identity and how much pride he took in each one, then he would have an accurate understanding of his identity hierarchy.

Person identities are usually highest in the identity hierarchy as they are salient or applicable in many situations while role and group identities are lower in the hierarchy as they have limited areas of application. One type of person identity is the moral identity. One's moral identity standard includes meanings of justice and care (Gilligan, 1982; Haidt & Kesebir, 2010; Kohlberg, 1981). Moral identity salience refers to the temporary activation of the moral identity in the consciousness. When a moral identity is activated frequently, it becomes more salient over time (Stets & Carter, 2012). Faithfulness to the moral self or identity (versus moral principles) provides the motivation to act in particular ways (Blasi, 1984).

If a person enlists in the military, for example, their moral identity would probably shift to include both a group ethos (i.e., always being there for their comrades) and an internalized view of war. The Geneva Conventions, which prohibit torture and hostage-taking, exemplify the principles that could influence one's moral identity in the military context.

Moral behavior is conduct considered right or good based on social consensus, for example, behaving in a just and caring way (Turner & Stets, 2006). Identity Theory assumes a moral identity continuum from high to low. When a person perceives a situation as right/wrong or good/ bad, this perception involves moral meaning and activates the moral identity standard. An individual's perceptions of a situation may be different and/or inaccurate (Stets & Carter, 2012, 197). As an example, a jeep misfiring could cause some soldiers to react with shooting a civilian because they misread the situation.

Behavioral output choices related to the moral identity influence actions across a number of situations controlled by lower level identities (Burke & Stets, 2009). Moral identities thus have wide influence to either change behavioral outputs of lower level identities in the short term (officer, friend, Marine) or activate moral identity standard changes in the longer term.

Exchange Bargaining is the interaction "between higher and lower level identities" (Burke & Stets, 2009, 179). The goal of the Exchange Bargaining process is for multiple related identities to become mutually verifying. For example, a Marine would want both his moral identity and his military identity to be verified. Sometimes these identities and their related standards are in conflict. This conflict could explain the veterans experiences of identity disruption in our study and their attempts to achieve the positive emotions of identity verification.

Moral Injury in Veterans of War

Military service confronts many soldiers with moral dilemmas but most are successfully resolved through dialogue, leadership and training. Sometimes, though, combat and operational experiences violate the deeply held moral standards of a soldier. These violations (or moral identity disruptions) may occur due to acts of commission or omission, other's actions, witnessing intense human suffering, failing to prevent immoral acts of others, giving or receiving orders that are perceived as gross moral violations or viewing the aftermath of a battle. Moral injury is defined as "an act of transgression, which shatters moral and ethical expectations that are rooted in religious or spiritual beliefs, or culture-based, organizational and group-based rules about fairness, the value of life, and so forth" (Maguen & Litz, 2017, 1). Thus we view moral injury as a specific type of moral identity disruption discussed in the Identity Theory literature causing non-verification that could easily occur in the military setting.

Moral injury may be associated with Post-Traumatic Stress Disorder (PTSD) and other post deployment mental health problems, but it is not the same. While PTSD is more fear-based, moral injury is more shame-based. Further, PTSD and moral injury differ in that moral transgression is not necessary for a PTSD diagnosis and PTSD does not necessarily lead to moral injury. Moral injury causes "shame, guilt, anxiety about possible consequences, anger about betrayal-based moral injuries, anomie (alienation) withdrawal and self-condemnation, self-harm and self-handicapping behaviors (for example alcohol or drug use)" (Maguen & Litz, 2017, 1).

Multiple studies demonstrate the link between killing in war and mental health and behavioral problems (Maguen & Litz, 2017). These studies find similar symptoms across wars from Vietnam to the Iraq War for those involved in killing. Even after controlling for the amount and type of combat exposure, taking another's life repeatedly predicted symptoms associated both with PTSD and moral injury. Some research has found that being the target of killing or injury in war is associated with PTSD while being the agent of killing or failing to prevent injury of others is associated with moral injury (Litz et al., 2009). Killing in self-defense is not associated with the same negative outcomes as killing that involves a perceived transgression that breaches either individual or group moral standards of behavior.

Certain war-zone events may lead to moral injury. These include the sense of betrayal by leadership or peers, failure to live up to one's moral standards, mistreatment of enemy combatants or civilians, inappropriate destruction of property as well as violence within the ranks such as rape, friendly fire and fragging (Maguen & Litz, 2012). Combat guilt from such behaviors is the most significant predictor of both preoccupation with suicide and attempted suicide among veterans (Hendin & Haas, 1991).

Another study finds that U.S. service members deployed in the wars in Iraq and Afghanistan are exposed to high levels of violence:

- 52 percent reported shooting or directing fire at the enemy;
- 32 percent reported being directly responsible for the death of an enemy combatant;
- 65 percent reported seeing dead bodies or human remains and
- 60 percent reported seeing ill or wounded women and children who they were unable to help (Hoge et al., 2004).

The Identity Change Process

Change in identities refers to change in the meanings within an identity standard for a person, group, or role identity. Identities change in two ways. First, they change in strength of the behavioral response on a given dimension (e.g., obedience of a soldier) and second by changes in which criteria are relevant for a given identity (e.g., changing what it means to be a soldier from unquestioned obedience to morally discerning) (Burke & Stets, 2006).

Individuals choose behaviors that hold meanings that correspond to meanings of identity standards. For example, a soldier may choose to do extra work to support the unit if he feels guilty about his inadequacy in combat. Our perceptions of these behavioral meanings or inputs are fed into the comparator to be weighed against the self-defining meanings of the identity standard. Differences between the two are registered as an error or discrepancy. The individual then adjusts one's social behavior to alter the environmental inputs. A soldier who is not seen as being a team member, for instance, may strive to cooperate more with his unit. This process of behavioral adjustment to make self-perceptions match the identity standard is called identity verification (Burke & Stets, 2009).

However, individuals hold multiple identities and identity standards. This multiplicity can complicate the identity verification process. The identity hierarchy determines how these multiple identities interact. Person identities are the highest level in the hierarchy and send input to the lower-level identities. The higher and lower level identities respond at different rates to discrepancies in order to create both identity verification quickly through behavior change and stability.

Behaviors adjust quickly to decrease identity standard discrepancies demanded by the highest level identities. A college student, for instance, could study harder so she can be a "good student" again. By contrast, identity standards adjust slowly and continuously to match self-perceptions of behavior until the error message is at zero. Dramatic identity standard change occurs only in unusual circumstances such as "joining a cult, living as a prisoner of war, and becoming a new parent" (Burke & Stets, 2009, 84). Combat situations may also cause a dramatic change in identity standards.

Identity change also occurs when people have multiple identities that share meanings and are activated at the same time. An example is the soldier, moral and Christian identities. Both the soldier and Christian identities may include an identity standard regarding compassion for those in need. As a soldier alters caring behavior to match standards for his Christian identity, this may create a discrepancy for the soldier identity that requires lesser treatment for enemy combatants even if they are injured. Theory suggests that identity standards for both identities shift slowly toward each other to become identical at some compromise position. The degree of change in the identity standards is dependent on the degree of activation, commitment and salience of each of the identities in a particular setting (Burke & Stets, 2009).

The research also suggests that for identity standards to change, discrepancy messages must persist over time and accumulate. Although identities act to resist change, it is clear that in response to persistent pressure or disruption, change occurs slowly (Burke & Stets, 2009). So, the soldier serving for a year in a combat zone may over time decrease his Christian standards of care for enemies in need in order to verify his soldier criteria to match his comrades expectations more completely. He realizes that losing the support and affirmation from his comrades is more important than acting on his Christian beliefs. His priorities and thus identity standards may change again once he is home and in a non-combat environment while attending college or church as we found with a number of the veterans in this study.

Burke and Stets (2009) identify four mechanisms of identity change. The first reflects *changes from a new environment* that disrupt identity standard meanings. Identity Theory says that in new environments such as prison, losing a job or boot camp, the new demands of the culture often can't be met by a lower level identity. For example, Boot Camp demands a high level of discipline and obedience to authority that may be underdeveloped in the new recruit from her high school years. A lower level identity standard for following the rules to stay out of trouble may be inadequate and thus over time the new Marine adopts a principled moral identity standard criteria for discipline and obedience based on the common good and success of the military unit. This new principled criteria may grow slowly to create identity verification from superiors.

The second change mechanism is caused by an *identity conflict*. When two identities share a common dimension of meaning and are activated together, they become more like each other over time. An example is the soldier, moral or Christian identities, all having standards for care of innocents and enemies. Every new group membership and situation creates potential changes in identities that share meanings. Because of this, individuals often avoid situations that require large identity change and engage in strategies to confirm existing identities through groups they choose to associate with. An example might be a veteran choosing to spend his time developing relationships at the Veterans of Foreign Wars (VFW) hall instead of at meetings and activities with Iraq Veterans against the War (IVAW). Each group may verify different political views and positions on the appropriate use of war and/or antiwar activism.

The third identity change mechanism occurs when *one's identity standards conflict with one's behavior*. There are some environments where we can't anticipate the consequences of all of our behaviors. For example when a soldier in combat is advancing on an enemy stronghold and accidently kills a civilian rather than an enemy soldier. The death may cause the higher level moral identity standard for protection of civilians to shift in the direction of one's behavior and make it more likely that the accidental behavior will be justified. Thus, the soldier may learn to accept the accidental killing of civilians as a necessary evil of war or even come to believe that all civilians are potential enemies.

The final source of identity change, *affirming other's identities*, occurs when seeking mutual verification with significant others in a group. At times, the soldier or worker must celebrate or commiserate with those who do or value things they don't value in order to remain in good standing. An example from our interviews was finding comrades in one's unit talking about all Vietnamese civilians as dangerous "Gooks" and thus less than human. The Gook label may then justify indiscriminate killing of women and children that is outside of one's moral identity standard as either a soldier following the Geneva Convention rules of war or a Christian.

All four of these mechanisms of change introduce a disruption that leads to or catalyzes either behavior change or identity standard change over time. Our research seeks to identify the catalysts or disrupters in antiwar activists to explain why some veterans become adamantly opposed to a war or all war in comparison to the majority of non-activist veterans who continue to support U.S. wars abroad such as the Vietnam War or the Iraq War long past the time when public opinion has rejected the legitimacy of a particular war.

FIVE STAGES OF IDENTITY VERIFICATION PROCESS

1. Comparator holds identities & standards & seeks verification between standards & behavior.
2. The verification of an identity creates positive emotions while the non-verification creates negative emotions such as guilt, shame, sadness, embarrassment, discomfort. Error messages motivate one to change behavior in order to create verification.
3. The individual attempts to reduce negative emotions & create identity verification when absent first through behavior:

   a. Changing one's behaviors
   b. Leaving a disruptive situation
   c. Confessing, denying or apologizing for one's behavior
   d. Going numb, addictions, or busyness keep disturbance from registering in comparator

4. The individual receives feedback on one's behavior from the environment and individuals.
5. The individual then evaluates the feedback and decides what information will go to the Comparator. When the individual evaluates their behavioral strategies as a failure and additional disruptions or non-verifications accumulate, the individual uses cognitive strategies (Exchange Bargaining) to create identity verification.

   a. changing the identity standard to match a new situational meaning
   b. conflicting identities and their standards shift gradually to become identical
   c. the higher moral identity shifts gradually in the direction of the disruptive action
   d. over time, the behaviors adopted to increase identity verification become part of the identity standard (Burke & Stets, 2009, 175–196).

Responses to Identity Disruption or Discrepancy—Identity Change

Persons have multiple possible responses to identity discrepancy: either behavioral or cognitive. A large discrepancy between inputs and the identity standard results in greater emotional turmoil and more attempts to create identity verification.

The behavioral approaches often occur quickly for soldiers during their service. When a moral identity is not verified due to a soldier's unfair or cowardly actions in combat, the soldier may change his behavior the next time. They may adjust their self-perception by demonstrating greater fairness, sacrifice or courage. Changing behavior is a rapid strategy for attempting to verify one's identities. But, when this is not possible or desirable, or the discrepancy persists or is significant, cognitive approaches are utilized to create identity standard verification.

Identity Theory can explain these cognitive approaches by assuming that identity meanings are "constantly although slowly in flux" (Burke & Stets, 2009). Cognitive strategies for identity verification include:

- changing the identity standard to match a new situational meaning;
- conflicting identity standards shifting gradually to become identical;
- the higher moral identity standards shifting gradually in the direction of the disruptive action; and
- over time, the behaviors adopted to increase identity verification become part of the identity standard (Burke & Stets, 2009).

These mechanisms are not necessarily mutually exclusive. Measured in months and even years, identity standard change is cumulative as opposed to immediate. Identity standards are relatively stable as individuals act to bring identity verification into alignment when it is threatened. A symbiotic relationship exists between higher-level identities and lower-level identities. Lower-level identities are influenced by higher-level person identities and they also serve the demands of the higher level moral and gender identities. The higher-level identities change at a slower pace and this brings stability to the system. The identity standards at each level engage in an exchange or negotiation process to create identity verification (Burke & Stets, 2009).

Military Sociology and the Soldier Identity

Studying soldiers and the inner workings of the military has been a difficult task for sociologists throughout history due to the tight knit association of people within the institution (Cockerham, 2004). Moskos (1970) was able to gain access to soldiers during the Vietnam War in part due to his status as an established journalist and sociologist, but also due to his prior military service. Other pivotal works by Cockerham (1973, 1978a, 1978b, 1979) and Dowd (2000) were possible only by the authors' prior role in the military as officers. This barrier to research serves to indicate how the military tends to reject perceived outsiders who do not fully understand the soldier identity and the structural meaning of being part of the military society.

What makes antiwar veterans a group worthy of study is the degree to which the military goes to create a strong soldier role and moral identity for each person entering the military system. Goffman (1961) discussed asylums as *total institutions*, meaning centralized socializing groups that maintain consistent authority and messages. Research on soldiers indicates the degree to which the military model works as a total institution, effectively aligning soldiers' role and person identities. Zurcher and Wilson (1981) demonstrated how consistent authority with a central message, combined with the exclusion of outsiders served to create soldiers with a common perspective and belief regarding their role in combat and military service. In addition, a great deal of literature indicates that although soldiers resent some parts of basic training, overall the training techniques of military institutions are successful in creating an Army that generally abides by the values and goals of their superiors (Faris, 1995).

This research is set apart from research on the public's changing views on war due to the military's power as a total institution to instill a pro-war identity in its members. Research confirms that military personnel are less likely than civilians to participate in protesting war (Langton, 1984). In addition, military personnel are more likely than the general population to be Republican, conservative and hold pro-war attitudes (Holsti, 1999, 2001). Thus military veterans had to negotiate competing identities in order to engage in their anti-Iraq War activism while supporting friends or family members in the military (Leitz, 2014, 18).

While the general population of the U.S. slowly changed its views regarding specific wars such as Vietnam and the Iraq War, it is remarkable when a soldier or veteran becomes an antiwar activist because of what the soldier role and military branch group identity represent. The soldier or veteran is the ultimate insider to war while opposing war risks losing the insider status. Our research also reveals the multiple identity changes that occur with the transformation to an antiwar activist identity.

The emotional context of war involves the belief in the morality, mission, selflessness, and collective protection, which serves as a consistent and stable perspective for soldiers to rely on during military service (Dowd, 2000; Padavic, 2001; Williams, 2002). Although everyone will not respond uniformly to the training of groups in which they are members (Passy, 2001), research indicates many members of such groupings will maintain this role for much of the rest of their life (Cockerham, 1979). This strong socializing process is what makes understanding the moral, group and role conflict faced by some military veterans important to study in the advancement of Identity Theory.

The Influence of the Collective Identity on the Identity Change Process

The strong socializing influence of the military and intense sense of loyalty and belonging soldiers feel to their units provide powerful inputs to the Identity Control Model for maintaining the pro-war moral identity. But, when the moral pro-war identity standard is disrupted within the military, the soldier or veteran may experience significant negative inputs for questioning the morality of war. Some veterans, when the disruption is strong and persistent, may seek a new group to identify with where they can receive identity verification. The impact of identity groups or group identities is best explained by the concept of Collective Identity.

While there is no one agreed upon definition of collective identity, social movement researchers agree on a number of characteristics of collective identity in social movements. Collective identity refers to a network of active relationships that include emotional involvement. Conflict provides the basis for the consolidation of group identity and solidarity. Collective identity regulates membership for joining a social movement group. Emotions and affective ties are vital to collective identity formation. These ties can keep activists committed through difficult periods in the movement. Boundary work or maintenance of the collective identity creates reciprocal identification between group members while simultaneously communicating differences from oppositional groups. Finally, a social movement group's collective identity is crucially linked to "a shared project of collective action" as we find in our study (Flesher Fominaya, 2010, 395).

The 114 veterans in our study were solicited primarily through three veteran's peace movement organizations (Veterans for Peace, Iraq Veterans against the War and Vietnam Veterans against the War) and the Mennonite Church USA. The veterans identified these groups as significant in the support they felt as they moved to their new pacifist and/or antiwar identities. The collective identity concept meshes well with the Identity Model as it explains the role of important group identities and their influence in the feedback loop that leads to either identity verification or an error message. Following identity disruption, there is a period of emotional turmoil, attempts to change behavior to create identity verification and if this is not successful, a period of seeking new understandings and behaviors to stop the turmoil. Groups with which veterans share a collective identity while in the military—that is, the Marines—may need to be replaced in order to find antiwar identity verification. The new peace and antiwar group affiliations meet this need.

The strengths of the Identity Theory Model combined with the concept of Collective Identity, are key to analyzing the veteran's transcripts and tracking their pathways to pacifism and antiwar activism. The following chapters will focus on the four disrupters that caused a lack of identity verification, especially for the moral, soldier, male, intelligent, patriotic American and religious identities. The Identity Theory was also helpful to trace the healing process many veterans describe in managing their PTSD symptoms and/or moral injury. As stated at the outset, the goal of the Identity Control Process is identity verification. This concept applies to tracing the veterans' descriptions of their life courses to a point of peace and integrity, their words for identity verification.

Chapter Two

Research Methods

There is something about soldiers' personal narratives, their story as they want
to tell it, that is particularly revealing about identity. (Duncanson, 2013, 57)

The stories we share and the conclusions we make throughout this book are
based on ten years of in- depth interviews. This research includes the narratives of 114 former military personnel. In gathering our data we sought to
uncover the lived experiences of the veterans in relation to their change in
views on war.

Like most qualitative researchers, we had to make choices about methodology during the project. First, we had to choose a specific research method.
Social scientists have many methodological options for exploring the social
world, including surveys and focus groups. We chose in-depth interviews as
our method for gaining an understanding of how former military personnel
adopted an antiwar identity. In-depth interviews are preferable when one's
research aims include describing a process, learning how events are interpreted, and/or understanding an event from the inside (Weiss, 1994). Stan-
dardized survey options simply cannot capture the rich details and thick
description that emerges from in-depth interviewing. We also decided that
individual interviews would yield richer data than a focus group because we
were specifically interested in personal narratives as opposed to opinions on
narrow topics.

Another decision concerned the theoretical approach for data analysis.
Our overall research approach was inductive and rooted in grounded theory
(Glaser & Strauss, 1967). This approach assumes that a theoretical explanation is given only after a researcher has gained in-depth information about a
situation (Charmez, 2006). So, while we eventually come to understand the
veterans' responses through the lens of Identity Theory, we did not begin

with this lens. As described in the preface, Author One began this project with an interest in understanding how and why veterans would adopt an antiwar position. At the start of this research it was not obvious that an identity change had occurred among our respondents. Based on her own "sensitizing concepts and disciplinary perspective" (Charmez, 2006, 17), Author One was at first interested in attitudinal change and its location in a social movement. As advocated by Charmez (2006), she used these questions as a starting point for the research. During the process of data analysis, though, we realized that the respondents were not merely describing an attitudinal change but rather a holistic identity change. Following this insight, we decided to employ Identity Theory for understanding both the catalyst or identity disturbance and processes of change among these veterans.

We attempt to provide an etic and emic analysis through the presentation of the veterans' stories and our analysis of these narratives. For our purposes an etic perspective refers to our application of the Identity Theory framework to the interpretation and analysis of the qualitative data. An emic perspective refers to the study participants' perspective and interpretation of the data. We attempt to provide the presentation and analysis of our qualitative interview data, although there are times when we are more successful.

The names that are used in the following chapters are pseudonyms. The veterans in the study were assigned a pseudonym based on the first letter of his or her name. So, for example if a veteran's name was Julie, we assigned her a pseudonym starting with the letter "J." We share deeply personal stories that often involve painful memories and therefore wanted to protect the identity of the veterans that voluntarily shared these stories. Additionally, given that some of our participants have died since the time of interview, it would be impossible to obtain permission to use their real names.

METHODOLOGY

This research occurred in two phases. Phase One occurred between 2005 and 2009. In this phase, Author One conducted semi-structured in-depth interviews with a purposive sample of self-identified antiwar veterans. She interviewed a total of 114 veterans. Seventeen percent ($n = 19$) of the interviews were face-to-face while 83 percent ($n = 95$) were phone interviews. Following our University's institutional research board approval and informed consent, each interview proceeded in a semi-structured fashion lasting from one to three hours and included demographic data collection plus a set of 17 open-ended questions. These questions focused on each veteran's change in thinking about war and the events, people, and situations that impacted this change. Additionally, veterans were asked to reflect on how they see the change process now and the impact of their change in thinking on war on others areas of their lives. (See a complete list of questions in appendix A.)

During the interviews, Author One reflected their answers, clarified their statements, and probed for additional details. She also hand wrote responses verbatim, and later transcribed the interviews based on these notes (no recording was made). Author One and two of her colleagues (a sociologist and an art therapist) analyzed and coded preliminary using a process of independent sorting followed by discussion to reach agreement on category placement.

Phase Two occurred during February 2013. During this phase, we selected a sample of 26 veterans from the larger sample of 114 using a quota system and re-interviewed these veterans. We chose the subsample based on a cross-section of four catalyst groupings we had identified, the researchers' interest in self-described identity standards at 18 and currently, masculine identity change, management of opposition to the identity change and the role of religion as a catalyst in identity change. The second phase of research was also approved by our University's institutional review board, including the protocols on informed consent. Every participant was told the purpose of the study and nature of the questions prior to the start of the interview and voluntarily agreed to participate.

Because Phase Two occurred after the Phase One interviews had been transcribed and analyzed, the interview questions in Phase Two were informed by the results of the Phase One Interviews. This method is congruent with a grounded theory approach (Charmez, 2006). Phase Two then, allowed us to clarify and expand on themes uncovered in Phase One. Using a speakerphone, Author One conducted semi-structured interviews that lasted from 45 minutes to 2 hours. We taped and later transcribed these interviews.

The interview schedule included 20 open-ended questions regarding these themes:

- Primary identities at age 18 and currently,
- Criteria of being a good man or masculinity at age 18 and at their current age,
- Experiences with and coping strategies for dealing with the new antiwar identity, and
- Religious background and experience. Interviews and construction of memories.

Our research design is cross-sectional and retrospective, hence the interviews required participants to reflect on past experiences. By nature of this design, we are essentially collecting memories, which we know are shaped by where the respondent is now. Memories are constructed and often do not accurately reflect the objective reality of the past. Soldier narratives and autobiographies have been especially criticized for their inaccurate retelling of history, as well as their unreliable accounts of self (Hynes, 1998).

Duncanson (2013), who makes a compelling case for the use of soldier autobiographies, readily acknowledges that soldier narratives are essentially soldiers "making sense of their lives," and are not at all unbiased or accurate accounts of war or its aftermath (55). She further argues that the "sense making" that occurs in soldier narratives provides a vivid window into the identity of soldiers. She states, "narratives provide us with insights into their identities—gendered, raced, class and national—how they are multiple, complex, contradictory and shift over time" (Duncanson, 2013, 60). Rather than the "inaccuracy" of narratives being a limitation, though, this writer argues that it is a strength of the research design because it gives the researcher access to the identity formation and change process through the eyes of the respondent.

We also acknowledge that reflections of the veterans on identity change are the product of memories shaped by past and present experiences. As such, we do not claim that these memories accurately depict the reality of the war or even the entire truth of the respondents past experiences. Since these memories are framing their current identity, though, they are not only relevant but essential to understanding our respondents. We believe it is more important to understand the respondents' perspective rather than some "objective" truth about what occurred in the past. Thus, the respondents' understanding of the past is central to their identity formation today.

The interviews began when Author One interviewed a pilot of 16 pacifists within multiple Mennonite congregations in 2005. Four of these pacifists were veterans. This group of 16 interviews aided in clarifying the research question and in refining survey questions. The four veterans in the pilot group are included as part of the 114 veterans in the study.

We were able to cross check 26 of the narratives as the Phase Two veterans retold parts of their stories in 2013. In addition, we asked all veterans to share anything they had written about their military service and adjustment to civilian life and approximately 15 percent of the vets sent narratives or newspaper articles about them that are at times utilized for triangulation.

Reflexivity Statement

Throughout the data collection and analysis processes, we were acutely aware of the potential for bias based on the relationship of the researchers to the research context and participants (Broom et al., 2009). Biases arising from one's relationship to the research context and research participants are necessarily a part of research, especially in qualitative research (Broom et al., 2009). However, it is suggested that such biases can be minimized through awareness of one's position and its potential impact on the research results throughout the research process (Foley, 2002). Some have even argued that qualitative research is "as useful as the reflexive nature of the researcher regarding his/her influence on data production and analysis" (Broom et al., 2009, 52). Reflexivity can be understood here as the critical and constant examination of one's own position in relation to the respondents, as well as the assumptions that pervade the research process (Foley, 2002).

We were particularly conscious of gender incongruence (female to male) and affiliation with an antiwar position (Pini, 2005). Author One conducted the interviews. She identifies as a female progressive pacifist Christian. While she identified herself primarily as a university professor to the interviewees, elements of her identity were sometimes revealed during the interview to build rapport. As a result of these disclosures, she occupied an interesting position in relation to the interviewees. She was simultaneously an "insider" in terms of understanding an antiwar position, and an "outsider" in terms of past military experience and often gender. The dual "insider/ outsider" position has been discussed extensively in qualitative research and offers both advantages and disadvantages to the researcher (see, for example, De Andrade, 2000; Kanuha, 2000; Larabee, 2002). Larabee (2002) argues that an insider position can be advantageous in that it can provide greater access to respondents, can allow for a deeper understanding of a phenomenon and can better facilitate cultural interpretation. Author One's "insider" position, specifically in relation to the pacifist community, did increase access to respondents. Aware of how her shared position could influence the respondents' answers, she intentionally avoided showing her "insider" status. For example, she would ask a respondent to clarify a term even when that term was familiar to her.

The second author identifies as a female and Christian, but is not part of the pacifist or antiwar movement and does not take an overtly antiwar position. She began to work on the project in 2012 and helped to create the interview schedule for the second phase of interviews. She was also involved in transcribing, coding, and analyzing the data. We believe this improved objectivity in the analysis by creating distance between the researcher and the researched. Additionally, the analysis involved multiple discussions concerning the impact of both the interviewer's pacifist position and the position of both researchers as females.

Recruitment and Description of Subjects

The first author solicited participants from three areas. First, she interviewed a snowball sample of 15 (13 percent of the sample) veterans within the Mennonite Church USA, a pacifist denomination. Second, she placed an announcement on the following organization's websites: Veterans for Peace (www.veteransforpeace.org), Vietnam Veterans against the War (www.vvaw.org), and Iraq Veterans against the War (www.ivaw.org). The announcements requested contact with veterans who had experienced a significant change in perspectives on war over the life course. This group includes 92 veterans (81 percent of the sample). Third, she identified veterans within and around a small Midwestern university that had no antiwar organizational affiliation as an informal control group. This includes seven veterans (6 percent of the sample).

The 114 veterans in this study included 89 percent men. As noted in Table 2.1, they ranged in age from 21 to 92. White European Americans comprised 88 percent of the participants. This is a highly educated group with 74 percent holding either a bachelors, graduate or professional degree. Only one veteran self-identified as homosexual although a direct question was never asked about sexual orientation.

Also, Table 2.2 describes other features of the subjects. Thirty-two percent of the group experienced combat and 22 percent had a diagnosis of PTSD from the Veterans Administration. The participants represented all

Table 2.1.   Description of sample

Demographic Characteristics of Sample	
Gender (%)	
Men	101 (89%)
Women	13 (11%)
Race/Ethnicity	
White	97 (88%)
Other	14 (12%)
Age at Interviewee	
20s	8 (7%)
30s	9 (8%)
40s	13 (11%)
50s	33 29%)
60s	41 (36%)
70–90s	10 (9%)
Highest Education	
High school only	5 (4%)
Some College	26 (23%)
Bachelor's Degree	35 (32%)
Graduate Degree	48 (42%)

branches of the military (with 50 percent Army) and had served in the following operations: World War II, the Korean War, the Vietnam War (43 percent), the Persian Gulf War and the Iraq War. Ten percent were career military. While we collected statistics on the number who were drafted or enlisted, it is not meaningful because of the number of Vietnam War veterans (43 percent of the sample) who described enlisting simply to avoid being drafted and serving in the frontline infantry. Enlisting gave them more options for type of service.

Measuring the Antiwar Position

Serving in the military does not necessarily mean that an individual is "pro-war." Furthermore, antiwar does not mean anti-military. For purposes of this book, we define antiwar as actively opposing a particular war due to its being unjust or unnecessary (a Just War position) or opposing the use of war as a response to violence or injustice in any situation (a Pacifist position). It was this antiwar position that we sought to measure among our respondents.

To do so, the moral position of the subject concerning war was first determined with an open-ended question asking what he or she believed at age 18 to be the appropriate use of war. This was followed by what he or she

Table 2.2. Description of the sample's experiences

Branch of Military	
Airforce	21 (18%)
Army	57 (50%)
Coast Guard	2 (2%)
Marines	18 (16%)
Navy	16 (14%)
Served During War Time	
WW II	5 (4%)
Korea	2 (2%)
Vietnam	40 (35%)
Iraq 1	7 (6%)
Iraq 2	10 (9%)
Career	9 (8%)
No war during service	50 (44%)
Conscientious Objector	5 (4%)
Served in Combat	36 (32%)
PTSD Diagnosis	25 (22%)

believe today. Next, Author One read an eight-point scale from militaristic to pacifistic and the subject identified the point or points on the scale that they were closest to at age 18 and currently (see appendix A).

This scale determined the moral identity on war for each subject at age 18 and presently. It also determined the degree of identity change for each subject. For example, a subject may have identified No. 1: It is appropriate for our nation to respond to offense or injustice anywhere in the world in any way it sees fit, as his or her belief about the appropriate use of war at age 18. If his or her belief about war today was identified as No. 7: Neither the Christian or the person of conscience, or the nation should engage in war because all human life is sacred; or No. 8: I believe that there are nonviolent means to resolve conflict peacefully without recourse to war, his or her identity change was scored as high on the scale.

We used guidelines from two Christian ethicists: John Howard (Yoder, 1992) and Dr. Duane Friesen, Professor of Bible and Religion at Bethel College in Kansas for designing the eight point scale from militarism to pacifism. The scale began with an indiscriminate pro-war perspective. Here the veteran believed that it was appropriate for a nation to respond to an injustice anywhere in the world in any way it sees fit. The majority of veterans identified this as their primary belief at age 18 prior to joining the military. The next three positions on the scale place additional conditions that must be met in order for war to be an appropriate response to an injustice anywhere in the world.

Position four on the scale includes eight criteria for a war to be considered a Just War. These criteria originate in Catholic thought and are cited widely today (National Conference of Catholic Bishops, 1983). The fifth position on the scale allows for the use of war by the nation/state but never allows the Christian or person of conscience to participate in war. Positions six and seven on the scale are two versions of Christian pacifism that were edited slightly to allow for persons from other religious persuasions to also adopt the position that war is never appropriate for the individual or nation/state due to the dignity of all life and/or the teaching of a religious figure such as Jesus that they believe forbids the use of violence for any reason, even against enemies or in self-defense. The final position eight could be adopted along with other positions and was stated in a way that both a religiously-affiliated individual and an atheist could adopt. It simply states that the individual believes that there are nonviolent means to resolve conflict peacefully without recourse to war or violence.

Data Analysis

The transcribed interviews from Phase One yielded approximately 450 pages and Phase Two yielded approximately 260 single-spaced pages of data for analysis for a total of approximately 710 pages of data. The coding process involved many decisions about how to narrow a large amount of data into relevant categories while maintaining the essence of the data (Westin et al., 2001). First, we developed a coding scheme. We decided on a grounded theory approach based on line-by-line or incident-by-incident coding instead of a pre-established system based on a prior theory.

The initial phase of coding was a type of incident-by-incident coding (Chamez, 2006). We read each of the transcripts line-by-line and "episodes" were identified and given a label (Westin et al., 2001). Episodes, as described by Weston et al. (2001), were used to "capture the context of an entire event of reflection" (393). We grouped these episodes in categories and identified themes that emerged.

In Phase One of the research, Author One focused on the questions: When did the change in your support of war occur, how did it happen, what did you do about it and how did others respond to your change (see appendix A)? After constant comparison, Author One combined categories and identified four common catalysts for identity change. These catalysts were: combat, betrayal, religious conviction, and education although there was evidence of multiple categories in about 20 percent of the veterans. When there was evidence of multiple categories, the researchers coded using the catalyst that first disrupted the moral stance on war and appeared to be the strongest.

As Author One examined the data from Phase One, she realized that the participants were describing more than a change in attitudes related to war. Instead, she found themes that indicated a holistic identity change. Respondents discussed changing not only their attitudes on war, but also their views of religion, the environment, their understanding of gender roles and minorities, and their interest in justice more broadly. At this point, she decided that Identity Theory would be the primary framework for data interpretation.

We then re-examined the transcripts by applying Identity Theory to the data. Additionally, we used Identity Theory to shape the interview guide for the Phase Two interviews (see appendix B). During the Phase Two interviews in 2013, we found that the themes related to Identity Theory in the Phase One transcripts were verified and expanded by Phase Two subjects. Because only the Phase Two interviews were recorded and transcribed verbatim, the direct quotes throughout the book are primarily from the Phase Two interviews.

During the transcription and coding of the Phase Two interviews, we grouped the responses into emergent categories through an iterative process. This involved expanding categories, eliminating categories, and collapsing categories based on their similarities (Charmez, 2006).

In this chapter we described our ideological and methodological approach. We detailed the methods used to collect the data presented throughout this book. Our intention throughout this text is to first give a voice to the veterans that that were willing to participate in our study. Identity Theory thus becomes a framework in which we situate the stories of their journeys to an antiwar identity. We primarily present case studies that are illustrative of the identity change process of our respondents as well as represent the diversity of ages, wars, and experiences of the veterans in our study. We include lengthy quotes in order to both give voice, as well as to ensure the accuracy of the narratives of our respondents. What follows in the next four chapters is an examination of each of the four disturbances to the pro-war identity that we call catalysts of identity change and opened a pathway to pacifism and/or antiwar activism.

Chapter Three

The Combat Catalyst of Identity Change

I used to believe it takes a strong Army to guarantee peace. The whole thing changed when I saw combat. It was obvious that this would not lead to peace. I went in one person and came out another. Combat was horrible. (Edward)

Among the four primary catalysts that disturbed the moral identity (combat, betrayal, education and religious conviction), combat impacted the highest number of the 114 veterans in the study (38 percent; $n = 43$). Experiencing combat initiated a complex and lengthy process of disruption and reconstruction of these veterans' moral identities.

This group of veterans named "combat and war" as the disruptive experience that was the first step to changing their moral stance on war. Veterans we placed in this category often described the reality of war as being "beyond description." These veterans used words like "wrong," "confused," or "ashamed" when explaining how the reality of war disturbed their moral criteria. As we examine their narratives, we see much evidence of conflict between the behaviors of the veterans and their moral identity standard. For example, one Army veteran was shocked by the valor of the enemy and the contrast in firepower between the United States and the North Vietnamese in 1967. "Bob" (pseudonym) held a moral identity standard that required the military to "protect women and children." He was shocked to discover that his fellow soldiers were not responding as he expected and that he could not stop their immoral behavior. The negative emotions he describes are typical of the many disruptions that eventually led these soldiers down a pathway to a new antiwar moral identity.

COMBAT CATALYST GROUP CHARACTERISTICS

Factors unique to the combat group included having the highest rate of combat experience (58 percent; $n = 25$). The combat group contained the largest number who had served in-country during a time of war (81 percent; $n = 35$) with 53 percent ($n = 23$) being Vietnam War veterans.

As expected, this group contains the largest number of males (95 percent; $n = 41$) as combat was restricted to males until 2013. The combat group contained the oldest veterans with 54 percent being age 60–80 due to the fact that so many Vietnam veterans served in combat and are in this catalyst group. As a whole, they primarily served in the Army (51 percent). The combat catalyst group had the lowest rate of bachelor's or graduate degrees (58 percent; $n = 25$) and the lowest rate of Career Military (5 percent; $n = 2$).

One critical point is that the combat catalyst group had the highest rate of diagnosed PTSD (42 percent; $n = 14$). The official diagnosis of PTSD was not made until the 1980s, fully 10 years post-combat for the majority of Vietnam war vets although symptoms recognizable as PTSD were described by the vets upon return from the war from 1967 to 1973. Most of the veterans in this group who had a PTSD diagnosis were receiving total disability payments from the Veterans Administration at the time of the study.

The interview transcripts indicate that their struggles with PTSD symptoms impacted their marriages and increased their rates of divorce and alcoholism. This group seemed to resolve their identity discrepancies by becoming heavily involved in antiwar activism through Veterans for Peace, Vietnam Veterans against the War, and Iraq Veterans against the War (83 percent; $n = 36$). Despite the fact that many of them live with daily symptoms of PTSD, most describe a sense of personal peace and meaning in their new antiwar identities.

Ninety-three percent of the Combat group began with a pro-war stance in the 1–3 range on the militarism/pacifism continuum (appendix C). This included such views as "it is appropriate for a nation to respond to an injustice anywhere in the world in any way it sees fit." By the time of their interview, 69 percent ($n = 30$) of these veterans adopted the view that "there are nonviolent alternatives to conflict and injustice short of war" or Just War Theory (37 percent; $n = 17$). Some veterans chose both of these perspectives.

Bob's Pathway to Antiwar Activism

As discussed earlier, Bob had been disturbed by his comrades' immoral behavior during the Vietnam war. He began life in New York City during the 1950s and 1960s, growing up in a "traditional Catholic" upper middle class household. He described his father as an opinionated Republican and an active alcoholic from the 1950s onward. At eighteen, Bob identified himself as a conservative Republican and a good student. Above all, he saw himself as a traditional "brave" male protecting others against bullies and being kind and considerate. Drafted into the Army in 1966, he served as a squad leader in an infantry unit for one year in Vietnam. In 1968, he returned to the U.S. and voted for Hubert Humphrey because of "his promises to end the war."

When drafted, Bob never questioned his belief that "the U.S. always helped and did good things abroad." When interviewed at age 62 (in 2009), though, his views on the use of war had changed dramatically. He believed that "the U.S. needs the military only for self-defense for real attacks on our soil. Our outreach to others should be diplomatic. We are woefully misled by our government." At age 18, Bob rated himself on the eight point militarism scale as affirming the first position that "it is appropriate for a nation to respond to an injustice anywhere in the world, any way it sees fit." By 2009, he related to number eight, "I believe there are nonviolent means to resolve conflict peacefully without recourse to war or violence."

As Bob describes some of his early combat experiences, we see evidence of his first moral identity disruption. According to Identity Theory individuals experiencing identity disruption first respond by changing their behavioral response to a situation in order to verify their identity. The following quote captures Bob's experiences of disruption during combat and his unsuccessful attempts to change the situations behaviorally:

> The most important event was just seeing real war. We walked endlessly and waited for someone to shoot us. . . . The first event was when we got hit by our own artillery and two guys were killed. The medics would pop morphine pills in the mouths of the wounded. I tried to carry one guy back for help and he died. . . . It's so bad . . . you can't imagine how bad it really is. I can't even explain it. . . . We were involved in the Tet Offensive on the third day. Our unit started with 160 men and was down to 60 by the end. We did a search on some people's land and eight of our guys were shot. The U.S. destroyed a village . . . bombing all day and all night. One hundred and ninety-two people were killed that day. Our unit was one quarter mile away from the village. I had to go numb during the bombing. I remember one 16-year-old girl came out of the village holding a baby in the air and no one tried to help her. There is no morality to war. We didn't even help orphans. Earlier in the day, 20–30 women came running out of the village and our soldiers were shooting and I yelled stop shooting, they are women and children but they kept shooting. . . . These are the people we were told that we were there to protect against Communist monsters . . . I was flabbergasted at other soldiers' bad behaviors but rarely said anything. . . . It was nine months from hell for me.

Not only is the intensity of war beyond his expectation but we soon find evidence of identity disruption at the level of moral injury. Bob describes his shame at witnessing the behavior of his comrades that transgressed his deeply held moral beliefs and expectations for treatment of women and children.

Interestingly, his memory of this battle also suggests trauma from the impact of continuous bombing, seeing many in his unit die and not being able to help. This type of experience often leads to PTSD.

> As a squad leader, I had to choose a point guy to go first on ambush patrol. One day, my point guy stepped on a grenade and died. He was a ghost for me for 20 years encouraging me to act. I kept secrets about the war for years, except from my younger brother [who also went to Vietnam]. My brother was shot in Vietnam and it made him a negative person.

This narrative reveals various identities with similar meanings emerging simultaneously in combat. During the Tet Offensive (a major battle launched in 1968 by the North Vietnamese against the South Vietnamese and U.S. forces that resulted in significant losses on both sides), it appears that Bob faced conflicting demands from his different identities: moral identity (i.e., kind and considerate), role identity (i.e., soldier as protector of women and children), and group identity (i.e., loyal and obedient to one's Army unit). Since person and moral identities are master identities, these should influence or change the lower level role and group identities in order to create identity verification (Burke, 2004a). In fact, Bob attempted to change his comrade's behavior (part of his group identity) by yelling at them to stop shooting because they were women and children but this is ineffective causing him great emotional turmoil that seems to haunt him yet today.

While identity verification is always the goal of the Identity Control Model, some situations make it impossible for a person to change one's behaviors to create verification or consistency. For example, non-verification of an identity may occur when one is drafted into the military and must perform actions that do not match one's multiple identity standards. A newly drafted soldier, then, might either go numb or live in a great deal of turmoil. He could also adjust to the stress by modifying his moral identity standards to comply with the role or group identity demands of a combat soldier. For example, Bob may have decided to set aside his moral standards (i.e., kind and considerate) in combat or life-threatening situations.

Research suggests though that such changes to the moral or master identities are slow and difficult. These changes are difficult because master identities are activated across many situations and roles. Because we frequently verify our master identities, they are the core of one's sense of identity and become more salient or important over time (Stets & Carter, 2012). Because of Bob's clear sense of right and wrong as expressed in his transcript above, it was easier to attempt to change his and other's behavior than to change his moral identity standards.

When experiencing non-verification of a master identity, another option was to exit the difficult situation even at the risk of rejection by one's comrades or punishment by military authorities. For example, some of the veterans in the study rebelled in the ranks, declared Conscientious Objector status, and were sent home (or exited the military sooner than planned). But, this type of exit was not a viable option for most of the combat catalyst group as they depended on their comrades to survive and would be considered cowardly for leaving. In addition, little was known of the Conscientious Objector status and process during the early years of the Vietnam War.

Another option for the conflicted soldier is to attempt to change the behavior of his/her group so that the group's behavior reflects one's own moral or role standards. Bob initially tried this option as a way to verify his "kind and considerate" moral identity and his "protect women and children" soldier identity standards. When he yelled at his unit to stop shooting, though, the other soldiers ignored him. This failure to change their behavior led to a great deal of emotional distress for Bob.

Once Bob returned to the U.S. in 1968, he knew that he had changed and that he needed healing. He describes finding support for his newly forming antiwar identity in an old friend. As he progressed in what he terms his "reintegration and healing," he gradually began to attend antiwar rallies. Later, he decided to actively participate in these rallies. During this period, Bob struggled to find stability in his community, career, and relationships. Although Bob was not diagnosed with PTSD until 1990, his description of his mental state indicates the symptoms started upon his 1968 return to the U.S. His statement that "I still think about the war every day, all day long" is a haunting description of both PTSD and moral injury although, Bob never mentioned the latter term.

It took Bob decades to receive total disability payments for PTSD caused by his combat in Vietnam (1990), since it was not until 1980 that PTSD was named by the American Psychiatric Association. The diagnosis of PTSD required understanding the concept of trauma as being an event outside the individual (http://www.ptsd.va.gov/professional/PTSD-overview/ptsd-overview.asp).

In its initial DSM-III (Diagnostic and Statistical Manual of Mental Disorders) formulation, a traumatic event was conceptualized as a catastrophic stressor that was outside the range of usual human experience. The framers of the original PTSD diagnosis had in mind events such as war, torture, rape, the Nazi Holocaust, the atomic bombings of Hiroshima and Nagasaki, natural disasters (such as earthquakes, hurricanes, and volcanic eruptions), and human-made disasters (such as factory explosions, airplane crashes, and automobile accidents).

Crippled by his PTSD symptoms for years, Bob relates how his healing journey began:

I had a co-worker from before the war who became my best friend. He invited me into his family and he was antiwar. When I returned, his family was supportive and we remained close. They helped me with reintegration and healing. . . . In 1970–71, I went to some antiwar demonstrations. . . . I did some counseling at different times. I became a hippy until 1981. I moved around a lot. I lost old friends. I lived on a commune for a while. I tried to back away from plastic people. I lived a life of poverty and anti-consumerism. I worked as an agricultural worker and kept moving and breaking off from people but I never returned [home] to NYC. In 1969, I got 30 percent disability for un-employability for shrapnel wounds. In 1990, I got 70 percent disability for PTSD. I didn't marry until 2000 and I have a daughter.

When Bob returned to the U.S., then, he had difficulty adjusting to civilian life and knew he needed healing. He describes a decade moving around the U.S., avoiding long-term relationships and running from his combat "ghosts." Over time, he sought disability assistance from the Veterans Administration. By 1990, drawing 100 percent disability payments from the war offered him both emotional and financial stability and the freedom to engage in more full time antiwar activism with other veterans.

Thirteen years following his return from Vietnam, though, Bob found support in an antiwar veterans group. He also became involved in activism opposing U.S. covert involvement in the wars in El Salvador, Nicaragua, and Guatemala during the Reagan Administration. In this excerpt, he expressed a sense of urgency that drove him to feel he "should be doing more (against war)."

From 1981 to 1983, I was in a Vets group for support. During the 1980s I worked against [U.S. involvement in] Central American wars. I was petrified of public speaking but I began to do it when I joined the Committee for Solidarity with El Salvador and Witness for Peace. I went to Central America with some vets groups. . . . I joined Veterans for Peace in 2001 and I'm pretty involved. I go to meetings. I write letters to the editor. I bring speakers to rallies and do some public speaking now. I carry banners in parades and I go to Arlington [Cemetery Vigil] Northwest at the Peace Park every year. I still think about the war everyday all day long. I replay scenes of the war all the time. . . . I always feel like I should be doing more [against war].

As indicated by this passage, his activism with veterans groups with "like-minded people" in the 1980s stabilized Bob's life. We suggest that these groups provided Bob with a Collective Identity that was essential to his antiwar identity verification and ultimately his journey toward peace and healing from both PTSD and moral injury. We believe that his drive to "be doing more" occurred to verify his moral identity. By becoming an outspoken antiwar activist and "nonviolent" protest leader, he could verify his new moral identity standards as a male who is "kind and compassionate, wise like

Jesus, acts on what's right and who questions things." His military socialization "to disrespect women and civilians didn't take with me. I was too nice." He reconstructed his moral identity by rejecting the Vietnam War and later the U.S. involvement in the Central American wars. He concluded, "What I saw in Vietnam was cruel and hideous and that wasn't what we were supposed to do." He was now certain that he "was brave compared to his fellow soldiers."

Later at age 65 (when interviewed again in 2013), Bob's primary identities changed in important ways—or more accurately, his standards for his primary identities had changed. According to Bob his role identities as a husband and father being fully "connected" to his wife and daughter instead of "thinking about the war all the time" were of primary importance. He considered moral identities of being loving and protecting them "to the maximum" and being "kind, brave and nonviolent" even when protesting and speaking out against U.S. involvement in current wars.

The contrasts in his pre-war and post-war identities also include his religion and politics. Bob started adult life at 18 years as a Catholic and Republican who believed that the U.S. "always did good things abroad." In 2013, Bob identified as a Deist who believes in the existence of a God on the evidence of reason and nature only, with rejection of supernatural revelation (www.dictionary.com) and as a Liberal/Progressive Democrat. He was a full time antiwar activist who believed that "we are woefully misled by our government." Despite his constant struggle with "daily flashbacks and emotions from combat in Vietnam," he still works actively "against war without fear." He surrounds himself with like-minded vets with weekly Veterans for Peace meetings and is "satisfied with who I am," an important sign of full identity verification.

Jake's Pathway to Pacifism and Antiwar Activism

Like Bob, Jake's pro-war moral identity standards were initially disrupted by the combat experience. Jake grew up during the 1980s as a "proud Texan" and a Southern Baptist with his mom and a stepdad. His parents were southern Democrats who were involved in "spreading the gospel" through their church. At age 18, Jake identified as a "macho-male motorhead" who fixed cars. This young entrepreneur had his own detailing business, besides being an artist and football player. At that time, he believed that the "fuckin' hippies were nasty civilian pigs" and that any U.S. intervention abroad was justified "at anytime and anywhere we saw fit."

After losing his job following high school because he "discovered alcohol," Jake joined the Marines. He had been jobless and homeless in New Orleans when he found a Marine recruiter. Joining the military corresponded with his "warrior mentality." By becoming a Marine in 1992, he received both economic "benefits" and the potential for a rewarding career:

> My early experience in the Marines was good. We jumped out of airplanes in deserts and jungles. I had great camaraderie with my fellows. I was a baby Rambo. . . . When I reached middle management and recruiting, things changed. As recruiters in 1999, there were competitions and prizes like guns and vacations for getting the largest numbers. . . . By January of 2000, I was concerned about fraudulent enlistments where recruits were coached not to tell the truth about medical conditions. . . . We were reprimanded if we didn't meet our recruiting quota and there was a three-strikes policy . . . I didn't meet my quota for three months and got an adverse fitness report.as a recruiter and was sent straight to Iraq.

As a career Marine (1992–2003), Jake had positive military experiences until he reached middle management and recruiting. There he witnessed "fraudulent recruiting practices" and morally could not comply with them. This witnessing and rejection of fraudulent practices in the Marine Corp he loved, suggests moral injury as he was unable to prevent policies and behaviors that transgressed his deeply held moral beliefs and expectations not only for himself as a Marine but for the Marine Corps. He was then "punished" for his refusal to follow the fraudulent practices by being sent into combat. Jakes description of this experience suggest his moral identity standard already included a strong sense of doing what is just. At this time Jake also described his Marine and soldier identities as primary. Once in Iraq, though, he grew ashamed of his immoral actions:

> They didn't prepare us for the Middle East culture very well. I was a platoon sergeant in charge of infantry and snipers. . . . I witnessed numerous violations of the Geneva Convention—which is our Bible. I personally took part in the killing of innocent civilians including older men, women, and children. It was easy due to our firepower. It wasn't anything to worry about. We could have leveled the whole country with our firepower . . . I was the second in charge of 45 Marines and when I began to voice my opposition, I was quickly labeled a rogue. At that point, I didn't care as I knew what they were doing was wrong. I knew the Geneva Convention was right and the Marines were wrong. . . . We were using depleted uranium, targeting known civilian areas, and destroying more than what the mission called for.

When the Marines placed Jake in a combat role, he was forced to reconcile the demands of two conflicting identities. His moral identity, based on the Geneva Convention standards for war, clashed with his platoon sergeant role that demanded strict obedience to orders. Jake's combat actions of "killing civilians" led to the non-verification of his moral identity standards, which resulted in emotional turmoil. He attempted to change the situation by voicing his opposition. As a result, though, he received non-verification of his Marine and sergeant identities from the officers to whom he voiced his concerns. Jakes language here suggests again that the moral identity disruption is at the level of moral injury as he appears ashamed of "what we did in Iraq."

> It was incredible what we did in Iraq as a military mission. We were also in shock and trauma. . . . We were asking, what are we doing here. . . . That's when I started raising concerns about the invasion of Iraq to my superiors and I was terminated. It was noted by my captain and he said that's it, you're done. I was transferred to another division and I continued to raise the issue. They asked me if I wanted to see a chaplain and be evaluated as a Conscientious Objector and then I needed to see a psychologist. He said I had post-traumatic stress disorder because of what I had witnessed in Iraq. and from there I was given an honorable discharge [in 2003].

Jake responded to the non-verification of both his moral and Marine identities in a number of ways. First, he voiced his opposition to the military actions that were "beyond our mission." When given the option, he declared Conscientious Objector status to remove himself from what he describes as a "morally abhorrent" situation where he felt trapped. Finally, he was discharged due to a PTSD diagnosis. He concluded, "In this war, the psychopaths were the so-called good guys." Jake arrived home feeling angry and betrayed by the Marines he loved. Now safe and out of combat, Jake engaged in a time of reflection and study. He appears to begin to heal and reconstruct a coherent moral and group identity once he meets members of Veterans for Peace.

> When I left for Iraq, I was going through a divorce and it was final when I returned [to the U.S.]. I was on my own and thinking, fuck, I just pissed away twelve years of my life for these fucking assholes. I felt duped. We [Marines] are supposed to be about honor. I realized it was a systematic problem after talking with others [Marines]. I had a psychiatric evaluation in Iraq and then in the U.S. They [the military] said, we can't help you as a CO so I hired a lawyer and they changed the diagnosis to PTSD—100 percent disabled. I was ready to kick back and fish [with the disability payments] and then I heard about VFP [Veterans for Peace] and found a bunch of like-minded people. I found docs, lawyers and priests in VFP and it helped break the stereotype of the peace activist hippy.

Like Bob, Jake describes how important being an anti-Iraq War activist and member of Veterans for Peace were to his moral and group identity. Jake reports speaking around the world and on college campuses with the peace movement from 2003 to 2006. After writing a book about his experience that was only published in France, he gave dozens of television and radio interviews. However, perhaps because he didn't take sufficient time for healing, he eventually felt "burned by some in the movement" and so he is "very careful who I talk to today."

We again see how a Collective Identity related to antiwar activism is important in Jake's attempts to verify his moral identity standard. In the following quote, Jake describes the losses he experienced with his identity change, which is a theme we observe in many of the stories of the veterans in our study who experienced moral injury. We also find here a strong and clear sense of moral standards for the Marine identity. In fact, Jake still identifies as a Marine but explains that they abandoned their own moral standards and although he tried, he was unable to change their behavior:

> I'm a professional Marine, I'm not a mercenary. We were doing borderline mercenary work [in Iraq]. Also, my faith in God tells me we answer for all our sins. It takes a true man to stand up in the face of wrong, to stand up for humanity. I lost everything and had to start over with nothing. It's been a difficult road. My lifestyle had to change.

Jake reported feeling good about the Veterans Administration as they have "taken care of me to this day." But he continues to feel "duped." though as there were "no weapons of mass destruction (in Iraq). We destroyed Iraq for nothing." This statement demonstrates that he has also been impacted by the betrayal catalyst (chapter 6). The combat catalyst, though, was the first disruption to his moral identity. Jake continued to affirm his moral identity with the "boot camp code for Marines" that includes the values of "obedience, judgement, justice, tact, dependability, integrity, decisiveness, initiative, endurance, unselfish, courage, knowledge, loyalty and enthusiasm." In light of these values, Jake concludes that the "U.S. lost their way in Iraq."

According to Identity Theory, changes in a higher level identity, such as one's moral identity can impact lower level identities. Jake describes a number of additional identity changes that we suggest illustrate a shift in lower level identities to find congruence with a new moral identity standard. In 2013 when interviewed for the second time, Jake was living in an isolated area with a girlfriend. While he began life at 18 as a "proud Texan, Southern Baptist, and Southern Democrat," now his identities include Socialist, liberal Episcopalian, and a deeply religious person. He also continued to see athlete and artist as important identities. To these he had added a new identity of "good earth steward" that included a vegan lifestyle while treating his body as "a temple of God."

Jake also describes a shift in his masculine identity standard. His perception of manhood at age 18 was the "macho image of a Marine, a team player and adventuresome." By contrast, his description of a good man in 2013 was as "a full time peace activist, a gentleman, a good listener, someone who has taken Marine values to care for others to a deeper level." He reminded himself "when talking to others with different opinions, I must respect them and listen. They haven't studied as I have, they don't have the same facts and understanding of history."

Despite his traumatic Iraq War experiences and living with PTSD, Jake appeared to be at peace with himself and his life. He stated that he had "no regrets, absolutely not" regarding the direction his life has taken. Instead, "It takes a true man to stand up in the face of wrong, to stand up for humanity." These statements indicate that he has finally found a place of full moral and masculine identity verification as his past and present behaviors are congruent with his identity standards.

Luke's Pathway to Antiwar Activism

Luke was traveling with an Iraq Veterans against the War bus tour across America when we met in 2007. He was planning to attend university in the fall to study International Relations and Electrical Engineering. Luke grew up in a middle class household in Vermont. His divorced parents exposed him to both liberal and conservative political views. He joined the Marines out of high school and at that time identified as,

> a Hawk with a romantic notion of war and the U.S. was a force for good. I thought of war as a necessary evil. By high school, I thought war was fought for resources and to intimidate. I joined the Marines to have a stepping stone to grow up.

Upon reflecting on his views post military at age 22, he stated, "now I believe the U.S. fights wars to project its will and get resources. War is disgusting, brutal and inhumane." Later, when interviewed at age 28 in 2013 as a college graduate, he stated,

> My views on war today include Just War Theory . . . but I lean to the idea that war is a failure of humanity, there may have been Hitlers to deal with but an ounce of prevention is worth a pound of cure and there is no reason to believe that we couldn't have prevented a Hitler.

Compared to Bob, Jake and others we placed in the combat group, Luke's shift in views on war is less dramatic. Luke's Marine service from 2004 to 2007 included tours in the U.S., Japan, Thailand and one seven month tour in the Anbar Province of Iraq "experiencing indirect mortar fire." Already skeptical of the need for the U.S. to invade Iraq, this is where he experienced significant moral identity disruption that meets the criteria of moral injury. Luke held high moral standards for both himself and for the Marines and concluded, once he witnessed the war in Iraq first hand, that multiple acts among his comrades transgressed his deeply held moral beliefs and expectations.

> Nothing changed in me about war in general-U.S. foreign policy changed. I thought it [the Iraq War] was wrong and for oil and this was confirmed when I got there. When I interacted with Iraqis, they were ruined and hopeless. I helped a Reserve Unit for four months and joined an existing unit that had been hit by an IED [improvised explosive device]. . . . My boss shot an Iraqi civilian in the shoulder and wondered if he would get an award. I couldn't believe it. . . . But I couldn't really share my skepticism in the fall of 2004. . . . Others from Texas exposed the reality of the occupation right away. We never had an instance where we made the country safer. We kept ourselves going by staying focused on growing from adversity. I tried to do my job well. Everyone there wanted to come home.

Luke had a strong sense of the war being "wrong and for oil," before seeing conditions on the ground that shocked him. We consider his observations as moral and group identity standard disruptions. Luke explains that these factors eventually drove him to take the risk to speak out and organize against the war during his service in Iraq. According to Identity Theory, this behavioral change allows Luke to achieve identity verification:

> Eventually, I took the step from being a talker to a doer when Navy sailor Jonathan Hutto came forward. Jonathan Hutto and Howard Zinn influenced me . . . the legacy of Martin Luther King had a profound impact. . . . I was emboldened by others.
> I organized my own men while in the military . . . I stepped out against the war during my tour in Iraq on *60 Minutes* [the television news program]. I appealed for Redress and started a petition in September of 2006. What I did was completely legal and the Military Whistleblower Protection Act okayed it if I was off base and off duty. I called it an appeal and not a petition.

Like Bob and Jake, we see the importance of significant others and the adoption of a new Collective Identity as important in Luke's description of personal transformation. His activism work promoting the "Appeal for Redress" online allows him to verify his moral identity standard while honoring the ethical guidelines demanded by the Marines:

> David Cortright [a leader with Vietnam Veterans against the War from the 1960s] was speaking at a meeting and said the military should be involved in working against the war. David Cortright stayed involved. We held a press conference and got the word out. . . . 2,000 have signed the Appeal for Redress. We submitted the first appeal with 1,200 names on it in January of 2007. It was exciting, and scary and a growth experience.

The Redress petition is a human rights organization that helps torture survivors (i.e., Iraqi civilians) obtain justice and reparations from governments like the U.S. and other groups. Redress (a remedy to set something right) works with survivors to help restore their dignity and to make torturers accountable (http://www.redress.org/about-redress/who-we-are). Luke refers to Jonathan Hutto as an inspiration. Jonathan is an antiwar Navy veteran who founded Appeal for Redress in 2006, one of the only active duty antiwar groups dedicated to ending the war in Iraq. The appeal is only three sentences:

> As a patriotic American proud to serve the nation in uniform, I respectfully urge my political leaders in Congress to support the prompt withdrawal of all American military forces and bases from Iraq. Staying in Iraq will not work and is not worth the price. It is time for U.S. troops to come home.

Luke's superiors and peers, though, did not support his efforts. Reflecting on the resistance to his antiwar activism while still in Iraq, Luke noted that "I was ostracized by senior career Marines and by peers in my unit . . . everyone treated me differently and people stopped talking to me. It didn't break me, though." Once Luke returned to the states and was discharged honorably in 2007, he connected with other Iraq War veterans and felt obligated to speak out. He joined IVAW (Iraq Veterans against the War).

> I was thrust into the spotlight. I got out of the Marines and started a speaking tour. I wanted to be able to contribute quality to the IVAW and galvanize. I shared [my views] widely through the media and the IVAW listserv.

Like other veterans, Luke made sacrifices to verify his new anti-Iraq War moral identity. He acted on his conscience despite the opposition he experienced. In 2007, He received a letter from the Marine Corps alleging he had violated the Uniform Code of Military Justice by wearing part of his uniform during an antiwar rally. They were recommending "other than honorable discharge."

Rather than silencing protest, the push-back from the military prompted Luke and other dissenting troops to explore creative ways to voice their disapproval of the Iraq War while remaining within military guidelines. Luke used language typical of many veterans when describing his antiwar activism as serving the mandates of his conscience. His drive to activism may also serve to heal the shame he felt being associated with an officer and unit members as they engaged in acts that transgressed his deeply held moral beliefs and expectations of Marines:

> I don't regret it. It puts a strain on my relationships. I get continually consumed by it but I think that people who are doing what they truly believe are

serving their conscience well. I always believed if you wanted to achieve something, you need to focus and do it well.

Luke's lower level identities also changed to align with his high level moral antiwar identity. He began with different primary identities at age 18 (religion and politics) than he holds today at age 28. He was raised as an Irish Catholic and his parents exposed him to both Democratic and Republican parties growing up. As an 18 year old he was a "physically and mentally strong, determined, strategic athlete." At 18, he identifies as a loving and supportive brother to his siblings. He deemed it important to be a good American and "to use our strength and power and influence wisely."

As an antiwar veteran in 2013, Luke described his primary identity as "divine energy, just like you. . . . My religion is love." As an "environmentalist" aware of his impact on the planet and a global citizen, he was working in the solar energy field. He considered himself to be a questioner: "so much of my identity is of someone who questions authority and that is an incredible responsibility." Although, Luke is being true to his conscience (a clear sign of moral identity verification), he is wrestling with the strain that full-time antiwar activism places on his relationships, time and energy.

CONCLUSIONS

The three stories in this chapter illustrate how the veterans in the combat catalyst group experienced an identity change process that was both emotionally difficult and socially turbulent. Perhaps this is due to the fact that their moral identity disruption often included witnessing acts by comrades that transgressed their deeply held moral beliefs taking it to the level of moral injury. These stories typify the identity change process of the other veterans in this group as occurring during periods of combat. Each vividly recalled times in which their moral identity standards were in direct conflict with the action they were either performing or observing in battle. The combat experience initiated an identity standard change that demanded years for full "processing." Indeed, the pathways to antiwar identity verification often solidified years post-combat, especially when untreated PTSD symptoms complicated the process of deep reflection and study. But whether identity verification took years or decades, the Combat Catalyst group adopted a a antiwar moral identity that dramatically impacted their lower level group and role identities.

Table 3.1. Summary of moral identity change of one combat catalyst group member

Catalyst Group	Moral Identity Standard at 18 years	Behavior at 20 Years in Military	Identity Disruption	New Moral Identity Standard	New Behavior to Reach Identity Verification
Combat Edward, 60 years	I have an obligation to make the world a better place, solve social problems, reach out & protect others. Regarding war: It takes a strong Army to guarantee peace. #3*	Joined Army & served in Vietnam. We killed, raped, & burned villages but I didn't know if war was a necessary evil yet.	Everything changed when I saw combat—it was horrible. It was obvious that this would not lead to peace. I went in one person & came out another. After VN, I built a steel closet of silence about my experience in the war.	I am an antiwar activist working to abolish all war. Regarding War: it is never appropriate. You can not simultaneously prepare for war and peace. War is not a path to peace. #8*	I organize and empower people for social change. I am systematically working through the courts to stop antiwar protesters from being arrested and arrest those who do war crimes. I am informed, knowledgeable and a good talker.

* Numbers refer to the veteran's position on the militarism to pacifism scale.

In comparison to the other catalyst groups as discussed in subsequent chapters, these veterans described extreme turmoil from the identity non-verification experienced in combat. While some of these veterans still struggle with symptoms of PTSD, activism played a key role in both identity verification and "healing" as defined by the veterans. Even among those that continue to struggle with PTSD, such as Jake and Bob, signs of identity verification are present.

Chapter Four

The Betrayal Catalyst of Identity Change

> When Daniel Ellsberg leaked the Pentagon Papers, this was my epiphany. I recall sitting on the pier in San Francisco thinking the hippies were right. I realized the government lied to us. I felt raped and screwed and could never trust the bastards again. (Kent)

Like the combat catalyst, the second catalyst of moral identity change was dramatic and painful . . . betrayal. The betrayal catalyst group includes 19 percent of the veterans ($n = 22$). The source of moral identity disruption for this group began with a profound sense of betrayal by the U.S. government, the military, or a particular U.S. leader. In this context, "betrayal" is viewed as an intentional deception, lie or harm carried out by an individual or group that was trusted to "do the right thing."

This profound sense of betrayal disrupted the veteran's patriotic pro-war moral identity, causing them to seek new moral identity standards regarding patriotism and/or the appropriate use of war. When these veterans entered the military around age 18, their self-described patriotic pro-war identity was based on the belief in the righteousness of their cause. Many describe their belief in the moral superiority of the U.S. government, the high ethical standards of U.S. leaders, and the altruistic motives of U.S. interventions in other countries. When these veterans encountered conflicting sources of information that they trusted and/or could not refute, they experienced a sense of betrayal that was both emotional and visceral. It was as if the breach of trust had assaulted their body, mind, and/or spirit. Applying Identity Theory to this experience, we call these assaults a disruption in the moral identity. Below are a few illustrations of the assault.

John encountered evidence of wrongdoing by the U.S. government. This Coast Guard veteran from the Vietnam era became a whistleblower in 1994 after learning that the U.S. Agricultural Department was involved in a cover-up related to Gulf War Syndrome. We find in his story a clear sense of moral responsibility to tell the truth about his scientific research on nerve gas despite the fact that his superior demanded that he halt his experiments. We suspect that this chemist's moral identity standard was set quite high due to the fact that he risked pursuing the banned research and initiated contact with a U.S. Senator who might be able to act on the veteran's findings regarding the mysterious set of symptoms found in Gulf War veterans that became known as "Gulf War Syndrome."

> I had been involved with laboratory research on nerve gas for the U.S. Agricultural Department. . . . In 1993, I discovered that Gulf War vets had been exposed to bug repellent in Iraq and bug repellent makes nerve gas more toxic. . . . This information helped to establish what is now known as "Gulf War Syndrome." I began to pursue this research on my own and my boss at the Agricultural Department told me to stop. . . . I decided to call Senator Rockefeller and was invited to testify before the Senate Veterans Affairs Committee in Washington, DC [1994]. . . . I felt morally obligated to pass on what I was finding. Soon after that, I lost my job. . . . When Bush began beating the drums of war in 2002, I realized that he was lying and I began attending protests. (John)

Some veterans felt betrayed post service by new revelations about the war in which they served. One Vietnam War soldier discovered that "the U.S. was bombing in Laos before the Gulf of Tonkin incident and I realized that the entire Vietnam War was a lie!" In this instance, it is important to note that the U.S. military used the Gulf of Tonkin incident in 1964 as justification to escalate U.S. military involvement in the Vietnam War although years later, U.S. Secretary of State McNamara admitted that the incident did not happen as originally claimed. This represents a profound disruption of the historical narrative that the veteran had adopted to justify U.S. involvement and escalation of the war. He concluded that if the U.S. had lied about this incident, they could have lied about others. His actions in the war, he reasoned, had cost precious lives of both U.S. soldiers and innocent civilians. Thus the revelation of lying at the highest levels of the U.S. military was an insult to his moral justification of the war.

Another veteran recalls that "while in Vietnam, I got in a conversation with a Vietnamese woman who was completing her doctoral dissertation and spoke English. I saw her as a human being! It ripped the veil of ignorance away and I felt ashamed." This Vietnam vet had adopted the label for all Vietnamese as ignorant "Gooks" who couldn't be trusted. His conversation with an intelligent and articulate Vietnamese woman forced him to reconsider one of his moral foundations for the war.

Decades later, a female Army Intelligence officer serving since 2001 discovered "our intelligence division kills more people than our infantry . . . and my colleagues would say these things and be proud!" In this instance, she realized that her moral identity standard for killing differed significantly from many in the military intelligence division that she served. It appears as if she felt guilty of the morally reprehensible act of killing civilians by association.

By contrast, some in the betrayal catalyst group experienced a moral disruption 20 years post military. These disruptions included the following:

• Realizing that there were no weapons of mass destruction in Iraq in 2003, which had been a primary justification for the U.S. invasion: "Bush fuckin lied to us!"
• Reading about "classified information that prior to the end of the Cold War in 1989 Russia was "in the stone age . . . we lived a lie."

Whether or not the betrayal experience occurred during one's service, these veterans sought to resolve the disruption by seeking moral identity verification. Most of them eventually found their way to an antiwar position based primarily on Just War criteria. Sixty-four percent of the group identified the eight Just War criteria (position 4 on the militarism/pacifism scale of 1–8 in appendix C) for their current moral stance on war, often adding, war must only be fought defending an invasion on U.S. soil rather than threats from abroad. Unlike the pacifists (positions 5, 6, and 7 on the militarism/pacifism scale in appendix C), who opposed all wars as contrary to a dignity of life ethic, the betrayal catalyst group often supported the U.S. war in Afghanistan but not in Iraq. Or, they believed in position 8 on the militarism/pacifism scale, that there are clear nonviolent responses to the aggression from other nations without resort to the violence of war. As a result, many in the betrayal catalyst group became outspoken anti-Iraq War activists, thus verifying their new moral identity with their actions.

BETRAYAL CATALYST GROUP CHARACTERISTICS

The betrayal catalyst group differ in a number of areas from the other catalyst groups. It included the largest percentage of women (23 percent; $n = 5$), the largest group of minorities (14 percent; $n = 3$), the largest percentage of career military (18 percent; $n = 4$) and the largest total number of Bachelor's and Graduate Degrees (82 percent; $n = 18$). This highly educated group of men and women became convinced of their betrayal by studying facts, figures, and history beyond what they considered the "indoctrination" or "lies" from U.S. government sources. They sought to develop their critical thinking ability so as not to be caught off guard again.

Other characteristics of the Betrayal catalyst group include: 50 percent (*n* = 11) served during a time of war but only 36 percent (*n* = 8) served in combat theaters. This compares to the combat catalyst group with 58 percent serving in combat. As a result primarily of combat, 36 percent (*n* = 8) had a PTSD diagnosis from the Veterans Administration. The Betrayal group ranged in age from 25 to 86 and served in World War II, the Korean War, the Vietnam War, the Persian Gulf War, and the Iraq War.

While 36 percent of the betrayal catalyst group experienced combat, battle itself was not the event that triggered the pro-war identity disruption. Instead, it was the raw experience of betrayal by the U.S. government they loved or a leader they trusted that led them to feel "raped, bitter, outraged, or ashamed." They usually described their response on a visceral rather than an intellectual level, as illustrated by Sam's story.

Sam's Pathway to Antiwar Activism

Sam's childhood began in inner-city Pittsburgh in the 1940s with a Jewish father and a Catholic mom. He respected his father who "challenged him to think and to work hard" in the family's restaurant. They talked politics, were liberal Democrats, middle class and believed U.S. "leaders were honorable and trustworthy." John Wayne movies served as the male role model.

Sam's journey to antiwar activism began with letters from trusted friends and former Army buddies serving in Vietnam. His journey to oppose war continued while in college as he attempted to fact check what he was hearing from Vietnam and from "watching the Civil Rights Movement" unfold on television in the 1960s. When interviewed in 2008 at age 63, Sam was a retired lawyer who was highly active with Veterans for Peace in opposing the Iraq War:

> I enlisted in the Army from 1963 to 1966 and served in the United States. I was a damn good soldier but wanted out after three years. . . . I worked and then went to college. In 1967, a spark came from an October letter from a veteran. The letter said that everyone in Vietnam hated us. I began to study the situation in the library. [I read] the historical information about the French in Vietnam and the U.S. oppression. I was shocked, angry and confused to learn about the U.S. oppression. I felt like I was psychologically raped. It shook me to my bones. I was out of control. . . . I felt I was enlightened, not rebellious. I trusted the literature because it "jived" with my buddies from Vietnam. There was a cross-section of Republicans and Democrats saying the same thing about events in Vietnam. . . . My friends in the military were victims and I had an empathetic conscience and felt I had abandoned them. I was very emotional

and withdrawn. . . . I also read [about Vietnam] from Noam Chomsky [an academic from MIT who spoke out against the war].

This new information in 1967 created the initial disruption in Sam's moral pro-war identity but did not result in antiwar activism. He graduated from college and then law school, married and divorced and became heavily involved in his law practice as well as with the community. Sam did not become an antiwar activist until 1987. He connected with other veterans who were concerned about U.S. preparations to enter another war, this time in the Persian Gulf.

Why did Sam's antiwar activism take decades to develop? Identity Theory might explain this lapse of two decades as due to changes in the political climate and Sam's social contacts. The morality of war regained salience with the build up to the Persian Gulf War and as he connected with other antiwar veterans. In addition, his moral pro-war identity was disrupted later in life when he had developed a strong community service ethic. This new ethic required him to speak out when he felt the nation was being led astray as it had been in Vietnam. His later connection with Veterans for Peace represents the period when he is able to construct a new collective antiwar activist identity as a veteran and weave this into his identity as a community servant:

> In 1987, I was in the Unitarian church and a veteran came up to me. He said I'd be interested in Veterans for Peace [VFP]. . . . In the early 1990s, I was an election observer in El Salvador. [Upon return], I flew to Maine to meet the leaders of VFP. I became a board member and soon President. The VFP went to Croatia [during the war there] and brought kids back who needed medical care. This turned the Pittsburgh [traditional pro-war] veterans around—they hated me.
>
> [Later]I began to work with traditional veterans on local war monuments. I recommended a monument to the veterans with kids playing and they went with it. I [told them] I felt our decision to go to war should be based on how it would impact our kids.

Neither Sam's journey to antiwar activism or the activism itself were easy. He spoke of multiple sacrifices, besides much opposition from his law partner, friends, acquaintances, and family. This opposition from significant others demonstrates the salience of his new moral identity, since he had to withstand input that challenged his position and behaviors against the 1991 Persian Gulf War. This quote also demonstrates the important role the VFP collective identity served in countering the significant opposition he was feeling:

> In the late 1980s, I became an activist with the VFP and radical. It was a perfect outlet and I loved the conventions and the conversations. Pittsburgh

[his home at the time] was pretty conservative, with strong unions, and they would beat up antiwar demonstrators. . . . In 1990, my law partner said that the bad press from my position on the Gulf War was bad for practice. I was suing the government and Senator Rick Santorum [PA]. The public resisted but I thought they were ignorant and I didn't care what they said to me. The secular epiphany [in 1967] about what was going on in Vietnam had shaken me to my bones.

The fact that Sam reflects back to his original moral identity disruption from 1967 to explain his 1990s activism attests to its power. Knowing that governments use "indoctrination" in order to justify their actions in war caused Sam to develop his identity as a critical thinker who questions everything. In addition, he now had the support of a moral community of veterans that he trusted, VFP. This collective identity would have aided his moral identity verification despite the fact that many in his community, including traditional veterans, resented his opposition to the Gulf War:

[Doing this work] is a heavy fuckin' burden. I share this burden with my buddies in VFP. Ignorance is bliss. . . . The horror of what the U.S. does overseas makes me ashamed and depressed. The trauma of wars are orchestrated by small groups of powerful people.

[To do this work] I gave up Camelot! I gave up a good time. I wouldn't change it though . . . as it gives me meaning and purpose.

Later, in his 2013 interview, Sam described feeling compelled to speak out against the Iraq War. "I am now teaching a course in critical thinking for high school students. There are a lot of people who are asleep. I did a bus tour last fall (2012) to military bases and gave information (on the Iraq War) to GIs."

Although Sam's activism has been meaningful for him, the behavioral demands of his new moral identity are challenging. These demands impact actions across a number of situations controlled by lower level identities (Burke & Stets, 2009). Moral identities thus have wide influence to either change the behavior of lower level identities or activate identity standard changes. As with many other veterans, Sam had a moral identity change (from pro to antiwar activist) that transformed other important identities in Sam's life. At age18, Sam describes himself as a "fisherman & hunter, a grandson, a hard worker in the family restaurant, a loner, an independent thinker who spoke the truth to adults, and as open to all kinds of people." As a male, "my image was John Wayne, the protector and all that crap."

This description contrasts sharply with his primary identities today. Sam states, "I am kind and try to help others. I'm a teacher of critical thinking; an activist/progressive/radical . . . being a good friend." This identity standard for a "good friend" requires "building community with people around you."

Although raised by traditional Democrats, Sam now crosses many political boundaries to demonstrate the importance of caring deeply about other's needs—even members of the Klu Klux Klan:

> Today, my hero is Martin Luther King Jr. I have represented the oppressed in my law practice and I have friends in many of those areas. I had contact with Klan members in Crawford County and they asked me to be their leader. They liked my progressive views. I helped them tackle problems with health care and childcare.

Sam took pride in his ability to relate with all kinds of people and not feel threatened by those who hold very different positions on politics, war, and human rights such as the KKK. However, he also referred to his antiwar activism as "a heavy fuckin' burden." He maintained his moral identity by explaining the differences between himself and pro-war Americans as:

> Well, they're all individual stories and I don't think you can characterize them all as being on the same intellectual level. In some of them, there may be denial because it goes against the way America is supposed to be. When they tell me if I don't like it [U.S. policy on war], I should leave, I say but people like Washington and Jefferson didn't like it either and they stayed and went to war to make it better. Part of the people know they're doing terrible things . . . and there are people who just don't want to know. Ignorance is bliss.

Max's Pathway to Antiwar Activism

At the time of the interview, Max was a 60 year old retired child welfare worker who served in the Army in Korea from 1966 to 1969. He joined the Army believing in the morality of the U.S. in its decisions to engage in defensive wars. The catalyst for disrupting his younger pro-war identity was a sense of betrayal during his college education, when he realized that politicians were lying to the American people:

> I thought war was an appropriate use of force to protect our country and kin. Military service was an honorable way to serve. . . . I was 18 years old and wasn't thinking much. Today, I see war as a failed option. Diplomacy, negotiation and defense of the homeland are the only appropriate uses today . . . but I'm not a pacifist.

Max's admission that he "wasn't thinking much" at age 18, is common among our interviewees when asked on their views of the appropriate use of war when joining the military. His comments suggest that his moral identity standards at this time were based on following the rules of those in authority including our government and whoever his group defined as "the good guys." Obedience to authority and external rules rather than thinking for oneself using moral principles would be typical for an 18 year old stage of moral development (Kohlberg):

> I enlisted in the U.S. Army from 1966 to 1969. The Army trained us to suppress all thinking and feeling. The regimentation of the Army didn't work for me; it caused questions . . . I served in Texas, New Jersey, Washington and then 13 months in the Korean demilitarized zone. We had some active fire with border disputes that was very stressful and we lost men. . . . The Army trained me to kill and not think.

Later we see early signs of moral identity standard disruption while serving both in the U.S. and abroad. Thrust into leadership at an early age and losing friends in combat made Max question the Korean War and helped him to develop a strong camaraderie and loyalty to his unit. This was not enough though to disrupt his moral identity and move him to seek alternatives.

> I started as an 18 year old in the wild west with alcohol and women. By 19, I was a leader with seven people in my unit. I cared only to get them home and came home a seasoned warrior. My service in the Army and Korea and losing buddies in the rice paddies greatly affected me.

While "the regimentation of the Army . . . caused questions," the dramatic sense of betrayal occurred only when he began to "think seriously" in college. Max traced his identity disruption to seeing that our leaders "lied to us . . . these fuckers lie to defend the interests of the U.S.":

> I married at 20 and had a son. I went to college at age 21 . . . and studied politics, economics and sociology because of the GI bill. I thrived with all A's. College changed me. I had my first serious thought at age 21 when I got out of the Army. I realized that the people who led our country lied to us to defend the interests of the U.S. . . . so I will never support the country because its politicians have to lie: These fuckers lie. I will never fight again for the country for this reason.

This feeling of betrayal impelled him to join the antiwar movement and provide leadership during the early 1970s in California. The support of the antiwar movement and his college classes helped to examine historical facts and form his new antiwar identity and to verify the new identity standards that required standing up for "what you believe in" rather than what the government told him was right:

> I joined the antiwar movement during college. I was welcomed in [as a veteran]. In 1970 I was active with the movement and traveled all over California for protests. My parents instilled a strong sense of standing for what is right and what you believe in. I realized I had been lied to by the government after the war. I felt betrayed.

Like other veterans, Max faced major opposition and non-verification to his antiwar activism but still felt driven to continue. He describes two motivating forces below: his guilt and his Catholic moral conscience to do "what's right and push back evil." This demonstrates the power of the negative emotions of guilt and shame resulting from identity disruption to stimulate changes in behavior.

Another inspiration was the 1960s liberation movements, which supported his activism and verified his new moral identity. This verification and camaraderie gave him the strength to persist despite major opposition and even threats against his life. This is congruent with findings that faithfulness to the moral identity provides the motivation to act (Blasi 1984):

> We [members of the antiwar movement] did feel like we were going nuts at times. I was working, attending college and had a wife and two kids. I was constantly threatened by the police. The guilt from what you did as a soldier was overwhelming. You turned into a killer; instead of helping old ladies across the street, we would kill them! My strength came from being a good Catholic boy. I am responsible for what's right to push back evil. I respected Jane Fonda. I was supported by the Antiwar Movement, the Southern California movements like Caesar Chavez and the Migrant Workers Movement.

The role of a strong collective identity from the antiwar movement in California and other rights movements appears to provide a great deal of social and emotional support. In addition, they provide identity verification to counter all the opposition Max faced from the U.S. government and public in his protest work:

> We [Vietnam Veterans against the War] provided support to returning veterans. We held and listened to their stories. It made me a man. My heroes were the guys I organized with. They gave up everything to stop the war. We were physically and emotionally attacked by U.S. politicians. They refused to take responsibility for the problems. At protests, Law Enforcement would attack you and rough you up. The traditional veterans groups are pussies, suck it ups, and commies. [Later] we made a blood oath that we would never allow this to happen to the Iraq veterans.

In addition to his fierce loyalty to antiwar veterans, Max expressed moral outrage due to law enforcement aggression against protesters as well as betrayal from the politicians' and "traditional veterans." His leadership in the antiwar movement drove him to continue his activism, start a career in Child Welfare, and advocate for the veterans of subsequent wars. Max eventually redefined his patriotic American identity standards to include opposing unjust wars and advocating for veterans:

I joined the Vietnam Veterans against the War and was armed but nonviolent I worked with Barry Romeo to start the Southern California chapters of VVAW. . . . He's still active in leadership. I formed rap groups for veterans. I was very active post Vietnam and today with Winter Soldier [documenting war crimes in testimonials from veterans]. . . . The core group over the years kept it going in low member periods. I fought for PTSD and Agent Orange treatment . . . I never gave up patriotism. We did this work because of our patriotism. After 9/11, I worked but failed to stop the wars in Afghanistan and Iraq. I feel so guilty about that [crying]. . . . I continue my involvement though because it carries with you the rest of a lifetime. I have long term damage. I hate chicken fuckers who don't even know war but promote it. They cause you to shit your pants. These young kids today are my family—the Iraq veterans. Because of this, the politicians have hurt my family and can't be forgiven. I am involved in making Winter Soldier II. I share it with high schoolers and it radicalizes them. . . . I feel so blessed today.

Despite his nuclear and extended families' opposition to his activism and their non-verification of his antiwar identity, Max remains strongly motivated to continue his work He valued his wife and children, but the demands of his antiwar moral identity seemed to trump his other roles such as husband and father. Max eventually found a career that verified the requirements of his moral identity standards that require him to protect his family who he identifies as today's Iraq veterans:

I gave up time with my family to do the organization. It did not hurt my career. My family relationships were pretty strained though. . . . My brother was involved with the CIA for his entire career and got a call about me.

As indicated by this narrative, the behavioral demands of the moral identity can impact actions across a number of situations controlled by lower level identities (Burke & Stets, 2009). Moral identities thus have wide influence to either change the behavior of lower level identities or activate identity standard changes. These significant changes in Max's lower level identities shifted from ages 18 to 65 because of his moral stand against war. At age 18, he characterized himself as a "practicing Catholic, an infantry soldier and warrior, a caring friend, and a sexual man with a strong work ethic." By contrast, at age 65 he considered his primary identities to be a loving and caring spouse, father, and grandpa. Also, he identified himself as a world traveler who was only limited by health issues caused by drug and alcohol abuse following his war experience. He identified as an activist who had turned his work over to the young, but he continued "to work against oppression, war and U.S. imperialism yet today." Max was "not religious today but I have a profound sense of spirituality." His politics drove him to support candidates such as Ralph Nader, who he explains were more progressive than the Democratic establishment.

His worldview, including the early formation of his moral identity, was influenced by his parents' modeling and Catholic schooling. By following his moral conscience, he had found his way to contentment and full identity verification. He could now speak with pride about his life's commitments and accomplishments:

> There was no one moment but it was the role models I had in my parents that clearly formed how I approached the world. Neither would give an inch on something they believed in. My heroes today are Malcolm X, Cesar Chavez, and Nelson Mandela.
>
> Today, I am an older man that is proud of my life history and kids. I am in love with life, enjoy my grandkids and I want everyone to experience this. . . . Every part of my life is congruent. My friends are running for political office. They are helping the profession. I have taken public service as a vocation. I do advocacy for abused adults and child welfare and am with like-minded people. I reject electoral politics as an avenue for change but I do vote I have achieved the American dream in my family and career.

Rob's Pathway to Antiwar Activism

In contrast to Max's story, the story of Rob's shift to antiwar activism took several years to develop. Rob enlisted in the Navy in 1961 "to avoid the draft." He served outside Japan for three years and on a patrol boat in Vietnam for one year seeing some combat. When enlisting, Rob believed that "what the U.S. was doing around the world was correct." By 2007, he was "convinced that "we [the U.S.] are wrong in Iraq" and U.S. intervention abroad must meet the full Just War criteria.

Following his discharge from the Navy in 1970, he taught in ROTC (Reserve Officer Training Corps) programs and at the U.S. Naval Academy thus solidifying his military collective identity. From 1984 to 1996, he worked as an electrical engineer in the defense industry serving McDonnell Douglas. It was not until 1989, that he experienced the outrage of being lied to by U.S. politicians about the Cold War. This disruption in his moral identity standard for truth initiated further questions and disruptions. The process of behavior change took place later when he became a whistleblower within the defense industry:

> I discovered my doubt in the early 1990s after the Berlin Wall came down and we [at McDonnell Douglas] were dealing with classified information so we could tailor missiles to meet problems and eliminate threats. When Russia opened up, I realized that rural Russia was in the Stone Age, that Russia was never a threat [to the U.S.]. The Cold War threat was a lie! We lived a lie! The propaganda was fed by our own government! Businesses and politicians benefited from the Cold War. [Following the Cold War], McDonnell Douglas had no one to sell its products to . . . like the Harpoon Missile. When I spoke out

about the lie, I was called a naysayer by the higher ups, the people who had never been in the military and those in junior positions from military backgrounds.

Through speaking out about the lie of the Cold War, he attempted to change his colleagues behavior. He was, by sharing this information with his engineering colleagues in the defense industry, attempting to build organized opposition and change the system that benefited from "the lies." When he was ignored and marginalized, he decided to take additional steps to verify his high moral identity standards for truth-telling. As we have seen in other veterans, faithfulness to his moral identity provided the motivation to act in ways that risk career and reputation (Blasi, 1984): "The change (in my thinking) was more about the reality of the U.S. foreign policy and the involvement of the defense industry. From 1991 to 1992, the opening up of the former Soviet Union. made me realize that the U.S. defense budget would be in the toilet."

Rob eventually decided to sacrifice his career and took other risks to be a truth teller about U.S. foreign policy, including the complicity of the defense industry in trumping up the threat of the former Soviet Union. These are good examples of attempting to change his behavior in order to affirm his strong moral and patriotic identities:

> I would voice my opinion [at McDonnell Douglas] and would be booed or hissed and taken off the stage. I'm not a yes man. Others who knew couldn't come forward. It was strangely silent. . . . I felt numb and didn't care. [Once I spoke out], the company began to give me unsatisfactory job evaluations after years of positive ones. I was in strategic planning and one employee told me they were cooking books at McDonnell Douglas. I needed to leave . . . so in 1996, due to seeing bad behavior [within the organization], I was able to get a bonus with retirement.

Although Bob often felt isolated and punished for voicing his concerns, here we find affirmation from another employee that gives him strength to leave. Gathering and studying the evidence and thinking strategically about best options for holding his former employer to accountability for their lies, he not only retired early but planned to use the legal system to call Mcdonnell Douglas to account before the law: "Then I filed a class action suit against McDonnell Douglas. I did the class action suit due to spite and a sense of justice. Yes, a few agreed at McDonnell Douglas. . . . I went to settlement out of court [in exchange for silence] and everyone got $1,500. It was worth $8.5 million but I settled for less to avoid more time in court."

Rob's story is especially interesting because it does not appear that he found a new collective identity or social movement organization for support and identity verification until after his lawsuit was complete. Now, he claims an affiliation with Veterans for Peace in order to defend the U.S. constitution: "I am not a crusader. If others ask, I tell them. [Now in 2007] I am a part of Veterans for Peace and I have a bumper sticker to impeach Bush. The U.S. is better than invading other people for no reason. The American republic and the Constitution are smeared by the current [Iraq] War."

Rob's "clean conscience" was more important than the sacrifices he made and the losses he experienced. His pathway to antiwar activism cost him job promotion, professional friendships, and the expense of lodging a class action suit against the major defense contractor McDonnell Douglas. He concluded that it had all been worth it. His assertion, then, clearly indicated that his antiwar activism and whistleblowing had given him the gift of moral identity verification today: "I feel good about the class action suit. I have had a good life. I have a clean conscience. I am proud of what I've done. I gave up advancement perhaps and there are people I don't talk to anymore but . . . I have gained a sense of doing the right thing."

Ann's Pathway to Antiwar Activism

Rob and Max spent a relatively short time in the military, but Ann devoted decades of her life to military and other U.S. public service. Ann was interviewed in 2009, at the age of 62. In 2003, she resigned from the U.S. Diplomatic Corps to voice her dissent against U.S. entry into the Iraq War. She served in either the Army or Reserves for 29 years and worked as a diplomat in Afghanistan, Central America, Africa and Asia. Beginning her army career during the Vietnam War, she believed that: "the people in charge will do the right thing." As a teen growing up in small town Arkansas, her self-described primary identities were: studious, intelligent and college bound, athletic and a small town girl who wanted to get out and see the rest of the world. She joined the Army when a recruiter visited her university and promised her the opportunity to travel. At this point in her life, enlisting seemed to be "a no brainer."

For 29 years, the Army served multiple purposes as Ann moved in and out of active duty, graduate school, and the reserves. Significant identity changes occurred through these years but these did not lead to antiwar activism until 2003. In 2009, when interviewed, she described her primary identity as an activist who encourages people to challenge the government's actions and information given to its citizens. In addition, she claimed the identity of organizer who forms coalitions of groups to challenge global injustices such as the Palestinians' situation in the Gaza Strip and the embargo against Cuba. Despite resigning from the U.S. Diplomatic Corps, Ann still identified as a diplomat who could negotiate with all kinds of people and who chose her words very carefully.

The transformation from naïve small town girl to professional diplomat and global antiwar activist occurred gradually. She spent years working abroad, besides obtaining a law degree and a master's degree in National Security Affairs from the U.S. Naval War College. Despite this immersion in the military milieu, she reached a breaking point in 2001 following the 9/11 terrorist attacks on the U.S. World Trade Center. In her 2008 book, *Dissent: Voices of Conscience*, retired Colonel Ann Wright and co-author Susan Dixon write:

> In December 2001, I volunteered to be part of the team that reopened the U.S. Embassy in Afghanistan. A month later, a few of us went to Bagram Air Base in Kabul to wish Afghanistan's interim leader, Hamid Karzai, good luck as he left for Washington to attend the State of the Union address. . . . Three days later, I was . . . watching President Bush's State of the Union address on a TV. . . . We were awaiting news of the President's plans for Afghanistan, but after he said a few words about Afghanistan, he began talking about Iran, Iraq, and North Korea, calling them the "Axis of Evil." The TV cameras focused on Hamid Karzai, in the gallery, and I could almost see him wince.

Ann agreed with many Americans as well as nations that there must be a response to the 9/11 attacks and she was supportive of targeting al Qaeda in Afghanistan. Her questions set in as she continued her work in Afghanistan but the U.S. failed to "clear out the Taliban, capture al Qaeda and help the Afghan people rebuild their country." Ann expressed concern as President Bush turned his attention to the "Axis of Evil" nations, especially Iraq, rather than provide military support to expand U.S. presence and begin economic development in Afghanistan. She decided to bide her time, though, since she was not required at this point to publicly support the possible U.S. invasion of Iraq.

However, she could no longer wait it out in 2002 as the Bush administration prepared for war in Iraq. Working in a diplomatic position, she faced a moral identity crisis because her diplomatic role identity required supporting President Bush's intention to bomb Iraq although she considered bombing to be "fundamentally dangerous and morally wrong."

This conflict between her moral identity and her diplomatic role identity was intensified by her group identity as a lawyer. She had enough expertise on the laws of warfare to know that an unprovoked war with Iraq would meet the requirements of a war crime. As the Identity Model suggests, at this stage of conflict, individuals attempt to change the situation by changing a behavior first and if this is unsuccessful, changing their identity standard.

After careful consideration, she rejected the Bush administration's claims that Iraq presented an imminent danger due to weapons of mass destruction. Her knowledge of U.S. history and policy in Iraq since the Persian Gulf War informed her thinking and identity as an experienced U.S. diplomat. While not expressing outrage at the government's betrayal like many veterans, she stated the logic of why the Bush Administration policy would meet the criteria of a war crime:

> I felt the claim that America and the world were in imminent danger from Iraq's weapons of mass destruction [WMD] was misleading. . . . During the decade following the first Gulf War, the United States and our allies flew 400,000 missions over two no-fly zones, taking photos the whole time. If there had been WMD in Iraq, we would have seen evidence of it, as would the UN weapons inspectors, many of whom were U.S. intelligence officials.

The above quote, then, shows Ann weighing her options and responsibilities to her diplomatic role identity versus her moral identity and her lawyer group identity. She finally realized that her only option of being "true to my conscience" was to resign. Again we find evidence of faithfulness to the moral identity driving the motivation to act even when it means losing a cherished job, friendships and reputation (Blasi, 1984).

> On March 19, 2003, the day before the bombing began, I cabled my letter of resignation to Secretary of State Colin Powell. The moment I did, I felt a huge weight lift from my shoulders. I was taking a stand, joining two other American diplomats who had already resigned in protest. In the days that followed, I received nearly 400 emails from State Department colleagues saying, in effect, we're sad you are not going to be with us, but we're proud of the three of you who resigned, because we think going to war in Iraq will have terrible consequences.

Ann, then, found widespread verification for her decision to resign and to publicly oppose the invasion of Iraq. As a result of her decision, she "felt a huge weight lift from my shoulders." As Identity Theory suggests, non-verification of our identities results in a series of negative emotions from guilt to shame. These powerful emotions can lead to physical symptoms of distress. Ann reported having symptoms of a stroke or heart attack prior to sending the Cable of Dissent.

Following the resignation, Ann shared her actions and perspectives widely starting with the *Foreign Service Journal*. She accepted invitations to speak at universities, peace conferences, and churches around the world. In 2009, she was speaking once or twice a week on issues of war, torture, and accountability.

Ann's book cowritten with Dixon about U.S. and other nation's government insiders speaking out against the war in Iraq, *Dissent: Voices of Conscience* was published in 2008. The book describes people who altered their behavior by dissenting and resigning their positions to verify their high moral identity standards as described by Identity Theory.

Table 4.1. Summary of moral identity change for one betrayal catalyst group member

Catalyst Group	Moral Identity Standard at 18 Years	Behavior at 20 Years in Military	Identity Disruption	New Moral Identity Standard	New Behavior to Reach Identity Verification
Betrayal Sam, 63 years	Independent thinker spoke truth to others & questioned adults. Open & interested in diverse others; didn't discriminate based on race, sex or religion. Regarding War: Trust U.S. leaders when they call us to war. War is honorable. #1*	Enlisted in Army & served stateside 1963–1966. Decided not to reenlist & go to Vietnam with my buddies. Decided to go to college & then to study law.	1966, got letters from my friends in Vietnam. I was angry when I learned the truth about what was going on there. They said everyone in Vietnam hates us. I studied the situation. I was shocked, angry & confused. I felt psychologically raped. It shook me to my bones.	Progressive Activist. Teacher of Critical Thinking. Kind to others all the time. Regarding War: Strict Just War Theory. War is only appropriate in self-defense on U.S. soil. #4*	In 1990s I became board member & then President of Veterans for Peace with first Iraq War. I spend time informing myself on the issues & then act on my convictions through Vets for Peace, teaching in high school & pro bono legal work. I'm also help bring resource people for worker owned businesses in town.

* Numbers refer to the veteran's position on the militarism to pacifism scale.

Like the other veterans in this study, Ann also chose to redefine what it is to be a patriotic American. This important identity now holds standards or criteria that require "dissent" even at the risk of losing "everything" for the sake of "real national security."

Finally we see the cascade of changes that occur as a result of Ann's activism against the Iraq War. This resulted from the behavioral demands of the moral identity impacting actions across other situations controlled by lower level identities (Burke & Stets, 2009). Moral identities thus have wide influence to either change the behavior of lower level identities or activate identity standard changes or both. For instance, Ann had to sever ties with her government friends because her "outspoken opposition to Bush would jeopardize them." She then embraced a "whole new set of friends in the peace community." She could finally "speak openly" about her views on all types of political issues. While she "has always voted Democrat" and would continue, she opposed President Obama's continuation of the wars in Iraq and Afghanistan. She considered herself to be not a pacifist but a very careful Just War Theorist.

CONCLUSIONS

The Betrayal catalyst group faced a visceral experience of moral identity disruption due to discovering "lies" from U.S. leaders or the military. Interestingly, these emotional experiences often occurred years after their service in the military. The veterans in this group reported changing their position on a particular war rather than all wars, usually adopting the Just War perspective. Few in this catalyst group seemed to experience moral identity at the level of moral injury although a few expressed "shame" for acts of the U.S. government. Perhaps the decreased evidence of moral injury is because they were more removed from front line combat due to their military branch (Navy, Air Force) or their officer status. Additionally, individuals in this group seemed better able to exit situations that violated their moral identity standard in comparison to individuals in the combat group. This control may have prevented the moral injury we observe among veterans in other catalyst groups.

Through resigning or retiring early and then joining antiwar activist groups such as VFP, these veterans could adopt behaviors that led to moral identity verification. Many of them maintained both a Collective Identity within the military as well as the antiwar veterans group as Just War Theorists. Speaking out against a particular war became part of their moral identity standard of "standing up for what is right." Additionally, there were fewer changes to the lower level of identities of veterans in this group. As evident in the following chapters, the differences between catalyst groups regarding the identity change process are striking.

Chapter Five

The Religious Conviction Catalyst of Identity Change

I came across that Sermon on the Mount . . . don't kill your enemies, love them, you know? And I began to look at the scriptures through a different lens . . . part of the context of that was how the Army trained you and the purpose of the Army . . . I began to realize, it was opposed to the ultimate ends of the kingdom of God. (Tom)

A third distinct catalyst group depicted in the quote above is Religious Conviction. Twenty-four men and women (21 percent of the 114 veterans) met the criteria for this group. Members describe their identity change process as initiated by new religious understandings or experiences that disturbed their moral pro-war identity. These disturbances included:

• New understandings of New Testament Christian biblical scripture about killing and the treatment of enemies;
• The biblical call for and option of nonviolent social change in response to violence and injustice; and
• A profound experience of God, forgiveness or peace.

As noted in the earlier chapters, the Combat and Betrayal Catalyst groups experienced moral identity disruption due to factors related to the military. For the Combat catalyst group, their experience with combat disrupted their moral criteria for treatment of others so profoundly that changing their behavior was not enough to achieve identity verification and thus they eventually redefined their moral identity standards for war and became antiwar activists.

For the Betrayal catalyst group, the disruption in their moral identity originated in a breach of trust by a U.S. political or military leader or in an understanding of U.S. history that was shattered. This new information so disturbed the veteran's belief in the moral superiority and righteousness of the U.S. that they began to critically question many of their foundational beliefs.

By contrast, the Religious Conviction catalyst group experienced a new understanding of their faith while studying within a religious setting, college, or seminary. Often moments of prayer or study exposed them to new meanings of Christian scripture, God, Jesus and war. As these veterans compared these new ideas with their moral identity standard for war and treatment of enemies, they felt such discomfort that they sought new beliefs and behaviors to achieve identity verification. For our purposes, religious conviction is defined as commitment to an organized system of beliefs, ceremonies, and rules for living used to worship a god or group of gods. The primary religious identification in this group is Christian.

Religious (group) identity is related to moral (person) identity as both include standards of caring and fairness and both are a higher level identity than the soldier role identity or Army group identity (Gilligan, 1982; Haidt & Kesebir, 2010; Kohlberg, 1981). When the moral identity standards change, the lower level role and group identities must also change for persons to feel internally consistent or true to one's self (Burke & Stets, 2009). Some veterans who became involved in faith-based groups, then, encountered new standards of compassion and love for all people—even enemies. The veterans' previous role identity standard of a soldier (i.e., being good to comrades and violent with enemies) often clashed with their moral and group identity standards as Christian. During their service, many of these veterans had had little time to consider moral questions from a Christian context because they were surviving from day to day and the military affirms the morality of Just Wars. Not until the veterans returned home from service did they have time to reflect on their beliefs and experiences and realize there was conflict between the identity standards of soldier and Christian.

After enduring moral identity standard disruption, 83 percent ($n = 20$) of the religious conviction group developed a new Pacifist identity: defining all killing as wrong and opposing all wars. The other veterans in this group (17 percent) developed a Just War position, which opposes some but not all wars by using strict criteria (e.g., self-defense) to weigh its necessity.

RELIGIOUS CONVICTION CATALYST GROUP CHARACTERISTICS

Besides the high percentage of pacifists in this group, additional factors make these veterans unique. The Religious Conviction group is dominated by men (96 percent; $n = 23$). They include the smallest number experiencing combat (4 percent; $n = 1$) although 46 percent ($n = 11$) served during a time of war. These veterans hold the second highest percentage of graduate degrees including PhDs, Masters of Divinity, MDs, and Law degrees (59 percent; $n = 14$) behind the Betrayal group.

These veterans also include the highest percentage of official discharge with the "Conscientious Objector" or CO status (14 percent; $n = 3$) although a full 46 percent ($n = 11$) would identify as COs today. Conscientious Objector is an official military designation that signifies that the individual has examined his or her conscience and believes that there is no war that could justify his or her killing of others. A CO application usually results in a period of evaluation and, if granted, an immediate honorable discharge from the military or an early retirement. Because many in this group were exposed to the Conscientious Objector position while in the military or afterwards, 83 percent of the Religious Conviction catalyst group identified with a traditional Pacifist position on war when interviewed. For example, they believed that "Neither the Christian or person of conscience or the nation/state should engage in war under any circumstances because it is contrary to the life and teaching of Jesus or another leader (followed by the person)" (see appendix C).

As opposed to the Combat catalyst group who experienced disruption of their moral identity during war, this group of veterans most often experienced disruption of their identity after leaving the military during a period of reflection and study. This reflective time often occurred within an academic or religious setting. Retroactively, these veterans applied their new beliefs about the appropriate uses of war to their own military experiences. Thus, it appears that religious identity disruption is more of an intellectual than an emotional experience.

In terms of activism in opposition to current wars, this group averaged the lowest involvement of the four catalyst groups. We believe this low rate results from the measurement of activism used in this study, which included involvement in secular groups such as Veterans for Peace, Vietnam Veterans against the War, and Iraq Veterans against the War. The Religious Conviction catalyst group included 10 Mennonites (a traditional pacifist church). While most Mennonites oppose war and participation in war, Mennonite veterans were more likely to focus their activism on church-related groups working on the prevention of war (Mennonite Central Committee, Every Church a Peace Church or Christian Peacemaker Teams) than secular antiwar groups such as Veterans for Peace. They also engaged in what we termed "lifestyle activism." This involved their descriptions of living more simply, involved environmentally sustainable household practices, supporting social justice and human rights efforts and using conflict resolution in relationships.

The pathways to pacifism and antiwar activism among the Religious Conviction catalyst group were diverse. The following three stories of veterans from different periods illustrate how diverse experiences can result in varied insights about peace.

Richard's Pathway to Pacifism and Antiwar Activism

Richard, a career Army Chaplain, described his process of moral identity formation, disruption and change in great detail. He was interviewed in both Phase 1 and 2, at ages 58 and 63. Many of the Religious Conviction catalyst group shared a powerful religious conversion experience in their teens or twenties that laid the foundation for their moral identity, and Richard was no different. He began his religious journey as a born again Baptist in his early twenties. Below is the story of how Richard "gave his life to Christ" in an evangelical church shortly after marriage:

> So I get by on three weeks of church and it was a very evangelical, fundamentalist church and Joe Williams was the pastor, who was a sweet-hearted man. He really preached on conversion experiences and I had the classic evangelical conversion experience in that Southern Baptist church in Tulsa, Oklahoma: I walked down the aisle and gave my life to Christ, big tears and the whole nine yards. It was a genuine, . . . it was a genuine conversion experience to where I remember to this day how it literally changed my life when Christ came into my life and I invited him in. And . . . it's been a perpetual change since then. So you know, that church, bless their hearts, they, they taught me the Bible:.. I ended up being the Sunday School teacher to young boys. I went visiting on Tuesday nights with one of the deacons . . . on Tuesday nights became a one-on-one discipleship time as we were in the car going around visiting people.

This conversion experience not only impacted Richard's group identity as a Baptist Christian but his role identity as a Sunday School teacher. He describes the changes as ongoing as his understanding of the bible is later challenged in college then seminary and adult continuing education within the military. Professors and texts studied raise questions that are difficult for him to answer within the fundamentalist framework that can be more literal in interpretation and view the world as good and evil:

> Over the years, some of my fundamentalism began to crack and break through college . . . but also in seminary because the Southern Baptist seminary I went to . . . it was before the . . . fundamentalist takeover of the Southern Baptist convention. So it was more the European form of . . . religious education. And

so . . . all of that began to crack some of that fundamentalist stuff for me . . .
but I was still pretty conservative at the time. . . . I guess I probably still am
but, you know, with a different definition of conservative. So that's how that
all came about.

Later, he joins the Army and is sent as a chaplain to German. The Army
recognizes Richard's intellectual potential and sends him for continuing education in military science that so profoundly disturbs his moral identity standards for right and wrong that he decides he's "not studying war anymore."
He is willing to risk his Army career on this conviction. This is significant as
his salary is now supporting his wife and three children:

And then . . . but that was part of my . . . peace conversion because as I was in
the Army . . . in Germany and they sent me back to Ft. Leavenworth, Kansas to
go through a, a three month long course . . . .basically it was studying . . . how
many bullets does it take to kill X number of men, how many gallons of diesel
fuel does it take per propeller in a tank from here to there. It was the study of
war, war-making and I remember leaving that class. I was, uh, I was a promot-
able captain at the time. I said, "I'm not studying war anymore. I don't care if
it's the end of my career. I'm not doing it. I'll just serve out my time as a
captain and retire or whatever happens but I'm not studying war anymore."

In this case, Richard was rejecting a particular pathway within the Army
that he didn't want to travel but not the Army or war itself. He did not
question his pro-war identity until he studied at the U.S. War College and
"learned how violent the Army could be." Years later, a seminary professor
introduced him to Just War Theory and Christian pacifist perspectives on
war. These two events initiated the disruption in his pro-war moral identity,
then later the disruption of the "Fundamentalist worldview." It was only after
exposure to the Christian pacifist position (a new collective identity) that
Richard was able to reject Fundamentalism fully and construct a holistic
antiwar pacifist identity. This new worldview was grounded in the principles
espoused by Jesus in "The Sermon on the Mount [Matthew Chapters 5–7]."
He concluded that "the kingdom of God is different" from the vision adopted
within his Baptist training:

But what became part of that was my old Baptist training . . . to believe the
Bible. Well, I came across that Sermon on the Mount thing, you know: don't
kill your enemies, love them, you know? And I began to look at the scriptures
through a different lens and . . . I guess part of the context of that was how the
Army trained you and the purpose of the Army was . . . I began to realize, is
really opposed to the ultimate ends of the kingdom of God and how hard
boundaries are established: you're either in or out, you're either with us or not,
enemy or friends, potential person to kill or not. And I came to say, "Well, it
looks to me like the kingdom of God is different."

The next step to solidify his pacifist Christian moral identity came when he realized there were lots of other contemporary Christians who viewed the bible as he now understood God's kingdom and treatment of enemies. He was introduced to Mennonite academics and theologians who were examining scripture and acting on their faith in a way that he had not been exposed to in the fundamentalist Southern Baptist worldview:

> And then what happened, in the Army's foolishness, they sent me to Duke University . . . for a year, in pastoral psychology to get ready to teach at the Catholic school and I ran into contact with Dr. Stanley Hauerwas and he gave me, he pointed me toward *The Politics of Jesus.* That's a dangerous book. And, and I read that and I said, "Oh my God, I'm not the weirdo. There's other people out here who think the same way I do!" And so what . . . uh, *The Politics of Jesus* . . . and being introduced to the other Mennonite world happened at Duke and that really opened up to me a system of Christian thought to think about religion in a different way and I began to understand that, that there was a, a whole new encyclopedia here for me to explore. And so I started reading and reading and reading and the more I read and the more I looked at the scripture for validation for what I was reading I began to say, "Ah! Fundamentalism is a contrived construct, a way of looking at, at the Bible, world and Christianity and I can construct my own worldview here!" And that's, that's kind of what I did. And as a result of that, I said, "What I'm doing, even if I'm a noncombatant, I'm still a Christian witness to the liability and the unacceptability of, uh, warfare." And I did not want to give that witness any longer. I could no longer bear to wear the cross on one collar and my rank on another because in so doing, I was validating the violence through military action. And so, I just said, "I can't do this anymore." And it was a struggle to get there and a real struggle to get there for my mind. But finally we [wife and I] worked through it, it was a real conversion experience! And I left, you know, I got out. I have . . . I don't get any . . . retirement benefits. I am a disabled veteran and so I do get, uh, that type of benefit, you know. But . . . nothing else.

In the above passage, we clearly see Richard's moral identity disruption. The intense contradictions and disruptions he was discovering to his moral worldview caused such contradiction that he could no longer bear to remain in the Army even as a Chaplain and noncombatant. His new understanding of scripture and what Identity Theory terms moral identity standards demanded his withdrawal from military service due to its connection to warfare. He makes the sacrificial decision to retire early and leave the Army without a pension. It is important to note that as he takes the leap of faith out of the Army, he has identified a new group with a collective identity, the Mennonites, that he can fully embrace and where he can receive identity verification.

Analysis of Richard's story suggests that his moral identity change involved multiple stages from disruption to reconstruction to behavior change and finally full moral identity verification only once he has left the military.

The first stage of disruption of his fundamentalist Christian ethics occurred when attending a more "European" Baptist Seminary. We define fundamentalism as a movement in 20th Century Protestant (rather than Catholic) churches that emphasized the literal interpretation of the Bible and the Bible as foundational for the Christian life and teaching (www.merriam-webster.com/dictionary).

The second stage occurred at the War College where he rejected studying the tools for war-making because they conflicted with his concept of building the kingdom of God. During the third stage, he discovered that he was not the only Christian questioning war; in fact, several groups of Christian pacifists agreed with him. He had found other believers who took the Bible seriously but not literally as did many Southern Baptists and understood its demands very differently. This discovery offered him the identity verification he needed to take the next step. Finally, he realized that fundamentalist interpretations of scripture were constructed by humans so he was free to construct his own worldview. He developed his own moral compass based on a Mennonite understanding of scripture. This new view was heavily influenced by pacifist Christian theologians like John Howard Yoder.

Richard's story exemplifies the transformation of the Christian group identity as well as his moral identity from youth through mature adulthood to the point where these two high level identities become mutually verifying. He then sought congruence between the moral and Christian identities with his lower level Army and soldier identities by leaving the Army and becoming a Mennonite Pastor.

We can see this transformation also in Richard's descriptions of his primary identities or characteristics at age 18 through his description of primary identities in adulthood:

> I was a student, not a good student to be honest. I was, um, drinking hard . . . and ran around and dated a lot of girls and so that was the kind of thing that I thought was . . . a man's role at my age, at 18, was to kind of explore those, those type of things. . . . And then of course I, the other piece that I learned from my grandfather, who was a farmer and. . . . You know, he taught me the value of hard work and, uh, a sense of integrity, you know? You had to, if you were a real man, if you said something, you would do it even if it cost you something, you know? . . . And so your word was your bond so those are the types of things that were in the mix when I was 18. Of course, toward the end of that time, a little bit later, that's when I met my wife so I guess there was some transition there . . . in my development that I would say that during that time my identity was primarily focused on having a good time [laughs].

By age 67, he had undergone a full transformation of both his master and lower level identities. However, he saw a clear connection between his earlier moral identity that involved "a sense of integrity, honesty, to tell the truth" and his primary identities that inform his decision-making today:

> I guess my, I think my primary identity is as a child of God, a member of the family of God. That really has changed my focus in life over the years and I think I've grown into that as I've gotten older. So my identity really is there as . . . a beloved person of God. . . . Part of the characteristics that I think came over from that early development on the farm is this sense of integrity . . . and I think that was part of what helped me to become a Christian . . . was the sense that there was . . . a, a need to be conscientious about your actions even though I struggled with that as an 18 year old. . . . But nevertheless you still needed to tell the truth, even when it hurts, and those type of things. I guess, one of the characteristics today is, is that . . . I want to be a genuine person, an honest person . . . a person . . . that is transparent when it's appropriate . . . a gentle person . . . a, a caring person and, and, and a loving person, I guess. . . . That's how I would describe myself.

The centrality of the Christian identity appeared as he reflected on the question, What does it require to be a child of God? The Christian moral identity required more than a set of beliefs for Richard, since he needed to act in accordance with his commitments. Richard's case demonstrates Identity Theory's position that when a moral identity is activated frequently, it becomes more salient over time (Stets & Carter, 2012). Faithfulness to the moral identity then provides the motivation to act (Blasi, 1984). Richard was driven to leave the Army and gained a sense of integrity through pursuing service to others, spiritual disciplines, and spiritual direction. To solidify his new identity, he earned a Masters in Peace Studies and became a Mennonite Pastor:

> Well, it requires a need to be in community with other people, other disciples, uh, of Christ. It requires of me to . . . be a perpetual student or a perpetual learner, especially about things spiritual. . . . It requires me to develop spiritual disciplines and maintain those. . . . Along the way, I have, I took a three year program in spiritual direction and am a member of Spiritual Directors International. Continuing my own spiritual life . . . is important and how to go about that.

One common theme in these veteran's stories was the suffering and sacrifice involved as they developed their new antiwar moral identities. Richard shared some of the sacrifices he has made because of his new identity in answer to the question, Do you ever wish that you hadn't gone through the changes in attitude or identity related to issues of war and peace?

> I do think of that from time to time . . . you know right now I could be retired, drawing four or five thousand dollars a month, you know? If I'd stayed in [the military] . . . you know, if I'd continued to get promoted and all that, which

was my track, that was my trajectory. I was a good chaplain. . . . But I, then I, I catch myself and say, "Oh, get behind me Satan." I feel good about where I am.

Here we see identity verification as Richard describes feeling good about where he is and is able to reconcile regrets about his identity change. Like many of the other veterans in our study Richard describes a sense of peace about his current identity.

Hank's Pathway to Pacifism and Antiwar Activism

In contrast to Richard, Hank enlisted in the Army at age 27 because of the terrorist attacks of 9/11. He believed that "if someone attacks you without provocation, you have the right to turn them into a collection of targets and attack." Hank served both in the U.S. and in Iraq as a mortarman in the Army Airborne Division for 10 months. When interviewed in 2008, he was 36 and living on 70 percent disability from PTSD in combat. He believed that "there is no appropriate use of war; peace is dealing with conflict without violence." Like many others in the Religious Conviction catalyst group, Hank was raised in a Christian household and described a series of significant religious conversion experiences that laid the foundation for his eventual Christian pacifist moral identity. He refers to the "red letters" in the Bible, which are often used to highlight the actual words scholars believe were spoken by Jesus, to describe his first identity disruption:

> Yeah . . . there was a time in Nashville when I was young [18 or 19] and I had just opened up in a Bible to a bunch of red letters and I put my hand on it and I had a . . . a feeling of such forgiveness and love that I, I, it brought me to tears and, and it was, it was, it was just really amazing. When I put my hand on the book, that was probably the most sudden [experience]. I mean that was like lightning striking.

Years later, Hank served as a mortarman "seeing lots of cities being bombed in Iraq along with dead bodies." He did not experience moral identity disruption, though, until home on leave. His pro-war identity was challenged when on leave from Iraq by his "new liberal girlfriend" and later in seeing the movie, *The Passion of the Christ* at age 28. This was a second conversion or identity disruption experience for him:

> I changed when I landed back in the U.S. and it wasn't all shot up like Iraq. We [here] have choices. I had a two week leave to be with my mom in Texas. I went to a party and saw the prettiest girl in the room. She was raised in Peru, but was a U.S. citizen. She was a liberal and revolutionary and politically aware. She debated with me about [the morality] of the Iraq War. We were

attracted to each other and we fell in love . . . but I couldn't understand her
perspective. . . . We stayed together for 10 months.

It is important to note that this conversion occurred during a time of
reflection and rest from the stress of combat that we identify as an important
step in the identity change process of the veterans in our study. In addition,
Hank was receiving non-verification of his pro-war identity from an individual
he loved, respected and debated about the morality of war, his "liberal
girlfriend."

> Then I saw *The Passion of the Christ.* [Afterwards] I was asking myself how
> can I be a Christian and in the Army at the same time? . . . I walk out of there
> and that was like a really big wake up call. . . . That was probably like the nail
> through my coffin of being in the military. . . . Walking out of that movie
> theater was as sudden as however long a movie takes.

While for most veterans placed in the Religious Conviction group, the
disruption is mostly intellectual, for Hank there was an emotional and physical component that demanded his attention. In addition, due to the serious-
ness of his physical response to the identity disruption, he acted immediately
to change the behavioral demands of his role identity standards of "mortarman" and to bring them into line with his new Christian identity standard.

> I went back to Fort Bragg and tried to deny my new feelings but had physical
> symptoms. I went to get checked out for chest pains and they said it was stress.
> So . . . I talked to my Sergeant and told him "I can't pull the trigger anymore."
> He was very understanding because I was a good soldier. . . . I talked to a
> Chaplain and he asked me if I was a Conscientious Objector and I went home
> and googled CO and found tremendous resources. Then, I went to a local
> Peace House and decided to apply for Conscientious Objector status. I was at
> the end of my tour and was honorably discharged 10 months later.

Although some of Hank's statements suggest moral injury including his
admission to being a suicide survivor, he does not seem to be struggling with
moral injury today. This might be explained by his summary of his frontline
experiences in Iraq and the fact that his strong and surprising reaction to
seeing the film, The Passion of Christ, came at the end of his tour when he
decided he couldn't pull the trigger anymore and he began his application for
Conscientious Objection. He was able to justify his and his units abuses
during combat as strategies good soldiers must engage in to protect each
other: "I took a good look at our actions [when I returned] and see abuses by
our soldiers but . . . I didn't feel I could speak up at the time and I needed to
watch out for my guys and needed to make it through my tour."

In other words, Hank was able to act immediately to verify his new
identity standard for Christian that forbade killing. Formerly, in Iraq, when

he was participating in killing, his moral and Christian identity standards permitted killing. In fact, his killing and even self-named abuses were verifying his soldier identity standards requiring care for and defense of his comrades. His soldier identity was obviously more salient and important during his time in Iraq.

Post military, at the age of 32, Hank changed his behavior dramatically by joining IVAW (Iraq Veterans against the War) and became involved in anti-Iraq War activism. This group of like-minded veterans engaged in activism, provided an important collective identity and verified his new Christian and moral identities. This was followed by a third conversion or "God experience."

> I spent a summer in Austin, [Texas] . . . at Barton Springs, just floating. I like, I sent out an email saying I'm fasting from the world and activism for the summer. I cut all my hair and rode my bike down to Barton Springs. And I blew up a floatie and floated and I just remember that summer, just really feeling one . . . I'd be reciting the gospel of Thomas because I was memorizing the book and it just kind of put me in a trance like.

With the freedom to take the summer off (as he was living on 100 percent disability from the V.A.), Hank has the opportunity to relax fully from his activism and relationship obligations and to engage in a period of biblical study and deep reflection. It is during this time that he describes what religious leaders often call a mystical experience of God and oneness with all living things:

> One time during one of my tunic walks in Austin, I was wearing a Jesus against war sign and wore a tunic and all that. It was hot, hot and I . . . go to Barton Springs . . . and sat underneath a tree and there's nobody in the water and the water had kind of like, a wave to it and just looking at the water it just seemed like everything became the water and then I was, I think I hypnotized myself. . . . I was just in this amazing, amazing, amazing place sitting under this tree. And, so I, I was over-amazed and was shocked and woke up and was there looking at the water. I was transported somewhere.

By providing him an avenue to act on his beliefs, IVAW fulfilled some of his identity verification needs, however, IVAW is a secular group so Hank sought an additional community of support for his Christian identity. It was his religious beliefs that had originally propelled him to question the violence of war and adopt his pacifist position on war. He soon found that the Gnostic Christian community supported his foundational religious beliefs:

> Well, I'm . . . a board member of Iraq Veterans against the War. . . . I'm also on their organizing team. I'm a counter-recruiter or informed recruiter [in high school classrooms]. [In addition,] being a Gnostic Christian that believes that

salvation comes through spiritual truths, it is an important identity . . . it's something that . . . for me it's not only reading Matthew, Mark, Luke and John, you know. You read [the books of] Thomas, Mary Magdalene, Phillip . . . you have a view of history that is, uh, that is not . . . rooted in mythology. Um, you have a kind of a, an affinity toward Buddhism. . . .

Besides his Gnostic Christian and antiwar moral identity standards, Hank experienced many lower level identity changes. These changes gave him a sense of peace and congruence about his life. At 18, Hank had self- identified as a devout Mormon, a disciplined athlete, a Karate practitioner, and an independent Texan. During his second interview at age 37, he identified as an active Board Member of Iraq Veterans against the War and also described himself as a "Gnostic Christian with an affinity toward Buddhism . . . so that every word that you say is prayer." His beliefs made him "a mad recycler, very politically active against poverty, racism, and ecocide."

Hank struggled with PTSD and flashbacks from the Iraq War reflecting, "fear can return too easily." Despite these struggles with PTSD and aliena- tion from his mom (due to differing religious beliefs), he claimed, "I am doing all the things I want to do. I am in charge. I am honest and disci- plined." We believe these assertions indicate full identity verification, acting fully on his moral identity standards or commitments. He has found mutual identity verification between his high level moral and religious identities while his lower level activist and environmentalist identities provide addi- tional congruence.

Tom's Pathway to Pacifism and Antiwar Activism

Unlike Hank, Tom had enlisted in the Army at age 18 (1987 to 1989) but like Hank he described a profound religious experience that caused a 180 degree shift in his thinking about peace and war. Tom was raised Catholic in Loui- siana and was highly involved with his parish youth group which helped to form his early moral and group identity standards. At age 22, he had a religious conversion experience that altered his understanding of Christian- ity, his practice of prayer and his life direction:

> At 1am on January 26, 1991, I was driving home from seeing a *Hamlet* video. It was about betrayal by friends and family . . . I began to think about the sin in my life and I didn't think I deserved forgiveness for my sins. I asked God what I could do for this forgiveness. I heard God reply, "Give your life to the church." After that, I spent hours a day in prayer . . . for two years. I would pray at all hours. I had a key to the church and went there to pray.

Later, Tom attended college and experienced a second "dramatic change" in his moral identity from pro to anti-death penalty. He attributes this to a profound experience during his prayer time. Interestingly, he is not aware of studying the pros and cons of the death penalty or of his moral identity standard change until after it occurs:

> Before that prayer experience, I am in a criminal justice class and a professor asked who is for the death penalty and who is against it. I was for it. After class he asked if anyone had any comments and I said yea, I am ashamed that the state wastes money to kill scum bags. They could actually make money. They could just auction them off to the highest bidder, whoever wanted to could kill them. I don't care if they shoot them or drown them. The classroom is looking at me like that guy is a sick bastard. The next semester I am in another class, it's still a criminal justice course. This other professor asks the same question: "Who objects to the death penalty" and my hand shoots up. And I'm looking at my hand thinking, when did this happen. I am absolutely sure there is no question that I am opposed to the death penalty. Between those two classes, I never read anything about the death penalty. I never had a conversation about it. I never spent a second thinking about it. What had happened is in that prayer, I spent a lot of time being open to love and I had changed. The professor even asked, "If I could show you that the death penalty actually deterred crime, would anyone still be against it?" and me and one other Catholic friend put our hand up. People are looking at me like is that the same sick bastard? That's a dramatic change.

Tom's story suggests that the moral identity disruption occurred without his conscious realization during those two semesters. He claimed that "his prayer experience" and acting on God's answer to his sincere request for forgiveness caused this dramatic shift to oppose the death penalty. Tom pursued his walk with God and life of prayer within various religious communities, which resulted in additional identity changes inspired by a powerful dream. It is important to note how his choice to spend time with various religious groups exposes him to a new peace oriented collective identity that would verify his new moral stances on war, the death penalty, and love of enemies. These periods of study would also provide an opportunity to test out some new behaviors in a safe environment:

> [More changes] happened from 1991 to 1992. I stayed with some Taize monks for a week in Dayton, Ohio and they talked about the realities of the war in Kosovo. In 1992, I had this dream. It starts off I am going to confession and there are priests there that I had never seen from some religious order—I didn't know. I am talking to one. Suddenly the dream changes and I am a soldier escorting refugees out of a country. And the enemy—we're walking along the road and on the right side of the road there is a field—there's no cover, no concealment. It's not a good place to be if someone is shooting at you. On the left side of the road is this forest and the enemy starts coming from our left side out of this forest and they are in this tank. . . . And they're coming and we tell all the people to get in a ditch and I run behind a tree and I'm

waiting for this big thing—this personnel carrier to come by and I jump on it and I'm holding on with my left arm and I stick my rifle . . . into the slot that the enemy is in so I can just shoot all the enemies. When I peek through that slot I suddenly have this realization that all of the men there are my brothers and they are children of God and there is no honor in killing them. And the dream is just blackness and I just feel . . . confusion and I was really an emotional wreck after that dream.

Tom's spiritual journey later led him to graduate studies in theology at Loyola University, a Catholic Jesuit University in Chicago. Professors, classes, and the Pax Christi ecumenical religious community continued to disrupt his primary identity standards as a criminal justice major and as a Christian. Initially he was reluctant to share his beliefs outside of the university or to advocate for changes in U.S. public policy. Fellow students and professors challenged Tom to move beyond his prayer life to learn more about social justice issues and to take appropriate political action. Taking action on one's moral beliefs was a new identity standard for Tom and it conflicted with his lower level soldier role and military group identities:

> Again because I had identified myself as a soldier, I began to question violence and war. . . . But I was questioning it for me personally . . . not is it wrong for everyone but for me personally and that's when my spiritual director put me in touch with some Pax Christi literature [an ecumenical group advocating for peaceful responses to injustice around the world]. So when I got to Loyola, I met people in Pax Christi. And also after that period of having that dream and spending a lot of time in prayer, I realized I could no longer be a criminal justice major. I was thinking of being a priest and I visited this awesome seminary in New Orleans and then Jesuits at Loyola. At Loyola I just saw all the different talks and lectures and spiritual happenings that were going on and decided to go there.

This is where Tom clearly connects with a new Collective Identity that both challenges his moral and soldier identities but also provides a coherent pacifist Christian identity that he can fully embrace. He is inspired to take his identity standards beyond mere belief into action and specifically action for social justice in Central America and the Philippines led by the professors and priests that he is spending time with:

> [Later] author Joseph Gazone, who wrote *Joshua*, helped me see the human side of Jesus. My spiritual director, prayer, Pax Christi, Bible study—specifically the gospels—and the Pax Christi peacemaker series on King and Gandhi [encouraged me]. I took a class at Loyola on inequality and injustice in Central America and was just starting to ask questions about the U.S. role and my role there. My professor and campus minister at Loyola was from the Philippines and taught social organization. He had moved from anger to nonviolence due to people killing his family.

Tom's religious studies, then, support the Identity Theory concept that when a moral identity is activated frequently, it becomes more salient over time (Stets & Carter, 2012). In Tom's case, this process of frequent activation of the moral identity pushed him to expand his standards of Christian behavior. His new antiwar activism and advocacy for social justice abroad helped him reach congruence between the requirements of his multiple identity standards. Like the other veterans in this group, Tom found that faithfulness to the moral identity provides the motivation to take risks in many areas of his life from religious to political to economic (Blasi, 1984).

> I became very active to close the SOA [School of Americas, a U.S. military base in Fort Benning, Georgia that trains military personnel from Central America] and in social justice issues. I became a war tax resister. I refused to pay my income taxes. I was active with the Peace Tax Fund. [Because of this refusal to pay my taxes that are used to fund our U.S. military] my wages were garnished and my assets were seized.

We find that Tom is now willing to not only take public actions that verify his Christian pacifist moral identity but he is willing to suffer the consequences of his action and does so willingly in order to achieve identity verification. His high level of political action also makes it difficult to hold down a fulltime job that reports his income for withholding income tax. Our income taxes, he explains pay for war:

> I am involved in youth ministry and social justice. I run a letter writing campaign to shut the S.O.A. I go to Veterans for Peace demonstrations. In 1994, I was very involved with Christian nonviolence. In 1996, I signed a vow of Christian nonviolence. From 1994 to 1999, I was at the S.O.A every year and was arrested once.

Like other vets who forfeited their military pension, Tom made a significant financial sacrifice to live true to his understanding of being a Christian. These sacrifices, as well as additional changes that have occurred in lower level identities, verified his Christian antiwar identity so that he feels a sense of peace and congruence:

> I let go of my career. I need to move from job to job [to avoid paying taxes for war]. I gave up the American dream of high school and college. I had to give up the idea of my criminal justice career. I gave up having a lot of money, owning a home, and having a bank account. I can't get student loans. I haven't had kids. I have some inner peace and some periods of fear. I listen more and question myself and the church. I partake in war tax resistance; I can't pay for war anymore. I am more progressive [politically]. I am putting love and humanity first. This means with work choices, environmental concerns, and dignity of labor. I am open to lots of different ideas and I treat all people with

dignity. I am no longer angry. I live in a cooperative [housing situation], living simply and share things with others.

Finally, Tom's journey of transformation mirrors other veterans in terms of the cascade of identity changes that occurred with his antiwar position. At age 18, he identified as a Martial Arts instructor, a Catholic, a friend, a big brother, and a conservative American. Later at age 43, he described himself as a good human being, a member of a housing community, a social justice advocate, and a warrior for conscience. While he began young adult life at age 18 as a proud member of the Army and a Black Belt Martial Arts instructor, he now associated with military pacifists. The former conservative Republican now worked for progressive causes around the world such as closing the U.S. School of the Americas (currently called WHINSEC or the Western Hemispheric Institute for Security Cooperation).

CONCLUSIONS

The stories of these three veterans (Richard, Hank, and Tom) share a sense of being at peace with who they are today. As expected in those experiencing identity verification, they now had congruence between multiple high and lower level person, role and group identities. After sacrificing their military careers and better incomes for their beliefs, they described a sense of identity verification using the terms "sense of integrity, I feel very right, the changes are a liberation, honest and authentic" to describe their new lives.

Perhaps more so than any of the other catalyst groups, those in the Religious Conviction catalyst group demonstrate a dramatic change in a high level person identity, namely their moral identity. These veterans engaged in both cognitive and behavioral strategies to reach identity verification primarily as pacifists. Unlike respondents in the Betrayal or Combat catalyst groups, the Religious Conviction catalyst group adopted extreme positions on war that demanded non-participation for themselves, others who called themselves Christians and the nation/state. Many of these veterans further verified their new pacifist moral identities through membership in the Mennonite Church USA ($n = 10$). As a result, the Religious Conviction catalyst group was much more likely to hold a collective identity with a Christian pacifist group than with a veterans' antiwar group.

Table 5.1. Summary of identity change for a religious conviction catalyst group member

Catalyst Group	Moral Identity Standard at 18 Years	Behavior at 20 Years in Military	Identity Disruption	New Moral Identity Standard	New Behavior to Reach Identity Verification
Religious Conviction Larry, 27 years	Open-minded, Military as merit badge. Regarding war: to defend recognized principles of freedom & justice, U.S. borders and people. #3*	Joined Army after high school & served for 6 yrs. (2000–2006) in U.S. & Iraq. Served in Forward Observer Quick Reaction force & saw combat.	I saw things in Army I disagreed with but didn't put it all together until the end when attending a New Testament class. I couldn't find support for the destruction we (U.S.) involved in. I decided Christians are not called to kill. In 2006, I had a vision from God to return to Iraq but without a weapon.	Duty to obey God versus Military superiors. I am honest, don't lie, a Christian Activist & Pacifist; Suffering Love is my model. Regarding War: There is no appropriate use of war as it destroys people's lives. #6, 7 & 8*	Applied for Conscientious Objector status while in Army but then discharged. Working on Masters in Theological Studies. As a Pacifist, I refuse to use violence in any form. I started an NGO, to assist Vets who are prematurely discharged due to conscience & in need of funds. I wrote a book about my journey to Pacifism.

* Numbers refer to the specific veteran's position on the militarism to pacifism scale.

We conclude that in part this catalyst group struggled less with their pathway to pacifism due to the fact that they experienced less combat (4 percent) and little PTSD (17 percent). Free of physical and emotional turmoil that may have led to addiction or psychological numbing, this group was able to enter a period of reflection and study fairly rapidly post identity disruption and thus begin to replace their military collective identity with a Christian group holding a coherent and holistic view on war and morality. But, perhaps due to their Christian identities emphasis on compassion and care of others, members of this group express empathy and understanding for both soldiers and veterans with differing views than their own.

In the next chapter, we will discuss the final catalyst group, labeled Education. This group like the Religious Conviction group describes a period of study and reflection but unlike the Religious Conviction group, the period of study usually lacks a spiritual component and they primarily identify with Just War Theory rather than Christian Pacifism in relation to their moral identity standard.

Chapter Six

The Education Catalyst of Identity Change

My history professor, a former Army sergeant had great credibility. His goal was to tell the truth. He was amazing at connecting the dots. I saw the complexity of the world. It was a life changing event—a breakthrough—an epiphany. (Chuck)

This quote from a U.S. Marine veteran who served during the Gulf War exemplifies the power of truth telling and critical thinking in moral identity change among the Education Catalyst group. In this chapter we examine the stories of three veterans for whom we saw higher education or study of U.S. history and policy as a catalyst for identity change. This education group includes 22 percent ($n = 25$) of the 114 veterans. The common denominator in this group is increased critical thinking related to issues of war and U.S. policy. This "new way of thinking" occurred through higher education and/or self-education by reading texts that analyzed U.S. history, society, politics, and economy. The critical thinking component includes an identity standard of questioning previous assumptions about the U.S. and war. This group heavily embraces Just War Theory versus pacifism, leading the majority to oppose some wars rather than all wars (76 percent; $n = 19$).

For the soldier completing military service and enrolling in college, the social environment includes the new student role with inputs from professors and fellow students without military experience. To excel in the university setting, then, new norms and identities become salient as the priorities and inputs of the student-veteran shift. The new identity of "critical thinking student" is near the top of the re-ordered hierarchy of identities. Usually, this leads to disruption of the moral identity criteria and a search for congruence between two standards: the critical-thinking student and the moral pro-war believer. To confirm both identity standards, these veterans compromise by situationally opposing wars that fail to meet the high standards of the Just War Theory criteria. In terms of Identity Theory, then, the student veterans gradually shift these conflicting identity standards to achieve congruence.

EDUCATION CATALYST GROUP CHARACTERISTICS

Most of these veterans served during periods when the U.S. was not at war (80 percent; $n = 20$) and experienced no disruptions in their pro-war moral identities during military service. The disruption for these veterans occurs post-military during a period of study or reflection. One Latino veteran admitted there were "some red flags" for him during his military service in Egypt. However, he loved the military and returned to college to become a Marine officer. During his period of study back in the U.S., he identified and addressed an important identity conflict as a Latino in a racist society. His studies made him see social injustices, such as unequal education for Latinos, for the first time. "By the end of my second year of community college, I was ready to get out of the Marines. I was eating up what I was reading—it was a new way of thinking" (Don).

Higher education, then, became the catalyst of identity change for many of the veterans in this group. Others, though, educated themselves outside the classroom by reading texts critical of U.S. foreign policy. The common denominator for both of these groups is developing their ability to think critically. One soldier explained:

> My first three years in the Air Force [63–66], I didn't consider the antiwar arguments [Vietnam] and went along with the President. I liked the macho culture and the *esprit de corps* and thought that I should go to Vietnam to prove my manhood. . . . When I left Vietnam, I immediately entered an MBA program and got married and started coaching college lacrosse. It wasn't wise because I didn't take time to think about the war for 15 to 20 more years. . . . In 1980, I met and married my current wife and we moved and became involved in our local community. In 1985, I began to read Noam Chomsky and Howard Zinn and this led to others [critical of U.S. policies that supported militarism]. I also began my involvement with Veterans for Peace. (Dick)

While this veteran admitted being uncomfortable with unnecessary military rules and structures during his first few years in the Air Force, he volunteered to go "to Vietnam to prove my manhood." While serving in combat, he "began to question the war" and described having "good relations with Senior Officers who shared my concerns about mismanagement and racial discrimination." Dick's red flags or disrupters were written off as mismanagement and never seemed to accumulate to the point where negative emotions such as guilt motivated moral identity change. However, in 1985, he found himself challenged by texts critical of U.S. foreign policy. These books led him to seek out a peace group and join Veterans for Peace.

Characteristics of the Education Catalyst Group

Compared to the other catalyst groups, the Education catalyst group is unique in a number of areas. They have one of the lowest percentages of combat experience (8 percent; $n = 2$) and the lowest rate of PTSD (4 percent; $n = 1$). Only 20 percent of this group ($n = 5$) served in a country during a time of war. Thus, the origin of their change was not experiential but rather intellectual. Their relative success in higher education (88 percent with a Bachelor's or graduate degree; $n = 22$) solidified their new critical antiwar identities. The Education catalyst group includes a large group of women (20 percent; $n = 5$) although the Betrayal group has slightly more at 23 percent. We find little evidence of moral identity disruption at the level of moral injury in this group.

Another unique feature of the Education catalyst group is the predominance of non- Army veterans. This group had the largest percentage of Navy, Air Force and Marines (84 percent; $n = 21$) as opposed to Army members. In terms of their antiwar activism, this group is the most involved with activism in the three antiwar groups: Veterans for Peace, Iraq Veterans against the War and Vietnam Veterans against the War used in our study. The Education catalyst group had the highest level of support for the Just War position as opposed to the pacifist positions on the scale (76 percent; $n = 19$) (see appendix C). These critical thinkers used specific logical criteria to support or oppose a war. Only five of these veterans identified a pacifist position opposing all wars and two of these men found their spiritual home in a traditional pacifist peace church.

Don's Pathway to Antiwar Activism

In 2008 (age 33), Don shared his story while studying for his PhD in sociology. He served four years as an active duty Marine and two years in the reserves. At age 18, Don believed that "it was our job as the United States to police the world. It was appropriate to go to war with any country that was a threat to us or broke the law." Fifteen years later, he stated, "War is the last means to an end but I can't think of any situations where war is appropriate."

As a Latino, Don grew up in Southern California in a mixed Mexican and white neighborhood. His parents, who had emigrated from Mexico prior to his birth, raised five children in a two bedroom apartment. Although from a poor family, Don was able to attend "an upper middle class school" where he was one of only three Mexicans. He was shocked to see the affluence of the white kids' homes. As a result, during high school he broke his ties with the white kids and "started hanging out with older [Latino] gang members." He rejected school and eventually dropped out altogether. When "one of my friends was shot and killed, I decided that if I stayed on this path, I would end up the same way." Don then enrolled in a new school, played football, and left the gang. Upon graduation, he joined the military for the "discipline, the toughness . . . and I wanted the biggest challenge." Don described two group identity shifts by age 18: during high school from Latino gang member to tough football player and during his early years in the military from teenager to adulthood as a Marine:

> After high school, I joined the Marines [1993–2000] to prove I was an American and I belonged. . . . I became a squad leader out of boot camp and I was so proud. Nothing could take this away from me. I was ready to make the Marines my career—they had my total loyalty. I was fit and trim and had no experiences with racism. . . . [Later] I volunteered to be in the U.S. Embassy Guard so I could travel. I went to specialized training and through special testing and intense interviews. I did well and graduated at the top of my class. They sent me to Cairo, Egypt. . . . My boss was the greatest role model one could ever have. He was Mexican American and I still stay in touch with him today.

As Don climbed the Marine hierarchy, he abandoned his Mexican identity in exchange for what he described as the elite, superior, and tough U.S. Marine identity. This shift required him to treat minorities with contempt. However we see a hint of identity disruption (or identity non-verification) during this time in what Don describes as listening to the voice "deep inside."

> I became quite arrogant and believed it was our [U.S.] job to police the world. If the locals didn't speak English and were dirty, the U.S. had the right to treat them like trash—they were inferior. We were told we were the top 10 percent of Americans and we could treat others as trash. My whole identity was as a Marine, not as a Mexican. I cussed them [Egyptians] out and treated them rudely but deep inside, I knew something was wrong, . . . but I set it aside . . . I dehumanized them. I couldn't wait for Egyptians to demonstrate against the embassy so I could do something.

Don further distanced himself from his Mexican roots when the diplomatic officers encouraged him to earn a college degree and become a career Marine. He admired the standard of living of the Marine officers and the diplomatic corps. Don's decision to return home for college, though, presented him with new questions, ideas, role models, possibilities, and identities. Some courses challenged his strong, proud U.S. Marine identity:

> Some of the diplomats there [Egypt] suggested I consider college . . . and I saw that the diplomats lived much better than me. I thought I would give college a

try and then come back as an officer. I left the Marines in 1998 to go to college. . . . I started at a Community College back home in California. I used the G.I. Bill. I never thought about a major, I just wanted a B.A. so I could be a Marine officer. I moved back in with my parents and saw old friends doing crystal meth. . . . I joined the Reserves—I needed it [the group support] and went to the base every weekend.

Upon returning home to attend college, Don is faced with his former Mexican group identity as he describes seeing old friends doing crystal meth. He appears to use his Marine group identity to distance himself from this former peer-group and explains that he still "needs" the reserves. However, his college classes cause him to reflect on his social location as a Mexican-American in a new way:

I took some Chicano Studies courses, and at first it seemed anti-American but it made me think about my own neighborhood. I thought about poverty and privilege. I started to wonder why my friends didn't go to college, why some schools were poor . . . I saw anti-immigrant rallies and saw Americans treat me the way I treated the Egyptians. I asked why we [U.S.] gave so much money to Egypt and not to my high school. I started to think that my battles were here in the United States and not in Egypt!

It is clear that Don begins to experience group identity disruption during his Chicano Studies courses. Don described trying to "fight the change . . . I felt I was betraying the Marines because it had given me so much. But I knew that the U.S. government could lie. I learned that in Egypt." We see evidence of reflected self-appraisal in Don's description of his change of thinking during his early years in college. It was during this period that he realized that it was time to end his military career:

By the end of two years of Community College, I was ready to get out of the Marines. I was eating up what I was reading—it was a new way of thinking. I studied a lot. I did well and had a 3.8 GPA. I was admitted to U.C. Berkley and got into the Puente [Bridge] Program. [This is a program designed to improve the college-enrollment rate of the educationally underrepresented (www.puente.berkeley.edu).] I saw Latino professors and they talked to us about a Master's and PhD I hadn't even heard of a PhD. When I came back from a trip with the Puente Program, the fog had cleared.

At this point, Don felt ready to abandon his Marine identity and career. He embraced a new vision and collective identity planted by his Latino professors and fellow students. Don now had the historical, political and sociological background to understand the statements of fellow Chicanos, who at first appeared as anti-American when criticizing U.S. policy. He embraces the more activist Chicano label along with being a Latino.

The 9/11 terrorist attacks on U.S. soil tested Don's new identities. By comparing the pro-war and antiwar positions, he took the full leap into antiwar activism and even joined an antiwar veterans group. Don's story once again demonstrates how faithfulness to the moral identity provides the motivation to act (Blasi, 1984). During the 2008 interview, Don was finishing his PhD dissertation in Sociology at a large public university. He had married a Brazilian woman he had met years earlier while in the Marines. He had solidified a new set of identities: husband, Latino, academic, critical thinker, and anti-Iraq War activist. As we have seen with the stories of other veterans, Don begins to form new group associations and a Collective Identity that is important to identity verification:

> I met people in the Chicano Movement, radical professors and moved much more left [politically]. I met Chicano students who were anti-U.S. and I asked why. Now I understand the larger context. After 9/11, I was reading and thinking in a more radicalized way. I had been at Berkeley for a year. During the invasion of Afghanistan, I was in Berkeley and didn't get the pro-war sentiment. But I was torn between friends going to war and the reality of the U.S. as a bully against Afghanistan. I did attend antiwar rallies in Berkeley. My political activism focused on the Latino community . . . I didn't join Vets for Peace until 2008.

Although Don verified his new moral antiwar activist identity standard by opposing the Afghan and Iraq Wars, this required significant sacrifice. He felt that he could not open up about his beliefs to some of his fellow veterans. As we have seen in previous stories, many of the veterans in our study faced loss with their identity change that required a period of adjustment, "Today, I am against war but not the Marines. I still use things I learned in the Marines today. I don't share my views with my Marine Corps buddies. The changes keep me from the Marine Corps and a happy go-lucky life. It's been a burden. It's made life more complicated."

While acknowledging the sacrifices and the reordering of life goals, he "relates the changes to God." He concludes that "I always felt things happened for a reason." Today it appears to be more important to both his moral and group identities that he has, "a purpose and there is something more powerful than me." These are clear evidence of full identity verification.

Steve's Pathway to Antiwar Activism

Unlike Don, Steve's pathway started in Vietnam as a forward observer, believing fully in the war. He served in the Marines from 1966 to 1967 in Vietnam, where he was injured. After being sent home, he spent the next two years in college "into sex and drugs" as he tried to cope with PTSD symptoms (which were not diagnosed until the 1990s). Steve volunteered for an interview in 2009 at age 63.

Steve's childhood begins as a poor Jewish kid growing up in Brooklyn, New York in the 1940s. His father fought in World War II and eventually divorced his mom. He and his mom moved to Florida where she remarried an abusive stepfather and a leader in the right-wing John Birch Society. Steve fought back against the abuse, moved out of the house at age 16 and soon after enlisted in the Marines.

Steve's story includes combat injury, losing his best friend in combat, killing Vietnamese soldiers and civilians, and being captured. Rather than causing moral identity disruption as we saw earlier with many Combat Catalyst veterans, these traumatic experiences only strengthened his support for the war as a path to revenge. Steve also expressed a sense of betrayal by God. He reflected, "I went to Vietnam and my mind was blown because a loving God wouldn't let that happen." He experienced further betrayal once home when he read the *People's History of the United States* by Howard Zinn (1980) challenging U.S. altruistic motives for military and economic intervention abroad.

Despite these experiences of combat and betrayal, he did not experience a moral identity disruption until returning to the U.S. and hearing a call from actress Jane Fonda. While speaking at an antiwar rally on his college campus, she invited any "patriotic veterans (in the audience) to come forward and tell the truth" about the war:

> I was throwing a Frisbee, not really paying attention. Fonda got my attention when she said, "This is supposed to be a democracy, and the people are supposed to be in charge. The people are not getting the truth, and without true information, a democracy cannot function. It cannot live. It's the duty of patriotic Vietnam veterans to come forward and tell the truth about Vietnam because the government is not." Well, I was patriotic, I was a Vietnam veteran, and I knew what we were really doing in Vietnam and I felt that the people had the right to know the truth.

Steve went forward to the stage and shared his story. A few weeks later Fonda invited him to film his testimony with other Vietnam veterans for the documentary *Winter Soldier*. He recalled, "I got to speak honestly and it transformed me . . . I had survivor's guilt-why did I get to live? John died and he was a friend from high school and dated my sister . . . I decided I was allowed to live to work against the war." Today, Steve uses his antiwar activism to make sense of his past experiences. Below is an excerpt of Steve's testimony from the documentary:

> My name is Steve, I was a sergeant attached to Charlie 1–1. I was a forward observer in Vietnam. I went in right after high school and I'm a student now.

My testimony involves burning villages with civilians in them, the cutting off
of ears, cutting off of heads, torturing of prisoners, throwing prisoners from
helicopters, calling in artillery on villages for games, corpsmen killing
wounded prisoners, napalm dropped on villages, women being raped, women
and children being massacred, CS gas used on people, animals slaughtered,
Chieu Hoi passes rejected and the people holding them shot, bodies thrown off
of helicopters, tear-gassing people for fun, and running civilian vehicles off
the road.

His background certainly did not prepare him for these experiences. Steve
grew up in a conservative Republican household where he believed that "war
was a legitimate form of conflict resolution" and he "trusted our government." He joined the Marines out of high school as the "ultimate place to
earn my manhood." Today, Steve "no longer accepts war as a legitimate
form of conflict resolution" but believes "that killing in self-defense is OK."

Steve, by sharing his testimony, was admitting his guilt and responding to
his moral identity standards to speak the truth. He listened to similar stories
of fellow veterans and experienced a whole new perspective on the war he
once supported so enthusiastically. Like-minded veterans joining with the
civilian peace community, led by Jane Fonda verified their truth-telling moral identity and helped the group move toward activism. Following the filming of the *Winter Soldier* documentary, life changed dramatically for him:

I started getting arrested [protesting the war] and my professors brought my
work to jail and it was incredibly empowering. They thought I was important. I
took psychology, philosophy, and history and learned about gray versus black
and white.
I helped organize the VVAW [Vietnam Veterans against the War] locally.
I was arrested for kidnapping [which was a lie] and was defended by Larry
Turner and was let off. I was always cool under pressure and still am today.
The newspaper was on my side, the veterans supported me, and my professors
helped me finish my courses and college.

Like many other veterans, Steve also dealt with significant opposition to
his antiwar activism although it seemed to strengthen his resolve which continues to this day. Throughout Steve's interview we see evidence of the
importance of public activism to verify his anti-Vietnam and later anti–Iraq
War identity. In addition, due to his PTSD diagnosis, he lives off of 100
percent disability affording him time for these involvements:

My parents were not supportive because they were right wing and hated "com-
mies." Federal agents attempted to kill me. I was charged with drugs. I defended myself and I was not found guilty but they [federal agents] were pro-
moted. I felt I was being effective when I was arrested. [Today] I'm involved
with United Voices for Peace which is an interfaith group in my city. I serve
on the. National Board of VVAW. I went to Central America with VFP and

met liberation theologists who were holy people and they touched me in terms of their ability to forgive those who killed and tortured their families. [Because of these role models] I was able to forgive my dad [for his physical abuse] before he died.

Reflecting on the sacrifices he has made in order to live and breath his antiwar activism, Steve clarified his moral identity and patriotic American group identity standards. He also describes a shift in his Collective Identity from groups like Veterans of Foreign Wars (VFW) to groups like Veterans for Peace (VFP):

> The hardest thing was to let go of my understanding of patriotism as blind obedience to the U.S. I gave up the U.S. flag and my love of it. I see it as an icon of corruption and murder. I gave up my recognition by right wing groups and people as a patriot . . . like the. VFW and American Legion. I have now transferred my loyalty to VFP and IVAW.

Like other veterans, Steve found it hard to let go of the violence he had done not only against Vietnamese soldiers but innocent civilians in Vietnam and to move on. One event that was especially helpful in dealing with his guilt due to what appears to be moral injury, was the opportunity to return to Vietnam in 1994 and speak the truth about his complicity in murder of villagers. Miraculously, he describes being forgiven by the survivors and family members who remain. This act of forgiveness from those one has harmed, is described in the moral injury treatment literature as vital to the healing process:

> I went back to this village where our battalion killed 272 people—old men, women and children. It's where I got my first Purple Heart from a Bouncing Betty [an explosive device]. There is a memorial in that village for the people we killed and I spent one day on my hands and knees and placed three burning incense sticks at each grave, one of which was a mass grave for 23 children. I made it a point to tell the people from that village that I was one of the guys who did this and there was absolutely no hostility against me. So now when I think about that place I have different pictures in my brain besides the people we killed and my buddies who bled with me. I have pictures of people who are happy there now, who are my friends, and who have forgiven me.

This dramatic scene exemplifies the concept of a moral identity. As noted earlier, behavioral demands of the moral identity impact actions across be-haviors controlled by lower level identities (Burke & Stets, 2009). As with other antiwar veterans, the transformation in moral identity standards created a cascade of other changes in Steve's lower level identities. He had begun at age 18 wanting to be a "greaser, partier, fighter, a real man and a protector," even writing a paper about being a career Marine in high school. Many of his primary identities, though, had taken a 180 degree turn by the time he was 63 and reinterviewed in 2013. However, Steve continues to see elements of his Marine identity in his antiwar activism:

> I am a total activist who is responsible, keeps my word and tells the truth and is well informed . . . I am an environmentalist and a part of the Sierra Club Executive Committee so my children have it better than we had. I am a peace activist who does counter recruiting in high schools and works for Veterans for Peace . . . I am a critical thinker which means being objective and looking at the other side, admitting mistakes . . . I am a man who is sensitive, able to cry, able to express myself. Standing up is still very important, especially for my people. I guess I'm still confused, I'm a lifetime member of the NRA [National Rifle Association] and have lots of guns—100 for sport and for security.

As a gun owner, then, he had not completely rejected the use of violence in self-defense or hunting. In reflecting on his identity as a critical thinker, similar to others in the Education Catalyst group, he also acknowledges his confusion and the paradox regarding his antiwar, anti-violence position when it comes to self-defense. He admits to losing patience with people who tell him to either love America or leave it. His male identity standard as a protector of the weak requiring physical force at times seems to trump his moral identity standard of non-violence and he still struggles to find identity verification for these two identities when activated simultaneously:

> The Marines is a macho culture and killing people is an acceptable source of conflict resolution that actually works. If you kill people, they can't hurt you. When we came home and we became antiwar, it took us awhile to become anti-violent and to try to adapt new strategies of conflict resolution. Like my basic attitude [toward people opposing my views on war] was, you inherited your rights under the Constitution by being born in this country, is that correct? I fuckin' bled for those rights so don't fuckin' tell me that I can't fuckin' stand in the street and demonstrate against fuckin' government policy. I volunteered to go into the Marine Corps. I volunteered to go to Vietnam and if I'm willing to go halfway around the world to defend the Constitution. What makes you think that I won't be willing to defend it right here on my own land. . . . So, I really, in all my public stuff, I try to be respectable, responsible, and win people over and I try to walk the walk but, if there is a threat, you're dealing with that Marine Sergeant again and I don't have the courage to turn the other cheek. I think it takes tremendous courage to do that and I can't do that.

When Steve faces resistance to his activism, especially from other men, his PTSD may impact his rapid resort to the fight response as he becomes combative both verbally and sometimes physically. He attempts to control his trigger response to potential threats with daily use of "weed." Although he identifies great demands and sacrifices that he has made as a peace activist, he had no regrets for the direction his life has taken as a full time antiwar activist and environmentalist. We see evidence that Steve found identity verification in answer to the question, do you have any regrets about the direction your life has taken?: "Oh, hell no, are you saying do I wish that I never grew up and I was still the same dumb old not-thinking for yourself person? . . . No, I'm extremely happy. What I'm upset about is that I didn't figure it out earlier."

William's Pathway to Antiwar Activism

William witnessed the Vietnam War not as a combat soldier like Steve but through listening to soldiers' stories right before they returned home. He shared his experiences in 2008 at age 54, having just retired as a U.S. govern-ment inspector of bridges. His military career began at age 17 as "a product of the John Wayne society." John Wayne was a popular American film star in the 1950s and 1960s who came to represent rugged American masculinity. William believed "what the U.S. government said." He was poor and figured "the Army was my only option to get out." Now decades later, William believed that "our government is completely corrupt. I don't believe in ag-gressive warfare. War should not be used unless we are attacked on U.S. soil." This opinion is congruent with a Just War perspective.

William served in the Army from 1971 to 1974 in Germany, the stopping point for many Vietnam soldiers prior to returning home. It was during his time in Germany that William experienced a disruption to this moral identity as he learned firsthand from the returning troops just how bad the situation was in Vietnam. William described the environment as taking a crash course in the History of the Vietnam War:

> I was an infantry weapons expert. My unit was full of [returning] Vietnam vets. We were in Germany and there were vets post-combat from every thea-ter. I was in at a unique time due to the GI resistance to the war. Literally my first day overseas, a bunch of Vietnam vets sat me down and gave me one of these "you're either with us or against us" kind of speeches. It was because of the resistance that I never really got to experience the robotic like thing they have now [in the military], where everybody just blindly and obediently obeys. The infantry, when I was in it, was just like a big private drug party and it was a war between the lifers and enlisted men.

We placed William in the education catalyst group, not because of the role of formal education in his identity change, but rather because of his description of his change occurring as a result of learning about the war from returning soldiers. The following quote exemplifies the importance of critical thinking in disrupting William's pro-war moral identity and resulting acti-vism:

> I learned explicitly about war and was all against the war in Vietnam by 1971. The enlisted men who were officers were still toeing the government line . . . I fed off the anger of the survivors and learning about the deaths of all the innocent people and the ruining of lives. I befriended and listened to them and they were all against it. .The military was deteriorating. GI's refused to follow orders. We organized against the war and started underground newspapers. We attempted to disrupt things from within by refusing orders. There was a battle between lifers and freaks. We had secret handshakes. You could fool the public but not the troops.

Serving in a unique leadership position within his company, he was tasked with handling discrimination complaints. This role required critical thinking because he had to balance the competing interests of individuals and the military. This position further sensitized him to complaints of injustice within the military:

> People were open to me and talked to me. I was the Equal Opportunity Human Relations person from 1972 to 1974. There was one person appointed in each company and it was me. People came to me with stories of being screwed. I was privy to daily complaints. I acted as a mediator and had a great impact. The grunts felt heard. It was the officers against the grunts.

Through these experiences, William quickly transitioned from the role of naïve grunt to providing "top leadership for the antiwar movement in Germany." He became more and more disillusioned with the military. He learned about the deteriorating situation in Vietnam, which made him doubt the U.S. mission of protecting the country against communism. Such knowledge disrupted his John Wayne moral identity of being the "good guy." He adopted a moral identity standard that demanded that he protect the troops from the Army hierarchy. Also, he took radical steps to disrupt the war he believed to be immoral, eventually fleeing his company without permission at the risk of court martial:

> Everyday there was an atrocity in the military. Dozens were killed each day. In the infantry divisions, everyone was radicalized. Nixon resigned in disgrace and the draft ended and battles ended, all in 1972. These successes spurred me on . . . Platoon members started wearing tie-dye T-shirts and the Army made a rule against it. I was ripe for this kind of opposition from my high school years. The military was a clusterfuck at this time. Officers rotated in and out of Vietnam for three months to get medals for combat infantry. They needed this to move up. Because of this, officers didn't know what they were doing and it cost lives. Because of this, the soldiers sometimes killed them.

As the war continued, William describes how the momentum switched from the collective identity of the officers to the soldiers and the antiwar moral identity standards of many of the returning troops expanded from opposing the war to obstructing the war. William describes the practice of "fragging" as the troops intentionally harming the military officers being sent into combat short-term in order to earn medals. The command structure was rapidly deteriorating as the troops themselves rebelled. Others engaged in extensive drug use as a form of escape according to William. In this chaotic environment, William sought escape through another route:

> I got in serious trouble on purpose, as did a lot of us. Four of us deserted together as a political statement. . . . We all got court martialed and were sentenced to hard labor. . . . And then returned to our unit. Then I got a second court martial which I beat completely and my commanding officer got repri-manded as well as my platoon leader for trumped up charges. I ended up leaving the military as a Corporal or as it was called a Spec 4 in the Army, with a full honorable discharge. So it was a huge victory on our part. The draft ended because of the GI resistance and a peace treaty was signed in Paris in 73. And my getting out of the Army prize was Nixon resigning in disgrace.

Despite opposition and resistance from Army officers and his family, William felt driven to extreme measures in opposing the Vietnam War on moral grounds while serving. But once home, his role identities and identity hierarchy shifted rapidly. "My father was ashamed of me. There was a lot of opposition from the officers in the Army. But when I completed my term, my activism declined."

After returning home from service in 1974, he got married and had two sons. His new family became the focus of his life adding role identities of husband and father. Since the U.S. involvement in Vietnam was finally over, he ended his antiwar activism that had been needed to verify his moral identity in Germany. Decades later, though, as the U.S. invaded Iraq, William's antiwar identity became salient once again. Now an empty nester, he had more time for activism. The Iraq War also reignited his desire to protect his fellow soldiers from the abuses by the military hierarchy. This time he felt driven to fight for a new generation of soldiers. Rather than working in isolation, he finds support and verification through the Collective Identity of Iraq Veterans against the War: "We organized IVAW in 2004 and it's up to 1,300 members [2008]. I'm on the board. Our total focus is on enlisted men. 40,000 troops are now AWOL. March 13–16, 2008, we orga-nized Winter Soldier II. Iraq soldiers gave testimonies and admitted to killing civilians in Iraq [for the documentary]."

Being true to his conscience with his anti-Iraq War activism forced William to make sacrifices once again. As with other veterans though, he claims the sacrifices were worth the peace of mind obtained through what we term identity verification. This quote demonstrates the lengths to which many veterans will go to affirm their moral identity standard demands for action and affirmation from like-minded veterans:

It's [antiwar activism] constantly a burden. There is a great sadness over the senselessness of war. . . . I would rather be really retired but instead I am working 10–12 hours a day on antiwar activism. I do have a sense of fulfillment and purpose but it's a huge strain on my personal life. It is slow depressing work. . . . Today, I am proud of what I do [in the antiwar movement] and my work as a leader and arbiter and photographer.

William's story shows that the behavioral demands of the moral identity impact actions across a range of situations controlled by lower level identities (Burke & Stets, 2009).The transformation from pro-war to antiwar had affected William's other identities. As a younger man, he had been a "rebellious hippy and wild man." He had also been a protective big brother and a talented athlete. Now he described himself as not only a proud activist leader, but as a successful father. Additional identities that formed to support his antiwar moral identity standard included being an environmentalist and feminist.

Adam's Journey to Pacifism and Antiwar Activism

William and Steve shared stories of their decades-long struggles with their war experiences. By contrast, Adam's story is much more recent. Adam was only 27 and a graduate student studying geography when he shared his story in 2009. He had enlisted in the Navy at age 18 (1999) right after high school. Coming from a lower middle class conservative Christian background, he believed that "war was necessary to defeat evil in the world." He served from 1999 through 2003, primarily in Puerto Rico. Ten years later in 2009, Adam stated that "there is no known justified use of war. Militarized solutions beget militarized solutions." Now declaring a Christian pacifist position, he joined a traditional pacifist peace church. We placed him in the Education catalyst group instead of the Religious Conviction group, though, because college professors and learning to think critically disrupted his moral identity initially rather than his religious convictions.

The first time he recalls thinking critically regarding the military was in Puerto Rico shortly after his basic training. He was exposed to racist statements from his colleagues and public protests by the Puerto Ricans:

There was an event at Vieques Island, Puerto Rico where a Marine pilot was dropping training rounds there and he killed a civilian contractor. This was a reason why the locals, who weren't supportive of the military, protested. I was stationed there on a boat. I watched the situation closely . . . I lived in town and was hearing lots of racist attitudes against the Puerto Ricans from the Navy. I was hearing both sides of the argument. . . . The U.S. military perspective was that we were using a tiny island and we protect them [the Puerto Rican people] *but* the locals didn't want them [the U.S. military] there. I was a conservative thinker but my local relationship with the Puerto Ricans caused tension [in my thinking].

The above quote illustrates what we would term an early discrepancy between Adam's moral identity standard and the behaviors he was observing. However, Adam describes his experiences after leaving the military and beginning college as central to his identity change process. Adam remembers two teachers in particular that taught him to think critically:

> In 2004, I moved back home and my time in the two-year college liberalized me. I began to see another perspective on U.S. foreign policy. Deaf studies were my introduction to oppression and systematic stuff [injustice]. My professor of signing was deaf and a lesbian and she was great. She brought together major contradictions. . . . Then, I had a group discussion class in modern articulate philosophy. The professor changed my life.

Clearly, multiple professors are challenging Adam's narrow worldview and demonstrating how to think more critically about both moral issues and social issues such as homosexuality and oppression of minority groups. He describes flourishing in this new environment but the identity disruption doesn't occur until he returns to the fundamentalist church of his childhood and teenage years. He could now compare his new insights supported by his professors with the narrower good and evil attitudes he identifies within his congregation:

> When I returned to my home [Baptist] church with my mom after the Navy, I saw the close-minded attitude about gays and abortion. . . . The debate about evolution bothered me. The girl I was dating at the time was so kind with everyone and also a committed Christian. We met in college in an interpreting class. She was apolitical but her parents were Democrats and supported Kerry.

It appears that Adam's new girlfriend provided a bridge that introduced a pathway to verify both his new desire to be a critical thinker and a compassionate rather than judgmental Christian. Her parents, also committed Christians, supported the political party that had been labeled as evil due to their support of the Democrats who supported not only abortion rights but gay marriage. As their relationship solidified, they sought a more politically progressive church they found via the internet. This demonstrates a period of study to identify new options that might verify all of his new identities:

> I went to a Mennonite Church in January of 2007. Everything I had dealt with to that time, everything made sense: the military was not OK, it was not OK to hate gays. I tried the Mennonite Church due to my positive experience with Mennonites in high school. I returned to the Puerto Rican Deaf School in 2008 and my old church there and could see how conservative it was.

Eventually joining this progressive Mennonite congregation provides a new Collective Identity that verifies both the critical thinking he has embraced as a college student along with a progressive Christian identity that is antiwar. Adam quickly moves from a bachelor's degree to a PhD program as he fully embraces both the student role identity standard of critical thinker and the Christian pacifist moral identity he embraces with his new wife, the compassionate Christian who served as a bridge.

The identity change in Adam is obvious. At age 18, his most important identities were "as a son, a Navy sailor who was smart, disciplined, responsible and fit; an older brother to three sisters who was a good role model, rebellious, a Christian evangelical with a social sense opposing abortion and gays but no political sense." By age 27, he identifies as a "Christian Mennonite with responsibility to the community and to nonviolence, as a follower of Jesus." Other identities were now as "a husband with dedicated commitment" and "a student with commitment to critique."

In response to a question about how the changes in his thinking felt at the time, he reflected, "I felt scared . . . but it was liberating. I never questioned my faith but I didn't know what it meant. I wanted to be able to ask questions and dialogue." His old church discouraged questioning while his new congregation and Adult Sunday School classes embraced his questions.

While many other antiwar veterans experienced major opposition, Adam only had to deal with his old Baptist friends who "pushed back . . . I had no real resistance from my mom." Upon further reflection, though, he realized that he had made some significant sacrifices for this new identity, "I gave up certainty. I gave up comfort. I used to be able to just write people off and say everyone thinks the same." He now acknowledged that there was a lot of gray and complexity to explore.

Despite these sacrifices, Adam received much support from his girlfriend/future wife as his Collective Identity changed from fundamentalist Baptist to Mennonite pacifist Christian. His new Mennonite Church USA helped him make sense of biblical scripture as applied to his life in a more complex and critical way. He appreciated the Mennonites' ability to dialogue about his critical questions because "they are not threatened by them."

He embraced the new set of Christian Mennonite identity standards that included not only pacifism but preferential treatment for minorities and the poor. This new Christian identity standard not only seemed consistent with a critical reading of scripture but raised serious questions about the Southern Baptist standards he was raised with of unquestioned patriotism and opposition to all abortion and gay marriage. He adopts the word radical to describe his new beliefs:

I think there's something radical about Christian theology that demands that you look to the margins. There's this parable of a worker who arrives late to a job and gets paid the same as people who are there early even though the people agreed to the wage that they had earlier. So Jesus has this parable and people become angry when someone gets something that people feel that they don't deserve . . . or we don't get as much as we feel we ought. . . . But I think once you become aware of difference and looking to the margins, it's pretty hard not to realize that this is a theme that runs through Christian theology.

In addition to his new primary identities as critical thinker and progressive Mennonite, we find his lower level political and career identities began to change in order to provide mutual verification rather than identity conflict. He also changes his career path, his environmental beliefs and his friendship circle:

> I switched from [majoring in] Chemistry to Pre-Pharmacy and finally to Geography. I had an experience in a geography class that explained things in a way that made sense [regarding poverty and other disparities between groups]. My friends changed; I lost my conservative friends. Politically, I identify as a Democrat now. My idea of good public policy is different. I have compassion and faith now. I am an environmentalist. My faith has moved to more liberal. I am more into process-oriented dialogue. I don't disrespect the military today but I don't consider it an asset and won't use it.

Adam expressed satisfaction with these identity changes indicating identity verification as the choices he has made align with his core identities. "Great, I love it. I feel happier being who I am. I respect the new people around me. I don't miss anything or anyone. I am doing the things that feel important. I feel important." He concluded, "I sought truth. I am a seeker and God's grace led me."

CONCLUSIONS

Stories such as Adam's exemplify the awakening of critical thinking as the disrupter of existing narratives of U.S. history or policy for the Education catalyst group veterans. This group is most likely to include truth telling as part of their pathway to antiwar activism. This antiwar activism, whether in an antiwar veterans group as we see with William and Steve or a faith and academic community as we find with Adam, provides a community of support to verify who they have become.

Table 6.1. Summary of moral identity change for one education catalyst group member

Catalyst Group	Moral Identity Standard at 18 Years	Behavior at 20 Years in Military	Identity Disruption	New Moral Identity Standard	New Behavior to Reach Identity Verification
Education Adam, 27 years	Smart, disciplined, fit, obedient, responsible Christian Conservative & apolitical Regarding War: It is necessary to defeat evil #1*	Joined Navy 1999-2003 & served primarily in Puerto Rico in Law Enforcement	In Puerto Rico a Pilot accidentally dropped a bomb on a Civilian Contractor. Locals protested & I saw the racism of U.S. military against Puerto Ricans. I stayed in PR to teach at local Deaf School & learned about systemic oppression. Later, in college I began to see a more progressive view of U.S. foreign policy that fit my Navy experience.	Christian Pacifist & follower of Jesus with commitment to church community. PhD Student concerned with issues of U.S. Immigration Policy Regarding war: There is no known appropriate or justifiable use of war. Violence begets violence. # 6, 7, & 8*	Left conservative church & joined a progressive traditional peace church congregation & became very involved in leadership. Dissertation deals with U.S. Immigration Policy regarding Hispanic populations. I speak out publicly about my views on immigration.

* Numbers refer to the specific veteran's position on the militarism to pacifism scale.

Collective Identity is especially important in the Identity Change Process of the veterans we placed in this group. Like the other catalyst groups, the Education group, once finding a social movement organization or church that verifies their new identity results in a profound sense of satisfaction and wholeness. This group appears to find a Collective Identity group that plays a central role in directing the identity change process and forming the new identity standards.

The Education group are also the most involved in antiwar activism but in a very holistic way. They are working for peace through a career in academia, teaching public school, providing counseling services, leading a church organization or coordinating a local peace group.

We see little evidence of moral injury among veterans in this group. Several factors might explain this absence. First, this group has experienced less combat than all other groups. Similarly, few individuals in this group report PTSD or symptoms of PTSD. Finally, like the betrayal group, it appears that this group had relative control in their ability to respond to instances of moral identity disruption and thus were not witnessing violations to their moral identity that could lead to moral injury.

Chapter Seven

Comparing Activist Veterans to Non-Activist Veterans

Why do identities (moral, group, and role) change over a person's life course? During a normal adult developmental maturation process, person, role and group identities often change. Another reason for an identity change would be a shift in priorities as people become spouses, parents, and/or full time workers. Crises can change a person's moral identity, such as a divorce or a severe injury. Encountering different environments can change a person's group identities, since new groups can uncover new dimensions of that person who may no longer be able to verify their old identities (for example, living in a foreign country).

For the veterans featured in the last four chapters, their identity change processes centered on their position on war. These veterans encountered one of four catalysts for change due to a disruption to their moral identity. The disruption or incongruence initiated a search for identity verification. Their stories illustrate both the uniqueness and commonalities of their pathways to pacifism and/or antiwar activism.

Further understanding of these pathways, though, requires a consideration of non-activist veterans who did not adopt an activist antiwar identity. By studying a comparison group of seven non-activist veterans, this study provides valuable insights into the identity change processes of both activist and non-activist veterans. Both groups have similar demographic backgrounds and military histories, but the comparison group do not consider themselves to be pacifists who opposed all wars. Nor did these non-activists join a traditional peace church or an antiwar group. Instead, the non-activists shared stories of their military service and return to civilian life that had less identity disruption and transformation than those of the activist veterans. Their collective identities varied also from that of the activist veterans and were limited to Christianity, the Democratic Party, or African Americans. Four of the seven experienced no combat and only one had a PTSD diagnosis.

Another focus of this chapter is the examination of the antiwar veteran's explanations for the reactions of those who had lived through similar experiences (combat, betrayal, education, etc.) but did not become antiwar activists. Some of their comrades, then, still supported the wars they had fought in and subsequent wars such as the Iraq War of 2003–2011 that was universally opposed by the antiwar activist veterans. By examining how identity change occurs over time among pro-war veterans, we will more fully understand the unique aspects about the identity change process of their antiwar counterparts.

CHARACTERISTICS OF THE NON-ACTIVIST VETERANS

In recruiting veterans to interview for this study, the researcher used a convenience sample that included acquaintances in Columbus, Ohio. Each veteran was asked if they would be willing to share their life and military stories and any changes they had experienced in relation to the appropriate use of war. They answered the same questions as did the antiwar veterans. Six of the seven were face-to-face interviews that took place in 2008 and 2009. These veterans had the following characteristics:

- 14 percent women ($n = 1$);
- 57 percent African American ($n = 4$);
- All seven had a bachelor's degree funded with the G.I. Bill;
- Ages from 35 to 80;
- All seven were married (some were on their second or third marriages);
- All seven had a religious upbringing (four Baptists, one Catholic, one Methodist, and one Pentecostal); and
- Five out of seven were still involved in a church, which was their primary community of support.

In terms of combat experience, four of the veterans did not serve in a country at war. The two oldest veterans had served in the U.S. and Europe, while two in their sixties had served in Vietnam. One of the Vietnam veterans had remained in the reserves and was called to fight in the Iraq War. Two of the veterans were in their forties: one who had served in the Persian Gulf War and another who had served stateside during the 1990s. Many of these characteristics mirrored those of the 114 activist veterans.

Post military service, three of the group worked in careers that they prepared for in college, including psychology, communications, and interior design. The others changed jobs more frequently. Only one veteran with

PTSD struggled with employment and currently lived on his disability payments. While all of the activist veterans in the study became associated with an antiwar veterans group (Veterans for Peace, Vietnam Veterans against the War, or Iraq Veterans against the War) or pacifist church, none of the non-activist veterans joined any of these groups.

At age 18, all seven believed that either "it is appropriate for a nation to respond to an injustice anywhere in the world in any way it sees fit or that at least war should have a 'Just Cause.'" By the time of the interviews (from 7 to 52 years later), all seven agreed with the Just War Theory criteria to determine the appropriate use of war. Three of the veterans added that they believed "that there were nonviolent means to resolve conflict peacefully without recourse to war or violence."

During the time of the interviews (2008–2009), the U.S. still had a military presence in Iraq. Four of the seven veterans had opposed the Iraq War but they were not engaged in any antiwar activism. Since faithfulness to the moral identity provides the motivation to act (Blasi, 1984), this non-activism may be the result of these veterans having had no disruption to the moral identity like the activists experienced. Although their views on war became more discerning with time to include Just War criteria, the veterans did not feel the same emotional turmoil due to non-verification of their moral identity. Therefore, the veterans showed no motivation to seek identity verification through antiwar activism.

Researchers hypothesize that the moral identity is a higher level identity than the soldier role identity or Army group identity (Gilligan, 1982; Haidt & Kesebir, 2010; Kohlberg, 1981). When the moral identity standards change, the lower level role and group identities must change in order to feel internally consistent or not hypocritical (Burke & Stets, 2009). This lack of moral identity disruption and change in the non-activist, then, also explains why none of the non-activist veterans identified significant shifts in their lower level group or role identities over time. Simply put, their changing beliefs on war did not always change their moral identity standards. Neither did they need to seek verification from a new collective identity group beyond the military or church.

Doug's Pathways to Opposing and Yet Serving in the Iraq War

Doug shared his story in 2009 at age 60. He had served in combat during Vietnam and again in Iraq in 2003 when his Reserve Unit was called. Raised by his grandmother and later his mother, he had enlisted in the Air Force "to get out of a bad family situation" and had always "dreamed of being a fighter pilot." His story indicates that Doug would fit into the Betrayal catalyst group due to his critical thinking abilities and "realizing our government really does lie on major issues and they do it under the guise of national security." However, his mild reaction regarding this breach of trust by the U.S. government contrasted with the deep anger expressed by the antiwar veterans who felt betrayed.

Once in the Air Force, Doug had what he termed "some significant paradigm shifts." Despite his realization about U.S. government decision-making, he still believed in the government's right to authority. He stated that if enlisted soldiers decided not to serve in wars they believed to be based on lies, "it would lead to anarchy and this (avoiding anarchy) is more important." In his mind, "We are a nation of laws and we need to follow them." Prioritizing law and order over being true to one's moral conscience distinguishes Doug from many of the antiwar veterans who volunteered for the study:

> Until VN, I took the U.S. government at its word. After being in Vietnam, I knew my government lied. I always ask why about things. When Nixon said that we weren't bombing Cambodia, I knew we were because I was guiding them. It was top secret. Later, I supported Operation Iraqi Freedom as the National Guard was mobilized. I saw Halliburton [a U.S. military contractor during the war] and other contractors [food, etc.] and some of [what the U.S. said they were doing] wasn't true. I was in Iraq for "Shock and Awe" [the name of the U.S. military operation that began the war] from February 2003 till the summer of 2004 [1½ years]. Every month of the first 6 months, we were told that we would go home. I was the command Sergeant Major of troops . . . I am still a soldier and gave an oath to defend my country and commander in chief.

It is interesting to note that Doug mentions an oath to defend "my country and commander in chief" as other veterans in the antiwar activist group differentiated between their oath to defend the U.S. constitution as they joined the military versus the President of the U.S. In addition, it is interesting to note that Doug is an African American who, being part of a minority group who knows the reality of racism both conscious and unconscious first hand, may feel greater pressure to conform to the culture of obedience within the U.S. military:

> [Today] my personal belief is that we should never have been in Iraq, Afghanistan yes, but Iraq was not part of it. It troubled and troubles me that we toppled a government and drew the ire of the people with 4,000–5,000 troops killed. I don't doubt Hussein and his sons were tyrants but these people are all over the world that require this kind of intervention. My biggest paradigm shift is realizing our government really does lie on major issues and they do it under the guise of national security. The average soldier has a greater degree of intelligence and can figure these things out.

Although Doug held strong opinions about the military, he described being cautious about sharing his views both within the military and his hometown community. His role as administrator in a state government agency and an Air Force Reserve soldier (until 2009) could explain his reluctance to be open about his political opinions. His discussion about his support for a draft, for example, could cause a negative reaction. He seems to want to avoid controversy despite holding strong opinions:

> I believe that the U.S. should still have a draft. I believe in the draft like they have in Israel. Freedom is not free and all citizens should share the burden. The military benefits youth. Youth could serve in many ways—military or civilian. Both men and women should serve. There is a danger with male's perspective on women. I mean the concept of men being the protector of women. The draft would help decrease crime, increase jobs, give youth time to mature and develop in a controlled environment with some independence.

Doug characterized his opposition to the Iraq War and his knowledge about government lies as "a burden." But he also is "glad for it" as this knowledge helps him "to prepare and to give advice to others." Similar to antiwar veterans, he realized that his insights have cost him. "I felt I was part of a lie and it screwed with my character and integrity. Trust became a big issue. . . . It is important to do the right thing." Despite this use of "do the right thing" language that suggests he is drawing on moral identity standards, he clearly prioritizes keeping law and order over the "anarchy" he imagines if every soldier who opposed war refused to serve. The antiwar activist veterans mentioned no such priority and were eager to challenge the status quo.

Unlike antiwar activist veterans who felt betrayed by the government, Doug underwent few changes in his lower level identities resulting from his opposition to the war in Iraq. He had always been and continued to be a Democrat and Baptist. His career changes did not occur from his sense of betrayal, but only from a natural progression in his work history and networking. He concluded that despite "knowing my government lies. . . . I am still a soldier and gave my oath to defend my country and the Commander in Chief." In addition to Doug's law and order ethic, his oath or his word trumps his opposition to the Iraq War.

Abe's Pathway to Just War Thinking

As an older veteran, Abe had experienced a different war from Doug. This 79-year-old veteran of the Korean conflict had begun his Army service at age 18 believing that "war was great, glamorous and macho." Today, he "dislikes war intensely" and claimed that "I could never go to war today . . . I couldn't even kill a robber." He was certain that "Christ would serve as a noncombatant." He opposed the war in Iraq due to his belief in the Just War Theory.

Abe's change in thinking about war was gradual, taking place over decades. Life experiences such as the Peace Corps and important friendships made him "a grateful and caring Christian." His story indicates that he had a series of small disruptions in his trust in the business world, the U.S. government, and the affluent U.S. lifestyle. His identity change, though, came within the religious setting. With each disruption of trust, he found various role models who were wise and/or religious and offered healing and resolution. He also discovered new ways of thinking that helped him form a new Christian identity. The church benefited from his volunteer commitments. Although he opposed the Vietnam War and the Iraq War, he took no overt action to oppose them as did the antiwar activist veterans:

> The first change came when I was in the business world with Wurlitzer Pianos [1950s and 1960s]. I traveled a lot all over the U.S. It was very demanding. I had to work Saturdays half days and went to the airport on Sundays to leave again. I worked with some Vietnam veterans and heard horrible stories. I was not thinking much in those days but in reading about Vietnam, I thought it was a bad war.

We found comments from both the antiwar activists and this small group of non-activists, like Abe, about "not thinking much" in their late teens and twenties. This explains the lack of identity disruption even in his opposition to the Vietnam War. In addition, Abe has almost no time for self-reflection due to his demanding work schedule. We identified a time of self-reflection as vital to the identity change process. Self-appraisal is vital to recognizing error messages or negative emotions that cause identity disruption and drive the need for identity standard change in order to experience identity verification. But we do find an abrupt change in career and environment in 1971 when Abe quits his vice presidential position, sells his home and makes a commitment to volunteer for two years in Brazil:

> My wife and I joined the Peace Corps in 1971 due to frustration with my work. I was at the point of promotion but I didn't have a life. . . . I experienced people who were poor, needy, and grateful for whatever we did. Sir Premo, the founding father of our town, was like a dad to me. I was in my 40s and he was in his 70s. . . . The biggest experience was coming back from the Peace Corps in 1973. It was a shock. I landed in the Miami Airport. I saw obesity, make-up, jewelry, and I knew we were ugly Americans.

Here we find real evidence of identity disruption. Abe had entered the Peace Corps as a proud and patriotic American and upon returning after two years of living among the poorest of the poor in northern Brazil, he sees

Americans through a new lens. He is now a disgusted American who idealizes the simple lifestyle of the poor and is ready to make a change in his own lifestyle. It is also important to note that his two years with the Peace Corps in Brazil offered the luxury of life at a much slower pace and ample time to reflect on his priorities and how he would spend the second half of his life:

> When we came back, we worked one year in VISTA [Volunteers in Service to America now called Americorps] on an Indian reservation south of Billings, Montana. I had to learn about Native Americans and the real history of the United States. It was such a shock. I asked what kind of government we really had. I realized the Bureau of Indian Affairs was there to serve the white people, not the Native Americans.

Abe fits the Religious Conviction Catalyst group primarily but also the Betrayal group due to his observations of U.S. versus Brazilian culture as well as his new understandings of U.S. history and politics that we see in his comments about the self-serving nature of the Bureau of Indian Affairs. These disruptions in his patriotic U.S. identity further solidify his desire for change in order to create identity verification. Rather than acting as another "ugly American," Abe sought to serve the Cheyenne community by challenging some of the systems of dependency that kept them poor:

> I started garden plots. The Native Americans had stopped gardens because after World War II they were given free commodities. We had a lawyer in our group who was working on legal issues related to corporations using their land. The Native Americans were getting a pittance for the mining and ranching on their land. They got five dollars an acre.

Native American spirituality was eye-opening for Abe as it introduced him to a mystical experience of God that was absent during his Christian upbringing and led during his early adult years to skipping church on Sundays even when his wife attended with their two boys. This "closeness to God" disrupted his Christian identity and assumptions and opened him in a new way to seeking God:

> In Montana I did Sweats with one of the Native American leaders named Fred. It was a religious-type ceremony. The setting in Montana made me feel close to God. During the Sweats, I felt close to God. [Following the Peace Corps and VISTA] we moved to southern Missouri and I worked for the U.S. Forest Service for 17 years and this is where I became stronger in my faith. I went to a small church that needed lots of help and so I took on leadership positions. . . . There was a great female pastor in Mountain View who put an emphasis on outreach [to the community] and kids. This changed my respect for the church and what it could do.

Finally, with his exposure to a new kind of Christian pastor that found ministry to the poor and outreach to kids core to the gospel, he embraced a new type of Christian moral identity that matched his moral identity that was shaped by the poor of Brazil. He was drawn into leadership and also in his work for the U.S. Forest Service, he was drawn into a strong environmental identity:

> Then we retired and moved to Hannibal, Missouri and went to a Methodist church and they asked me to be Treasurer and this increased my involvement. I saw the workings of the church and it was good. Mike K. was a lay leader and he encouraged me to take a course on the church and more classes and then I started preaching in our church. I had to do written sermons but I liked giving them the most. I felt like God was helping me [write them].

Here we see that his Native American experiences with God are influencing his leadership and preaching in the church. He senses God's presence in helping him write his lay sermons and fully embraces his Christian identity as it is congruent with his moral and environmental identity standards. He is so energized by this work that when asked, is willing to volunteer for even more demanding community service. We might also hypothesize that his role identity standards of lay preacher require significant volunteer work to those in need:

> My neighbor Earl W. was a part of "Industrial Chaplain Ministries" and went to a two-day training with continuing education to prepare him to serve in local businesses. He said "come and try it" and so I did and I liked it and I had the time. It was easy work. I worked at Dura Corp and they had three shifts a day. I went in a couple times a week on all shifts and talked to the workers and had resources to help them with personal problems. This Dura Corp work helped me to see people were hurting and often sick and in need but they were still working. I met different kinds of people. I went to their funerals. I got close to people . . . [weeping as he speaks].

Later we see evidence of full identity verification and life satisfaction in his retirement years. The changes are dramatic considering he began his adult life by avoiding anything having to do with church and spends 20–30 hours a week during retirement preaching, providing church leadership, plus acting as a chaplain in the local hospital as well as for a local factory. His emotional displays attest to the power and rewards of this work for him:

> Also at that time, Reverend Coleman got me involved as a hospital chaplain and I really enjoyed that. People were hurting and in need. When I visited the patients in their rooms and asked if they would like prayers, ninety-nine out of hundred would say yes, I want a prayer. Some would call me at home. They would ask for prayer because they felt lifted up by my prayers. . . . After

meeting people in the hospital or at Dura Corp they would stop me at the drugstore in town. It created a new sensitivity to people for me. It has changed my life. It was so rewarding [crying]. I learned not to judge people based on appearances.

Abe's story demonstrates that like the activist antiwar veterans, he made sacrifices to move in a new direction regarding his beliefs about U.S. corporate culture and the good life. "I gave up my job status, the pace and the challenge of a professional job with Wurlitzer." He was also acutely aware "that with the changes in career and lifestyle, my headaches and migraines left."

Abe summarized his life and identity changes by reflecting, "It was a spiritual journey. It was a slow, gradual process of change. It was probably just the people that surrounded me that encouraged me." As a result, he became more giving and generous with people and changed careers but unlike the antiwar activist veterans, neither his politics nor his willingness to actively oppose war were changed.

Carl's Pathway to a Liberal Political Identity

Growing up during the Cold War like Abe, Carl also believed that "if we're not strong, the communists will win." He came from another generation, though, since he joined the Army from 1985 to 1987 serving stateside as a mechanic and marksmanship trainer. At age 18, he had been "proud to defend the U.S." doing "well in (the Army) in a short time." It took several years for him to shift his opinion on war. Sharing his story in 2008 at the age of 40, Carl felt that the "military is a necessary function of our society but there's a lot of gray. War should be the very, very last option." His story began with the image of a young man who needed a chance to escape from a working class neighborhood with friends who were going nowhere fast:

> I joined the military at 17 years old with a 1.6 GPA. The military was life changing. I grew up in a working class neighborhood and I had few options. I joined with six other friends. I took the most training in the least amount of time. I liked the Army; boot camp was hard but very beneficial. It taught me self-discipline and self-respect. I formed a relationship with my Captain. He served as a mentor and I had few of them [Carl's dad died when he was five]. It was different mentally; I had more confidence at the end because I made it.

Later in college on the G.I. Bill, Carl's thinking about war and identity as a "Young Republican" started to change. This transformation accelerated when he found his "birth mother" for the first time at the age of 21. His mom was a "liberal artist from California who helped me to think in new ways"— an insight that fits with the Education Catalyst group. His opinion shift on abortion "felt like an epiphany" but otherwise "it was a natural progression": "During college I got interested in politics. I joined the Young Republicans and was an officer. I got lots of recognition. [At one meeting] a Pro Life person came to give a presentation and it was very manipulative so I got up and walked out. . . . Kent State was overall very liberal."

Here we find an early disruption in Carl's prolife moral identity as he strikes out against being manipulated by pictures of aborted fetuses. Since he associates being a Republican with being prolife, his commitment to his conservative political identity is also disrupted but this was not enough to cause changes to his pro war moral identity. His positive Army experiences and role models continue to verify this portion of his moral identity. Identity change requires continual disruption and this only occurs with the new and continual exposure to the well-developed moral identity of his birth mother who was apparently anxiously anticipating contact from her son who she gave up for adoption as an unwed mother while attending Kent State in the 1960s:

> In 1988 I went to the adoption agency that handled my adoption asking for contact information for my birth mom and I called her. She was in San Francisco and she was a liberal. We talked on the phone for an hour and then she came to see me at Kent. She was 39 and a funky artist. She had a B.A. in Art from Kent State and helped me to think in new ways. I began to see the wisdom of some social programs and I am now against the death penalty. I believe that bearing arms should not include AK47s. [As I developed my relationship with my birth mom] my adoptive mom was a rock and good to the core. She was OK with me contacting my birth mom. I aspire to be like her.

Moral issue by issue, we see Carl's questioning foundational Republican policies related to abortion, gun control, social programs and the death penalty as he sees them through his birth mother's more liberal political identity. The questions and disruptions in his Republican group identity continue with his move to a new state. New liberal ideas about the environment and natural foods fit with early interests from childhood in conservation. Moving away from his conservative adoptive mom in Ohio allowed his birth mom to further verify his budding environmentalist and natural foods identities while also receiving verification in the liberal environment around Denver, Colorado: "In 1994, I moved to Colorado after college to live near the mountains. I lived there for a year and picked up on the environmental movement. I had wanted to be a conservationist as a kid. I began to shop for organic foods, I recycled, and I had a lot of interest in the area of food and the environment."

His political identity, then, shifted to become more liberal as he said he was proud to be a CSA (Community Supported Agriculture) member buying organic food directly from the farmer and "I love Obama." Aware of resistance from old friends regarding his new commitments and lifestyle, he stated that "people chide you all the time for your environmental views." Raised Baptist, he now was a marginal participant in the Catholic Church due to his wife and children. He worked as a successful regional sales manager for a national company.

Carl's moral identity changes unfold gradually with new experiences and people. What is missing or different from more antiwar activist veterans is significant moral identity disruption causing negative emotions and a desire to reduce feelings of guilt or shame through changing behaviors or identity standards. As some of the non-activist veterans demonstrate, the changes are more of a natural progression in thinking than responses to moral identity disruption.

To answer the theoretical question: why do some veterans experience dramatic identity changes while others like Carl do not is important to us. The stories of all seven of the non-activist veterans showed evidence of one of the four catalysts (Combat, Betrayal, Religious Conviction, and Education), but none of these vets chose to work against the Iraq War even if they did not consider it a Just War. In this section, we will share both our own conclusions to this question and the important insights from the antiwar activist veterans.

During the second wave of interviews in 2013, we asked 26 of the 114 antiwar veterans how they explained the differences in views of war and activism among veterans who have served beside them in the military. Their explanations were both insightful and diverse. The explanations summarized below represent veterans from each catalyst group, period of war and arm of the military.

Insights about Pro-War Iraq War Veterans

The first group of explanations focused on the antiwar vets having different life experiences than the pro-war vets. Larry, one of the Religious Conviction veterans, from the Iraq War reflects on the role of different combat experiences or the absence of combat experience for explaining why many veterans have not changed their pro-war stance.

Different military experiences explain the differences in pro-war and antiwar veterans.

> I wonder what kind of experience that they had that failed to challenge. . . . I mean you can't go to Iraq and not be antiwar. . . . If there were veterans that had combat experience and went and remain pro-war for lack of a better word, I really wonder what's going on internally, what it might require to maintain those allegiances. Is it family stuff, is it political stuff? I have friends that are trying to hold on to that [pro-war] identity. They won't tell other people but they tell me, "I lied about military service on camera. I told them this, that or

the other thing." Like there is something they are trying to accomplish that I
don't know.

Bill, a Vietnam combat veteran with PTSD believes that the difference
may be the raw experience of seeing death, especially of civilians up close as
he did. When he finally stopped running and then numbing from his memories with alcohol, they so disrupted his moral identity that he continues to
struggle to create a normal life. He finds that antiwar activism is vital to his
ever making things right and preventing this type of unbearable carnage from
haunting others:

> Well, in very large measure it's because they haven't seen what I've seen and
> been where I've been. I've seen all kinds of violent death. Besides being a
> Marine, I was a Police Officer and I drove an ambulance and to me, the
> destruction of property in war is regrettable but the destruction of life is un-
> thinkable. The idea of killing combatants is repulsive but killing of women and
> children is beyond my ability to imagine that someone would do deliberate-
> ly . . . but you know I have neighbors who say, you know we can make peace
> in the Middle East by just dropping a few bombs and making glass of all of
> them.

*Coping strategies for dealing with the guilt from actions in war differ
among antiwar and pro-war veterans.* A second group of explanations for
the differences between pro-war veterans and antiwar activists and non-activists focused on various psychological factors often related to guilt. Bob, in
the Combat catalyst group, is clear that veterans who remain very supportive
of war in general or the Iraq or Vietnam wars in particular struggle with guilt
from their actions during war. In order to live with themselves or verify their
moral identity, they must also affirm the necessity of war:

> Well, I don't know, I have to guess. I had to accept that I wasn't as brave as I
> should have been but. . . . The thing about veterans who are still unwilling to
> say that the war was wrong, they can't quite separate the war being wrong
> from themselves being wrong.
> Some of them, I think this is a minority . . . some of them have done really
> awful things that they have to justify. So, they are stuck. I've heard them say,
> the war was the highpoint of my life. It was the last time I was a part of
> something bigger than myself. This is only a guess but if they admit the war
> was wrong, then they have to admit that what they did was wrong. Maybe
> that's what they can't figure out. Certain people say the Pentagon Papers were
> wrong. A lot of people say that we [the U.S.] didn't start the war, we just went
> to help.

Edward, another Vietnam era combat veteran, believes that there is a "non-
combat syndrome" related to survivor's guilt that motivates vets to maintain

a pro-war position. He believes that some veterans will even fabricate stories in order to live with themselves:

> Realistically I think with a lot of the veterans it's part of the non-combat syndrome. The combat vets suffer from PTSD, the non-combat vets suffer from what I call the non-combat syndrome and it's closely aligned to survivor's guilt. Umm . . . so they have to deal with this issue and some of them do it by creating combat stories and some of them deal with it by believing . . . internalizing all of the pro-war nonsense.

Psychologically, many people cope with internal fears and pain by projecting them on enemies and thus remaining pro-war maintains one's sense of wellbeing. Bruce, a Vietnam combat veteran who became a psychologist, suggests that facing one's internal fears is the difference between antiwar activists and either non-activists or pro-war veterans. Fear may also prevent vets who oppose the Iraq War from taking a public stance against the war as many veterans describe the tremendous opposition they face on the protest line:

> Fear, I see that as the main thing. There is a general fear that people have that leads to war and it's a fear that's based on their own unresolved stuff inside. Everyone has their demons and you've got to look at the demons and if you don't, you're tendency is to project them outside. . . . The war is within us and we need to deal with it in a way that is loving and not destructive. Also the military industrial complex [corporations in the defense industry] is so strong, so there is a focus on how we need to make the world safe for democracy . . . but it's based on greed and greed is based on fear.

Malcomb, a Vietnam combat veteran, who has needed a great deal of healing for his PTSD and moral injury is clear that when truth threatens one's belief system, people must deny it. "You begin to betray yourself and society when you begin to talk about this stuff [from the war]." Malcomb asserts that "You need to understand that PTSD is about emotional silencing." He helps vets heal and recover from PTSD by helping them feel the pain behind the betrayal [by the U.S.]. He believes that only then will they find meaning in their lives.

Individuals have different intellectual and motivational abilities to deal with complexity and contradiction within U.S. history and policy. A third group of antiwar veterans explained the differences between pro-war and antiwar veteran's views on war as due to intellectual abilities. Sam, a lawyer from the Betrayal group, who served stateside during the 1960s believes that the differences are due to operating on a different intellectual level:

> Well, they're all individual stories and I don't think you can characterize them all as being on the same intellectual level. In some of them, there may be

denial because it goes against the way America is supposed to be. When they tell me if I don't like it, I should leave, I say but people like Washington and Jefferson didn't like it either, and they stayed and went to war to make it better. Part of the people know they're doing terrible things but it makes life easy for them and there are people who just don't want to know.

Jake, a career Marine from the Iraq War in the Combat catalyst group believes that without doing your homework, it is difficult to understand the complexities of U.S. history and foreign policy. On the surface war is often described as the good guys against the bad communists, Germans, Iraqi's or terrorists but in reality, vets like Jake find that the evil enemy has a story to tell also:

> What we have to remember is that the stage was set a long time ago for the events that took place in Iraq. Before the Iraq War, there was the Persian Gulf War—I had to do a lot of reading first to understand it. Some people don't have that level of understanding and so I just have to be courteous rather than say something negative.

Steve, from the Education group and a Just War Theorist, believes that the difference is having an open and curious mind and thus being able to integrate more either/or thinking. As a philosophy major, he learned to look at an issue from multiple perspectives and believes many pro-Iraq War vets are unable to think for themselves:

> I think that I'm very able to question authority . . . think for myself . . . that basically I've always been a kind of nosy person, I want to know stuff . . . and in high school it wasn't like that because it was blind obedience but when I got to college, I learned to love learning and I had these wonderful professors reading these great books that really opened my eyes. And because I have a degree in philosophy, it is the epitome of a subject to allow you to open your mind. Like before, everything was black or white. I never even heard of gray. You were either with us or against us. Our way was right and yours was wrong and in philosophy, I learned to look at something from five or six different points of view that all could be right. . . . Because we have a very authoritarian kind of society, you're not encouraged to think for yourself or question authority. I'm not like that but today we still have too many people like that.

Dave, a Marine veteran from the 1980s who did not experience combat identifies multiple differences between pro-war and antiwar activist vets. Some of these have already been described but Dave adds to the list that those who can't empathize with other's and see things from another person's perspective baffle him.

> I'm just gonna sound like a jerk but I'm just going to say IQ, mental curiosity and a failure of empathy. I don't know how people cannot put themselves in

the same position as the person they are launching a grenade or drone at . . . it baffles me, it makes me feel insane. My father-in-law says just kill them all and it blows my mind.

In attempting to understand his former friends, Christians and Navy sailors who remain pro-war, Adam concludes that they view war as a necessary evil that responsible citizens must volunteer for. But he is certain that

> this depends on the view that Americans and America is sort of the center of the political universe. And it's, in my view, paternalistic to view it that way and I'm very skeptical that the U.S. or any country for that matter, is very good at determining what kinds of interventions are responsible or right.

Pro-war and Antiwar vet's perspectives are best explained by the cultural environment they are exposed to including collective identity group, news sources and friendship circles. A final group of veterans focus on exposure to a cultural environment to explain the differences between pro and antiwar veterans, those who become activists and those who while against the war don't actively oppose it. David, an Air Force veteran who served during the 1970s believes it's all about the culture you're exposed to. The VFW or Veterans of Foreign Wars halls hold different expectations for patriotic behavior than Veterans for Peace. VFP members often describe patriotism as synonymous with actively opposing an unjust war such as the Iraq War:

> I think it's their culture. If you grow up in the military, then your maturation stops. But that's no way to grow up killing people. Most of us grow up and do what we're told. We go fight the war and then go on. They just do what they're told. Unless you're a real masochist, you're going to feel bad about it. It's easier to go down to the VFW and drink with your friends.

William, an Army veteran from 1971 to 1974 who did not see combat but spent three years volunteering with vets returning home from Vietnam believes the difference in pro and antiwar vets is due to believing the extensive U.S. government propaganda about war. William is in the Education catalyst group:

> Well I just say they are misguided. And in this country since Vietnam, we have been subject to propaganda like the world has never seen before. It was actually during Reagan that movies like Rambo came out, a government sponsored movie. The real storyline of that movie was to kind of rewrite the history of Vietnam. Like we would have won if it weren't for the hippies and Jane Fonda. If you go and look at those movies, there are four of them that are pure propaganda—they sort of rewrote the history of Vietnam. The pro Vietnam vets now, they are just brainwashed.

The antiwar veterans in our study provide a variety of explanations for the differences between pro versus antiwar activist veterans and those who oppose the war in Iraq but fail to register their beliefs publicly. These include such psychological factors as guilt, denial and fear. A number of veterans named differences in mental capacities based on intelligence levels and the ability to think critically and move beyond either or thinking related to moral development. Quite a few veterans attribute the differences to varying life experiences, especially in seeing combat up close and struggling with the emotional silencing caused by PTSD. Finally they offer explanations related to cultural exposures and propaganda. It appears that these explanations help the veterans in our study to further verify their antiwar activist identity. In separating themselves from others, they justify their identity as antiwar activists as well as achieve congruence between their own identity standards and actions.

CONCLUSIONS

Our examination of the non-activist veterans reveals that some veterans experience both an identity-disrupting catalyst and a change in their position on war without dramatic identity change that leads to antiwar activism. While qualitative cross-sectional interviews cannot provide causal explanations, we do see some striking differences in the non-activists. First, these veterans do discuss change in attitudes and behaviors since leaving the military and for some, such as Abe, this includes adopting a personal pacifist perspective that permits others fighting in a Just War while he could not. However, their opposition to the Iraq War does not appear to be a result of a disruption in their moral identity. The non-activist veterans have shifted their belief that the Iraq War is a Just War but this change in political opinion failed to disrupt the moral identity or the lower level role or group identities. In addition to failing to disrupt the moral identity, group associations are key to the differences between both antiwar activists and pro-war veterans and antiwar non-activists. Group associations provide a collective identity needed to reconstruct coherent group and role identities that verify their higher level antiwar moral identity.

While only a few veterans identified cultural exposure as important to differences, it is clear that the majority of antiwar activist veterans either sought out or were asked to join Veterans for Peace, Vietnam Veterans against the War or Iraq Veterans against the War. We believe that the collective identity and accompaniment of veterans from one of these groups in the post military period of reintegration and meaning-making as a civilian was central to the differences we seek to explain.

The Role of Collective Identity in Social Movements

Collective identity, as described more fully in the Identity Theory chapter, refers to a network of active relationships. These relationships include emotional involvement, a system to regulate membership, support through difficult periods in the movement, maintenance of boundaries through differentiating with oppositional groups and a shared project of collective action.

The 114 veterans in our study solicited primarily through the three veterans antiwar movements and the Mennonite Church USA identified these groups as significant in the support they felt as they moved to their new pacifist and antiwar identities. Sixty-two percent drew support from Veterans for Peace. Fourteen percent noted the importance of Iraq Veterans against the War, a percentage limited by specific membership guidelines for those who served in Iraq. Vietnam Veterans against the War provided continued support, 30 years post war, for fourteen percent of the group.

In describing these social movement group affiliations, veterans used similar descriptors. Steve describes how after telling his story for the filming of Winter Soldier I documentary, he "transferred my loyalty" from the Marines to the Vietnam Veterans against the War organization. This group enabled him and in fact encouraged him to "get honest about what I did in Vietnam." Another Vietnam vet actively involved with VFP found veterans with "similar backgrounds and profound change. I found adults who expressed what I felt. My friendships changed to committed peace people."

One of the female Air Force veterans from the 1980s describes her close affiliation with an older member of VFP. "He adopted me and guided me and showed me the way." She also describes multiple friends from within the veteran's peace movement organization VFP. She describes how VFP, IVAW, and SWAN (Service Women's Action Network) members have supported her in her extensive antiwar activism, protest, advocacy, and speaking engagements.

Another Vietnam War vet, interviewed at age 63, describes himself as an activist for the last 30 years post sobriety and hospitalization for depression. Just prior to the Persian Gulf War in 1991, he attended an antiwar demonstration and met members of VFP. He says, "I met my community, we get together yet today and continue to process Vietnam." Today he speaks to groups across the United States and around the world about war. VFP members honor those who are arrested and jailed for social movement actions as he has been.

A vet who grew up traveling around the world in his career Air Force family joined the Airforce in 1972. Upon return to the U.S., he attended college and joined VVAW because, "They were the only group looking at Agent Orange. They wanted to fight the Klan in Mississippi. I fell in love

with the VVAW in 1979." This vet has devoted his life to counseling veterans and getting them the help and services they need.

Of the criteria for collective identity, we find evidence that the veterans
peace groups provided emotional support, a strong sense of solidarity, criteria for joining each movement, boundary work in terms of who is in and who
is out and finally a shared project of collective action. Veterans discussed
multiple examples of their "shared projects of collective action" through
annual conferences, legislative advocacy work, counseling and other support
for returning veterans, healing work for veterans with PTSD, regional protests and vigils as well as counter military recruiting in high schools.

We found that the 15 Mennonite veterans were rarely involved in the
three veterans peace movement groups in the study but they also drew on a
collective identity, that of being Mennonite pacifists. One of the areas that
this was most pronounced was in how the Mennonite men described their
changes in masculinity once they adopted the pacifist Mennonite identity.

They were primarily in the Feminist Masculine group naming opposition
to macho men, the importance of nurture and emotional expression as who
they are as good men. These vets were rarely involved in public protest or
counter military recruiting, vets conferences or legislative advocacy. We find
that their collective identity demanded other guidelines for membership and
boundary work. These vets were clearly pacifists opposed to all wars and
even opposed to using lethal violence in self-defense. Their collective identity rewarded further theological education and church leadership. The Mennonite collective identity, much more than the non-Mennonite vets mentioned lifestyle activism such as living simply, active membership and service to the church and wider community, and practicing of spiritual disciplines such as prayer, spiritual direction and bible study.

We also found other group memberships that provided a sense of collective identity for a minority of the veterans. These included religious groups
such as Buddhists, Catholics, Quakers, Presbyterians and Lutherans. These
groups served as important support and identity verification systems for 28
percent of our group. For the seven non-activist veterans who served as a
type of comparison group, five of the group were heavily involved with their
Christian faith, often Baptist. Of the other two non-activist veterans, one was
heavily involved in the Democratic Party and the other with the environmental movement. Thus we find that some source of collective identity was
important to each of our veterans. The collective identity group they affiliat-
ed with helped to explain their level and type of antiwar activism more than
any other factor.

Chapter Eight

Renegotiating Masculinity for Antiwar Veterans

It challenged me every time I had to get up and say I was antiwar and antiwar very publicly. I constantly had to present myself as a person that . . . did this very archetypally masculine role but in order to say in so many ways that I was opposed to what that role was doing, I had to like manufacture this side of me that was still masculine. (Luke at age 28)

Becoming an antiwar veteran was not an isolated event for the antiwar veterans in our study, but rather a life change that permeated many of their other identities and social relationships. In the process of adopting a new moral identity in relation to war, the veterans had to redefine themselves in many other ways. As we illustrated in previous chapters, for some this included shifts in the identity standards of certain role identities such as spouse or patriotic citizen. For others this included changes in group identities such as their political affiliation from conservative Republican to a progressive Democrat. In this chapter we examine how, over their life-course, these antiwar veterans altered their meanings of their masculine identity standard to bring them in line with their antiwar position. We argue that given the strong connection between the military and masculinity, men that adopt an antiwar position may be marginalized during the renegotiation of their masculine identity upon reentry to civilian life. In doing so, two striking themes emerge. First, we find, similar to the themes found in previous chapters, that activism was the key factor in the renegotiation of masculine identity. Second, the process of renegotiating masculinity was also impacted by social location such as age, career, marital status, and education.

MASCULINITY

In order to understand the importance of masculine identity among antiwar veterans, we must first provide some background on masculinity itself. Many gender scholars, since West and Zimmerman's (1987) seminal article "Doing Gender," accept that gender, at least in part, is something that is "done" (i.e., actively shaped and performed in numerous situations). From this perspective masculinity lies at the intersection of macro-level social structures (age, race/ethnicity, class) and micro-level interaction. It is constructed and maintained as individuals interact within various social contexts (Christensen & Jensen, 2014; Messerschmidt, 2008).

Masculinity is not a single or fixed category, but rather there are multiple masculinities, which are constantly compared against what is considered feminine (Connell & Messerschmidt, 2005). These multiple masculinities are defined and ordered in relation to an idealized masculinity (what scholars refer to as hegemonic masculinity) (Connell & Messerschmidt, 2005). Thus masculinity is inherently relational (Lusher & Robbins, 2009, 391; Messerschmidt, 2012). Men construct and maintain their masculinity by confirming that differences (i.e., non-hegemonic masculinities and femininity) are inferior. That means that the "rules of masculinity" are such that men act in ways that distinguish them from what is considered feminine. An example of this would be holding a belief that "men don't cry" as displaying one's emotions is associated with women. These rules will change based on contexts and situations. For example, the rules for masculinity may be different in a rural and an urban setting, or different within the military (Connell & Messerschmidt, 2005; Filteau, 2015).

At the micro-level, individuals work to verify a self-meaning of being masculine or feminine. Stets and Burke term this self-meaning of masculine or feminine, one's gender identity. However, it is important to remember that gender identities can be fluid, multiple and fragmented. Furthermore, micro-level identity work is intimately connected to the larger social structure. As Stets and Burke (1996) state, "We see the status of gender and the identity of gender as simultaneously produced and maintained" (193).

Here we are interested in understanding how the identity disruption and change experienced by the veterans in our study impact their self-meaning of being a man. We argue that how they "do gender" as a result of the moral identity disruption, has important implications for how they understand their masculine identity.

The Military, Masculinity, and Antiwar Activism

We choose to focus on the masculine identity of our veterans for a number of reasons. First, there is a clear and strong connection between the military and masculinity in the United States. In many ways, the military plays a primary role in shaping images of masculinity (Kilshaw, 2009). Both "military" and "war" are dominant symbols of masculinity (Barrett, 1996). Military masculinity is one privileged form of masculinity in the United States and many western societies, and thus a type of *hegemonic masculinity*. Hegemonic masculinity is defined as the privileged masculinity that is set in opposition to "lesser" forms of masculinity and femininity within a particular time and place. A distinct benefit of joining the military for men is "access to resources of a hegemonic masculinity" (Hinojosa, 2010, 180).

Military masculinity includes "a set of beliefs, practices and attributes that can enable individuals, men and women, to claim authority on the basis of affirmative relationships with the military or with military ideas" (Belkin, 2012, 3). While there are multiple forms of military masculinity that vary across time and place, several common descriptors of military masculinity exist, including being physically fit and powerful, mentally strong, unemotional, heterosexual, as well as endurance and loyalty (Barrett, 1996; Woodward, 2000). By applying the workings of hegemonic masculinities, militaries build cohesion with an "idealized" model of the military member contributing to a shared sense of pride. Hegemonic ideals also motivate particular behavior by "feminizing" undesirable behavior (Belkin, 2012; Duncanson, 2015; Goldstein, 2001).

Second, a key challenge for individuals leaving the military is defining and verifying one's identity outside of the military organization. Recent research suggests that this exit can lead to identity conflict (Smith & True, 2014). Adopting an antiwar position upon leaving the military can further complicate identity definition and verification. Reentry into civilian life requires soldiers to assume an "ex-soldier" or civilian identity (Smith & True, 2014). This identity may generate conflict in several ways. First, the growing divide between civilians and the military often means that systems of military, such as forms of recognition are not acknowledged or fully understood by civilians (Collins & Holsti, 1999). Additionally, the feedback of being a hero that many soldiers receive is at times incongruent with their own identity standard (Smith & True, 2014). Finally, the military aims to shape a soldier identity that emphasizes order, obedience, and collectivism. Combat further shapes a soldier identity, in part, by solidifying mutual dependence and trust among members of a combat unit (Smith & True, 2014). These collectivist traits are not necessarily valued in the civilian world where individualism and autonomy are prized.

Given the strong connection between the military and masculinity, men who adopt an antiwar position may be particularly challenged in the renegotiation of their masculine identity upon reentry to civilian life. For instance, people may question the masculinity of a soldier or veteran who has adopted an antiwar position. This social reaction (which the Identity Theory would call an "input") could affect his own reflected self-appraisals and even lead to identity non-verification. Denigrating a man's masculine identity standard, then, could cause a conflict between two identities, being male and being an antiwar veteran.

The third reason for choosing masculinity as a central theme for antiwar veterans, is the radical shift of status that often occurs from privileged to stigmatized. For many veterans, adopting an antiwar identity meant potentially losing their privileged status of white male by choosing a potentially stigmatizing identity. Past research on masculinity has demonstrated that privilege is not an all or nothing binary. Rather, categories of men may experience privilege to a greater or lesser extent as a result of other components of their social identity, such as class, sexuality or disability. Various identities can intersect with masculinity and cause men to be seen, at least, as "lesser men" or "not real men," and at worst, "not men." Coston and Kimmel (2012) note, "What is interesting is how these men choose to navigate and access their privilege within the confines of a particular social role that limits, devalues and often stigmatizes them as not-men" (99). Since being antiwar among a veteran population is often stigmatized as not-male, most of these men move from meeting the hegemonic masculine ideal (Hinojosa, 2010) to a marginalized masculinity (Coston & Kimmel, 2012) and must then revise and prove their masculinity with others.

Our exploration of masculine identity was based on in-depth interviews conducted with a subset of 26 men chosen from the initial study of 114 veterans in 2013. Note that while people who identify as women may hold or attempt to hold a masculine identity standard, we are only looking at individuals that identify as men. The data collection and analysis were considered Phase Two of the study and are outlined in detail in chapter three. We focused on the veterans' response to the question "what did it mean to be a good man at age 18 and what does it mean today." As we demonstrated throughout the catalyst chapters, these 26 veterans currently self- identify as antiwar and/or pacifist and experienced significant identity change since age 18 in relation to their position on war. Here we focus specifically on how they understand this identity change in relation to their masculine identity standard and how the way in which they currently "do gender" impacts their identity verification.

Connecting Antiwar Identity Change and a Masculine Identity Standard

The connection that the veterans in our study make between their views on war at age 18 and their understanding of what it meant to be a good man are striking. As 18 year olds, these veterans believed that U.S. leaders were knowledgeable and fair and thus could be trusted to do the right thing in response to violence and injustice in the world. Finally, most veterans at age 18 believed it takes a strong military to guarantee peace and justice against "bad guys" around the world. Whether their heroes were their fathers who fought in "the Good War" (World War II) or symbols such as John Wayne, these men wanted to emulate them. They, too, wanted to project strength and aggression in response to "bad guys" thus masculinity meant being fair and protecting others. For example, Gary, a 67-year-old former Air Force pilot and chaplain describes military service in terms of wanting to do the right thing as both a Christian and a good man:

> I went into the Vietnam conflict because the church thought being a good Christian was doing what the community wanted you to do like be in Vietnam. Because I was a man, I had the responsibility to defend the community and to respond in places where there would be danger. As a man, I had been conditioned to fight and defend those who were less capable. I would never have chosen to be a soldier without that context . . . I was bold and courageous and was shot at and saw people blown up and I didn't back away. . . . When I realized my actions had an impact on the lives of other people, it was important for me to not harm others. From that place, I began the transition of asking what is the practical way that that works itself out? So what choices do I need to make now?

In changing their position on war, many veterans were challenged to consider what it meant to be a good man. Identity Theory would explain this as a disruption to the gender identity standard (Burke & Stets, 2009). An antiwar position and a masculine identity standard may conflict, especially if one's masculine identity standard aligns with a form of military masculinity that values aggression, dominance and violence. If the two identities become salient simultaneously, creating identity verification for one may invoke a large discrepancy in the other. As illustrated in the above quote, many veterans at first considered a "good man" as somebody who should serve his country during difficult times. Then their positions on war shifted. Veterans' discussion of what makes a good man today, then, often involved a reflection on their changing perspective on war and how that impacted their definition of masculinity.

Many antiwar veterans positioned themselves against what they termed a stereotypical form of masculinity that was advanced within the military. The following quotes illustrate how men discussed their masculinity using comparisons between their current identities and the image of masculinity that was presented in the military:

> I feel like it [the military] emasculated me; it put all the emphasis on the machismo and physical strength and umm, it's kind of a caricature. For me it made me feel constantly not good enough, not manly enough. I think because, I'm small, I don't take up a lot of space. I'm 5 feet 8 inches and 155 pounds.

I'm not frail or out of shape but I'm not the John Wayne image of a man and manliness that got ingrained in my head.—Luke at age 22

The link between toughness and accountability and fortitude, the link between that and violence is severed for me. And I think the kind of fortitude and resilience and work that it takes, those values are only loosely, only become connected to violence in particular situations. There's nothing inherently violent about them . . . accountability does not necessarily have anything to do with violence. They become connected when we imagine that being a good man means being able to defend your home. So I'm a good man because I can protect my wife or I'm a good man because I can protect my kids or because I know that if we're out somewhere I'm going to be tougher than the next guy and so I'm going to hurt them before they hurt us. Absolutely no connection between that and masculinity.—Adam at age 27

Some described their definition of masculinity while in the military as an "old way of thinking" or a "wrong way of thinking". For example Richard, a 66-year-old former Army chaplain and current pastor, explained his change in thinking about masculinity in the following way:

Being a man, I think, now for me recognizes that there are differences in gender but they're; the differences I see now are less stereotypical . . . than they have been. Being a man still includes integrity, being honest, and those types of things, standing up when you need to stand up. It takes on a different method or form or expression in the sense that . . . I don't know how to describe this, it becomes, um, more gentle? . . . But it's, it's, I guess it has less machismo in it or something.

Many of the men's responses still reflected traditional and/or stereotypical masculine characteristics, but in a new sense. For example, men still considered themselves the protectors, leaders and providers, but they expanded their definition of these characteristics. For Dan at age 45 there was a clear juxtaposition between his old way of thinking about masculinity and a new "enlightened" form of masculinity:

You can be present enough to understand the cultural idea of what a man is and that it's largely at odds with what is good for you and your family and society in general. And that you could be strong enough to sort of ignore that and you know, do what you need to do like be reliable and have a job and umm provide for your family. I still have an insane battle and guilt about the whole providing for your family because my wife has to work and I feel like a total slacker. I know many moms and dads have to work but there is that lingering thing from my dad that the mom shouldn't need to work but that's just pollution that sticks with you forever.

Similarly, leadership was redefined in terms of veterans' antiwar position. Veterans described leadership in terms such as "standing up for what you believe in" and "responsibility to self and others." Men were to be leaders but the leadership of men was often described by veterans as a "servant leadership." The quote below illustrates how one man changed his thinking about leadership after assuming an antiwar position:

> Two things I learned as a leader: take care of your people and get the job done. The initial, stereotypical demanding thing gave way to taking care of your people and getting the job done.—Bruce at age 71

Activism as Key to Identity Verification

The activism of many of our veterans allowed them to verify their masculine identity and solidify their antiwar identity, thus providing congruence between these identities. Fifteen out of the twenty-six veterans identified activist as one of their top five primary identities today. All but two of our veterans were heavily involved in activism. For five of these men, antiwar activism was through a lifestyle which included leadership within a Mennonite or another traditional peace church. To some extent, all of the veterans make sense of their masculinity through their social activism for peace and social justice and the integrity of acting on their beliefs.

Many of the veterans adapted terms from within the military to define masculinity in their new identities as antiwar activists. This adaptation allowed the men to do what some call "reconfiguring a localized hegemonic masculinity" (Duncanson, 2009). This means that what is considered the "idealized" or most privileged form of masculinity looks different at the local level. For example within a particular organization or community, masculinity may look different than it does at the regional or society level. Duncanson (2009) observed a reconfiguration of localized hegemonic masculinity in his study of peacemaking missions of British soldiers in Bosnia. While challenging traditional hegemonic understanding of the soldier as "killing machines," this reconfiguration still required an "inferior other." British soldiers described their peacemaking efforts as the way to be a "real man." This localized hegemonic masculinity, in which peacemaking soldiers were rational, controlled and civilized, was positioned in opposition to Balkan male soldiers who were emotional, irrational and weak (Duncanson, 2009).

By verifying traits such as courage, service to country, and responsibility through their activism, the veterans in our study appear to "reconfigure a localized hegemonic masculinity." Among our veterans, activism was a way for men to continue to position themselves against an inferior other. The "inferior other" appears to be those that are less enlightened or those still buying into the traditional military masculinity. The following quotes illustrate the use of activism to reclaim elements of hegemonic masculinity such as strength:

> Yeah well I think it takes a lot of courage to some degree to be an antiwar veteran, especially after 9/11. We really had a lot of . . . it took a lot of courage to have those vigils after what happened with 9/11.—Brian at age 70

> I think that, it takes more to be an advocate for peace than it does for war. War is the easier avenue than peace. It's so difficult.—Mark at age 54

Luke explains that his activist work actually requires him to manufacture a "masculine" side. Doing so allowed him to gain legitimacy in his activism:

> It challenged me every time I had to get up and say I was antiwar and antiwar very publicly. I constantly had to present myself as a person that . . . did this very archetypally masculine role but in order to say in so many ways that I was opposed to what that role was doing, I had to like manufacture this side of me that was still masculine. I didn't want to be perceived as someone who wasn't really deserving of that role.—Luke at age 22

For Tom, taking an antiwar position gave him a sexual edge among women:

> It didn't threaten my manliness [talking about taking an antiwar position]. I'll say one thing where it actually helped to improve my perception of my manliness. I'm embarrassed to admit this but at the time, I found that a lot of women found it incredibly sexy that I was resisting. I was in Japan at the time and the women tended to find it very attractive. I don't know if it was that I was taking a stand or what but they found it very attractive. . . . I started hanging out off base a lot more.—Tom at age 33

Perhaps one of the most vivid connections between activism and assertion of masculinity is illustrated in a quote by Steve at age 66. Here we see a man verifying his masculinity by protecting women with physical aggression in a protest setting. His contradictory feelings of pleasure and regret illustrate this struggle to make sense of his masculinity in light of his desire to be nonviolent:

> For example, at one of our demonstrations, a guy came once and started taking signs away from the women, ripping them up and pushing the women and I got physical with the person. I pushed him to the ground and if he would have gotten up, I would have hurt him. I both regret it and feel good about it so I guess I'm still confused.

Social Location and Negotiation of Masculinity

While many of the veterans drew on activism to make sense of their masculine identity, we found some significant variations in the ways that veterans renegotiated the meaning of masculinity and their own idiosyncratic position within the gendered hierarchy. Some men overtly protested and/or resisted hegemonic masculinity. Others, while rejecting specific wars or war all together, remained complicit in the hierarchy of masculinities but no longer allowed masculine military ideologies and icons to define their positions in the gendered social order. By categorizing these responses, we found three distinct types of masculinity among our veterans: Feminist Masculinity, Responsible/Accountable Masculinity, and Enlightened Male Masculinity. Interestingly, the differences in men's definition of masculinity were closely related to the men's social status. Here we present the masculinity scripts within these typologies, as well as patterns occurring within each type.

Feminist Masculinity

The first type of masculinity, which we call "Feminist Masculinity," is characterized by clear language in opposition to what veterans identified as traditional masculinity or being strong, dominant and alpha. These men described a good man as one who is able to embrace "feminine qualities" including nurturing, cultivating, and empowering others, while rejecting traditional masculine qualities such as aggression and dominance.

Veterans in the Feminist type generally had the most privileged social status. These veterans were best able to challenge conventional, regional hegemonic masculinity and thus free themselves to embrace person identity standards such as nurturing, good listener, and empowering. These veterans discussed masculinity with clear language in opposition to what veterans identified as traditional masculinity or being strong, dominant and alpha. Among this high status group, the change in definition of a good man at age 18 and today was spoken of in terms of a conscious turn from a traditional definition of masculinity to one that embraces femininity:

> A man at age 18 was the opposite of being a woman, and masculinity was the opposite of femininity but today I have so many feminists that I'm working with who are so fucking strong that my idea today is totally different . . . being a man was being strong, not showing emotions, not crying, being willing to do the things that sissies wouldn't be able to do . . . being hard, a fighter, keeping your word. . . . There wasn't anything more important to me growing up than being a man. Today, a man is . . . I'm a very sensitive person, I'm able to cry now. I'm able to cry in front of other people. I'm actually very good at expressing myself and my emotions just flow.—Steve at age 66

> At age 18 a good man was an alpha male.—Brad at age 61

Table 8.1. Characteristics of respondents by masculine type

	Responsible/ Accountable (n = 7)	Enlightened Male (n = 10)	Feminist (n = 9)
Age (%)			
20–39	71	20	0
40–59	14	20	67
60–86	14	60	33
Occupation (%)			
Blue Collar	57	50	11
White Collar	43	50	89
Student	29	10	0
Retired/Disabled	29	50	44
Education (%)			
High School	0	0	0
Some College	43	50	22
Undergraduate Degree	57	40	11
Graduate Degree	0	10	67
War Served (%)			
Vietnam	29	60	44
Iraq I	0	0	11
Iraq II	29	20	0
No War	43	20	44
Military Branch (%)			
Army	29	60	44
Navy	57	0	0
Airforce	0	20	33
Marines	14	20	22
% Career	0	20	22
% with Combat Experience	43	80	22
% with PTSD	14	30	11
Marital Status (%)			
Married/Never Divorced	29	40	67

	Responsible/ Accountable (n = 7)	Enlightened Male (n = 10)	Feminist (n = 9)
Divorced/ Remarried	14	50	33
Divorced/Single	0	10	0
Single/Never Married	57	0	0
Catalyst Change(%)			
Combat	43	50	0
Betrayal	0	30	0
Religion	29	20	77
Education	29	0	22

This veteran used the imagery of the chalice (cup) and blade to explain traditional masculinity and femininity. He describes himself as striving to be more nurturing and like the chalice than the blade (referring to the book title *The Chalice and the Blade* by Riane Eisler). The book contrasts the male violence of using the sword in response to injustice and violence throughout history with the more feminine nurturing of offering the cup in order to care for others including enemies:

> I feel like the male has the blade and I gravitate toward the chalice and I feel . . . I don't know if impotent is the word . . . I don't want to be an alpha male and I struggle with that. . . . To be nurturing and to be facilitative and to empower people and to invest in people and . . . to make people feel like they are more than they ever could have been you know.—Brad at age 51

> being secure enough that I don't need to be a male chauvinist or think I need to be in charge.—Will at age 45

The masculinity scripts within the "Feminist Masculinity" type, more so than the other two types, overtly challenge hegemonic masculinity. Men in this group were also aware of their privilege as white men:

> Being aware of the power and privilege that I hold and trying to help those that don't have the same privileges find their place in life and in our culture and society. Particularly paying attention to non-white cultures, women. So having more of a service approach, a more holistic approach to who I am.—Leland at age 64

> You can be present enough to understand the cultural idea of what a man is and that it's largely at odds with what is good for you and your family and society in general.—Dan at age 45

Nine out of the 26 veterans discuss masculinity in this way and shared several characteristics. Religion was the catalyst of change for all but two of the men in this group. All of the men, except for one 49-year-old, were part of the baby boomer generation. Five of the eight men in this type were pacifist Mennonite pastors. As such, their activism was primarily a lifestyle activism rather than a traditional protest activism as is seen among other veterans. All of the men were married and all but one has children. Only two were ever divorced. While seven of the nine reported some form of conflictive relationships during childhood, often abusive, these men were more likely than other veterans to describe some kind of healing experience post abuse.

Responsible/Accountable Masculinity

The second masculine type we called "Responsible/Accountable" masculinity. This type includes being strong, wise and aware of one's relation to others. A key feature of these men's responses was an emphasis on the necessity of taking responsibility for your actions because actions have consequences. Men in this type occupied a lower social status due to youth, educational attainment, job status, and/or being disabled or retired.

Men in the Responsible/Accountable group were more likely to discuss masculinity using characteristics that were part of their military training such as loyalty, responsibility, and accountability. Similarly, there was less change in how men described masculinity at age 18 and today:

> I think to feel like a man in my experience is to feel strong, like I'm a presence, to be acknowledged and to be a good man at 18 umm, I don't think it was a conscious topic for me. The word that comes to me right now is strength and to use strength wisely. That's kind of a cliché among military folk but to use strength to protect others. To be a male today is somewhat similar but it's expanded to include not just strength but to be a person that is responsible and acknowledge your role with others.—Luke at age 22

The masculine scripts within this type appear to reflect what Niva (1998) identifies as a shift in the hegemonic masculinity of the military which occurred during the time of the 1991 Gulf War and embraces a "tough but tender" position. However, for these men, masculinity is intentionally disconnected from the activities of the military as an organization. Men in this group also appear to redefine and display their masculinity through their activism and often describe this activism in terms of responsibility to others:

> [Describing masculinity at age 18] Sexual and warfare prowess. [Describing masculinity today] Today . . . I'm still trying to work that one out . . . umm

honest, firm and caring. I don't know, it's kind of hard. You can say the same thing about all of humanity . . . responsibility to the whole.—Hank at age 32

> I think a good man is someone who is able to do whatever it takes to get the important things done whether that's putting food on their family's table or getting the job done when people are counting on you. I think being a man is not making excuses when you don't want to do it . . . you can find an excuse . . . if you really want to do it, you can get it done. I think being a man means really just keeping your word. If you say you are going to do something, do it. A lot of this would apply to all humans. But I think this makes me highly accountable and I think it means, while I don't necessarily think it means to be violent, I think it means to recognize that we have a lot of aggression and assertiveness and don't deny that.—Tom at age 38

Seven out of the 26 veterans described masculinity in this way. The catalyst of change for the men in this group varied more than the other two groups. Three of the men were in the education group, one in the religion group, and two in the combat group. This group of men were predominantly Generation Xers (5 out of 8), or young Baby Boomers. This group had the highest percentage of veterans that were never married, however, it also included more fathers with children at home than the other two groups. While their antiwar activism levels today range from low to high, all but one of the men in this group named activist as a primary identity today. Additionally, four of the men in this group would identify as conscientious objectors if asked to serve today.

Enlightened Masculinity

The third type is the least rigidly defined of the masculine typologies. The veterans describe their masculinity as being strong, caring, wise, supportive, loving, and listening. We call this group the "Enlightened Male" group because the descriptions of a good man were mostly "gender neutral" and might be used to more broadly define good human behavior. While some terms seem more closely aligned with a traditional feminine role, this group did not explicitly contrast these feminine characteristics against traditional masculinity. Unlike the Feminist Masculinity type, there is less resistance or protest language in this type. Change in masculinity from age 18 to today was described as movement toward becoming a better person:

> Still, a good man goes to work. . . . But there's more to life than what you do for work. I think I've gained some degree of wisdom. At least I know what I don't know. I'm not as idealistic but more patient than I once was.—Mark at age 54

Strong loving, leading still, the change is less macho—not that I was a macho kid but there is less emphasis on being a male and its more now about being human. That's something that I can see growing throughout my life.—Bruce at age 68

Ten out of the 26 veterans described masculinity this way. Three of the veterans in this type were in the religion as catalyst group; however, this group had the highest percentage of men for whom combat (4/10) and betrayal (3/10) were identified as their primary catalyst of identity change. In fact, this is the only masculinity type in which any of the veterans had betrayal as their catalyst of change. Eight of the men in this group were Baby Boomers. All but two of the men in this group had a lower socio-economic status than the men in the Feminist Group. Additionally, this group had the highest percentage of divorced veterans. Activism was a primary identity for eighty percent of the men in this group. Six of 10 in this type described experiences of trauma in war or childhood, with eight experiencing combat while in the military. Additionally, only five expressed a religious identity, which is much lower than the Feminist Masculinity type.

The clearest examples of experiences of masculine identity non-verification are seen in the group we label "Feminist masculinity." The regional or societal level hegemonic masculinity is not verified in the feedback received from those with whom the group most often interacts. This included spouses, progressive peace church congregations and their fellow pastors. Because feedback from their primary groups of interaction allowed men in this group to receive identity verification for masculinity standards that did not align with regional or societal level hegemonic masculinity. Additionally, this group had the highest social status. Their relatively higher status (well-educated professional, married, middle-aged, white) allowed them to challenge hegemonic masculinity.

By contrast men with lower status positions were more likely to assume a Just War Position, opposing some wars but not all wars rather than a Pacifist position against all wars. The antiwar identity and masculine identity of being a "better human" are able to align. Additionally, men in the "Enlightened Masculinity" group more likely to verify their masculinity from a position of subordination due to their lower social status positions relative to other men in the study. Thus this group may be less able to protest or resist hegemonic masculinity.

Recent scholars argue that hegemonic masculinity has the potential to be "unraveled" with resulting forms of masculinity that legitimate gender equality, as opposed to inequality. For Duncanson (2015) this "unraveling" occurs as men construct their identities in terms of equality with others, rather than through relations of opposition or domination (3). It appears that the group with the most privileged social location comes closest to "constructing their identities through recognition of similarity, respect, interdependence, empathy and equality with others" (Duncanson, 2015, 3). The masculinity described by men in this group may best represent what Messerschmidt terms "equality masculinities," which "legitimate an egalitarian relationship between men and women, between masculinity and femininity, and among men (2012, 73).

CONCLUSIONS

As we explored how antiwar veterans alter their meanings of the masculine identity to bring them in line with their antiwar position, we found that activism and social location were essential in understanding how men defined their own masculine identity. We found that men had various ways of re-negotiating the meaning of hegemonic masculinity and their own idiosyncratic position within the gendered hierarchy. Some men overtly protested and/or resisted hegemonic masculinity. Others, while rejecting specific wars or war all together, are still complicit in the hierarchy of masculinities, but no longer allow masculine military ideologies and icons to define their positions in the gendered social order. However, to some extent, all of the veterans make sense of their masculinity through their social activism related to peace and social justice and integrity of acting on their beliefs.

These findings highlight the continued importance of intersectionality, specifically how social status impacted men's definition of their own masculine identity and their ability to challenge or reformulate hegemonic masculinity. Additionally, understanding identity formation and change in the process of leaving the military and entering civilian life, whether as an antiwar veteran or not, must continue to acknowledge multiple-ranked masculinities. By exploring the impact of the antiwar identity on masculinity among male veterans in our study, this chapter demonstrates how complex and consequential identity change can be, profoundly altering one's master identity standards and activist behaviors.

Chapter Nine

Findings

In this chapter, we will identify common patterns found among veterans in their journeys to pacifism and antiwar activism. We will further illuminate periods of the identity change process as seen through the lives of veterans emerging from military service.

Our research finds four common catalysts of moral identity change regarding war among antiwar veterans: combat, betrayal, education and religious conviction. These four catalysts disrupted the veterans' thinking about the reality of combat (combat group), the trustworthiness of U.S. leaders to tell the truth (betrayal group), the public narrative of U.S. history or policy (education group) and/or the position of religious scripture or religious organizations on war and treatment of enemies (religious conviction group). We find that once their identity was disrupted, the antiwar veterans followed an identity change process that includes nine distinct periods:

1. Moral identity disruption from combat, betrayal, religious conviction or education.
2. An immediate attempt to change one's behavior to gain moral identity verification. If successful, the process of change stops here. If the corrective behavior does not create identity verification and the individual is unable to block out the error messages and discrepancy messages persist over time, a lengthier search begins to find moral identity verification through transforming identity standards.
3. A period of deep reflection and movement toward healing. This includes a quieter time for reflection on one's military experience (usually) post military service within a new setting such as work, college, family, therapy or a Twelve Step group for recovering addicts. This

differs from self-appraisal, a continuous component of the inputs portion of the identity verification process.

4. A period of study about war, U.S. history, and/or faith in order to construct a new congruent identity. This may or may not include contact with a new group that introduces a new Collective Identity.
5. A period of replacing the Collective Identity of the military unit with a new Collective Identity that verifies their moral identity as opposing unjust wars or all wars.
6. A period of testing the new identities by taking a public stand with antiwar or lifestyle activism in order to verify one's new moral, role and/or group identities with one's behavior.
7. A period of adjustment to loss and/or opposition resulting from the new moral, role and group identity standards that include activism.
8. A period of shifting of the lower level identities (group such as political party affiliation or role such as male or career) to become congruent with the new moral identity standards (Exchange Bargaining) in order to experience full identity verification.
9. Full identity verification, which results in a sense of freedom and integrity that is maintained through their antiwar or lifestyle activism.

Not all veterans in this study experienced their identity change process with all nine periods and some veterans returned to earlier periods as inputs changed in new environments but this process model serves as a useful framework to understand their pathways to pacifism and/or Just War perspectives. In the following section, we will describe specific examples of each of these periods from the veteran's stories.

FIRST PERIOD—MORAL IDENTITY DISRUPTION

The first period, moral identity disruption from combat, betrayal, religious conviction or education, is fully discussed in chapters 3–6.

SECOND PERIOD—ATTEMPTS TO CHANGE BEHAVIORS FOR IDENTITY VERIFICATION

The second period, which involved the soldiers' attempts to change their behaviors so they could verify their moral identities, sometimes resulted in a soldier's refusal to participate in future combat, behaviors that they deem as immoral. For example, one story in the Combat Catalyst chapter stands out. Bob tried to stop his comrades from shooting Vietnamese women who were running out of a village. "These are the people we were told that we were there to protect against Communist monsters . . . I was flabbergasted at other

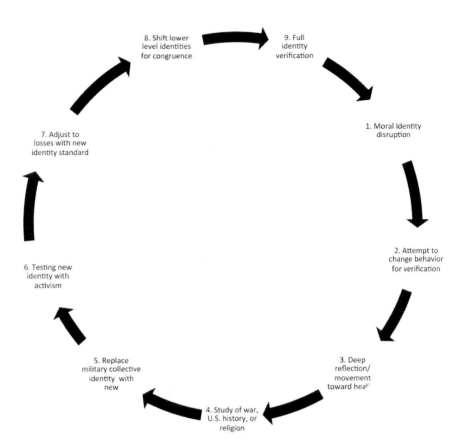

Figure 9.1.   New identity change model.

soldiers' bad behaviors but rarely said anything . . . It was nine months from hell for me."

Another example of this period comes from the Religious Conviction Catalyst group. Hank was home on leave from the war in Iraq. He saw *The Passion of the Christ*, which prompted him to ask himself "how can I be a Christian and in the Army at the same time?" Once Hank had this epiphany, he told his superior that he could return to Iraq but could not "pull the trigger anymore" and took concrete steps to change his situation by applying for a Conscientious Objector status.

THIRD PERIOD—DEEP REFLECTION AND MOVEMENT TOWARD HEALING

We find both reflection and healing present among these antiwar activist veterans following the initial identity disruption once they were in a safe space. Time to reflect on the war or military often occurred only once they were home on leave or out of the military. Sometimes they were recovering from injuries, in counseling, or attending a Twelve Step Alcoholics Anonymous group where they were sober engaging in "a fearless moral inventory." In other cases, their lives slowed down enough for reflection because of disability or retirement. It appears that without this time to reflect on their experiences, the identity non-verification error messages may not be addressed. Without this awareness, the negative emotions of guilt, shame, anger or confusion were not felt. Reflection, then, is vital for the mind's Comparator to weigh one's behavior against one's identity standards and to either verify the identity or to send an error message and a set of negative emotions.

One returning veteran, Dick, admitted to not reflecting on his service when returning from Vietnam in 1967. He got married, started an MBA Program, and began his career. Not until decades later did he take time for reflection. Although he was disturbed by the issues of "mismanagement, arrogance and radical racism against Vietnamese" while serving, "there was no time to think about the war for 15 to 20 more years." In the late 1980s, he started reading Howard Zinn's *A People's History of the U.S.* and Professor Noam Chomsky's critique of the U.S. Only then did he begin to question U.S. foreign policy. Dick soon met and became involved with Veterans for Peace, becoming very active as an officer in 1998. At this time, he had the privilege to return to Vietnam with wounded vets from both the U.S. and Vietnam for a 1,200 mile bike ride together. Sharing experiences and feelings about the war, these veterans ended up "making lifelong friends." During this time of reflection Dick reports, "I began to feel shame about what the U.S. did in Vietnam. . . . Today, I am inflamed by U.S. leadership in our history."

A second Vietnam veteran, Steve, also pinpoints the reflective period before his identity change. At first he was "gung ho war," serving multiple deployments even after being wounded. He had lost a good friend and half his unit to the Viet Cong and "made the decision to be ruthless and get them back for what they did." He "killed [Vietnamese] women and children. I killed all of my prisoners . . . I hated all Orientals until 1971."

Steve returned to the U.S. in 1966 and attended Florida State where he was exposed to a radically new perspective in his history and philosophy courses. He read Howard Zinn's *A People's History of the U.S.* but "ignored the evidence because I was too self-absorbed." Then in 1971, Jane Fonda came to campus. She said we live in a democracy and this requires "access to the truth." Further, it was "the duty of patriotic Vietnam Vets to tell the truth." Steve responded to a call to tell his story on video and heard other vets testify for the *Winter Soldier I* documentary. This experience made him see a "bigger picture." He gathered with other vets following the filming because "it was a safe environment to share," They soon joined forces to form a new chapter of Vietnam Veterans against the War.

Besides bearing witness to war, going on disability also provided an opportunity for some veterans to reflect on the war. Twenty-two percent of our veterans were receiving 100 percent Veterans Administration disability payments for PTSD incurred during war time service. Living on disability meant that they had more free time, besides gaining access to counseling and medical services to treat their PTSD symptoms. These veterans reflected on their military experiences and processed feelings of guilt, shame, rage, anger, fear, and sadness.

A period of reflection after military service, of course, is not inevitable. A number of situations may keep veterans from this kind of deep reflection and healing. Some found escape from their difficult memories in sex and drugs/ alcohol, while others found themselves distracted by marriages, families, and/or careers. For the veterans with untreated PTSD, living was a daily struggle with symptoms that did not allow time for reflection on their actions in the military. In fact, reflecting on and talking about combat often exacer- bated symptoms of anxiety, depression, and suicidal ideation. Other veterans avoided reflection by spending time with pro-war veterans and friends. These veterans took comfort in a narrative that justified U.S. policy and the "neces- sary evil of war" while feeling honored for their valor.

When reflection did occur, the veterans who had fought their addictions and/or PTSD symptoms began a time of healing. Malcomb described "peri- ods of treatment and healing from PTSD over 20 years that I continue to process today." A trip to Vietnam in 1994 contributed to his healing because "We met wonderful Vietnamese people. They are everything I wish we were." Today he is able to travel globally, speak in high schools, attend conferences, protest outside of military recruitment centers and write for publication. He concluded:

> I feel extremely good about what I do. Victor Frankel says, "Suffering ceases to be suffering when it has meaning." Today, I have a sense of meaning, my life is improved. It's a spiritual journey. You must tell the truth and that's so powerful. Now Vietnam has meaning for me. It's so rewarding when high school kids tell me they're no longer going to join the military.

Other descriptions of deep reflection and healing began with readings from religious leaders from many traditions: Mother Theresa, Mahatma Gan- dhi, Martin Luther King Jr., Thich Nat Han, Leo Tolstoy and Catholic Priest Daniel Berrigan. Many vets reported that their reflection and healing was a

continuation of their spiritual journey. One veteran summarized the healing
journey as, "this is about being true to myself." Another concluded on a
similar note, "I'm never turning back. . . . I'm finally genuine to who I've
always been."

FOURTH PERIOD – STUDY

During the periods of study, the veterans sought new perspectives on war,
U.S. history, and/or faith to construct a new coherent moral identity. This
period helped to construct a different worldview by reading common texts,
finding professors who challenged their thinking, and responding to new role
models. Whether or not these new perspectives were the main catalyst for
change, all of the veterans in this study had engaged in a period of study in
their pathways to peace.

The veterans studied the works of historians, linguists, sociologists, phi-
losophers, political figures, theologians and religious leaders. One major
work often cited by the veterans in the Education and Betrayal Catalyst
groups was Howard Zinn's *A People's History of the United States* (1980).
Zinn's book disrupted their view of the U.S. and aided in the reconstruction
their identity. The textbook depicts the struggles of Native Americans against
U.S. expansion beside the battles of slaves, women, and unionists against a
powerful system. Zinn's military service during World War II included dropping bombs on civilian targets in Europe, thus sensitizing him to the ethical
dilemmas of soldiers.

Another popular author among the veterans was Noam Chomsky, a professor of linguistics. He authored dozens of articles and textbooks critical of
U.S. policy and the war in Vietnam. Beside his significant contributions to
the field of linguistics, his works are also read by the general public. Perhaps
he is best known among antiwar activists for his 1988 book and 1993 documentary *Manufacturing Consent: The Political Economy of the Mass Media*,
which exposes the role of the mass media in the propaganda-model of com-
munication. He proposed that because the U.S. media is heavily dependent
on the U.S. government for news, the media must advocate the anticommu-
nist perspective of the Cold War.

A film star also captured the attention of many veterans in this study. Jane
Fonda was often mentioned by Vietnam War veterans in the Betrayal and
Education catalyst groups. In the 1960s and 1970s, she had toured college
campuses to call on veterans to tell their stories about what was really happening in Vietnam. Her activism not only disrupted the veterans' moral
identities, but also encouraged an alliance between peace activists and disen-
chanted veterans to work for peace.

Veterans also turned to theological writings during their period of study. One Mennonite theologian, ethicist, and Biblical scholar had a strong influence on some veterans in the Religious Conviction group. John Howard Yoder's 1972 text, *The Politics of Jesus*, challenged the veterans' thinking about war. The text argues for a radical Christian pacifism as the most faithful approach for disciples of Christ. Asserting that Jesus took a nonviolent political stand against the oppression of both the Jewish religious hierarchy and the Roman occupation of his day, Yoder encourages Christians to follow Jesus' example.

Another influential religious leader was the theologian and ethicist Stanley Hauerwas, an author and longtime professor at Duke University. Veterans also named John Stoner, a Brethren Christian leader in the *Every Church a Peace Church* movement and Old Testament scholar Walter Brueggemann. Liberal theologian and author Walter Wink in his text *Engaging the Powers* was instrumental for some veterans in examining the violence of the Old Testament and promoting active nonviolence for social change as the way Jesus confronted the violence of his day.

Other significant books were Leo Tolstoy's *The Kingdom of God Is within You* and Father John Dear's *Our God Is Nonviolent*. Christian activist Shane Claiborne, a leader in the New Monasticism movement, wrote works that helped some veterans to build a new pacifist identity. Buddhism also provided some insights, such as the ministry of Thich Nhat Hanh. This Buddhist monk and peace activist writes, travels, and offers healing retreats especially for veterans.

Beyond reading, several films and documentaries helped the veterans to consolidate their new antiwar identity. They frequently mentioned *Sir! No, Sir!*, a 2005 documentary about Vietnam War soldiers opposing the war. Another documentary was *Winter Soldier* about Vietnam veterans testifying in 1971 about their actions in the war. (The Iraq Veterans against War organization also conducted a Winter Soldier: Iraq and Afghanistan event in 2008.)

Social Movement leaders were also pivotal in the veterans' construction of their new identities. Cesar Chavez of the United Farm workers Movement and Martin Luther King, Jr. of the Civil Rights Movement were often mentioned as role models. The Chicano movement in California in the 2000s motivated one Latino veteran to become an activist. Pax Christi, an ecumenical peace organization, as well as Daniel Ellsberg were inspirations for other veterans. Robert Bly and the Men's Movement were also mentioned. Leaders and their movements, then, provided modeling and education for activism.

FIFTH PERIOD—REPLACING THE COLLECTIVE IDENTITY OF THE MILITARY UNIT WITH A NEW COLLECTIVE IDENTITY

Veterans sought to replace the collective identity of the military unit (Army, Navy, Air Force, Marines) with a new collective identity that verified both their military past and their antiwar activism. This is difficult as Leitz (2014, 122) points out due to "being separate from a broader peace movement identity" and being an outsider from veteran's groups who remained supportive of war. The most common veterans group affiliation cited among our 114 veterans was Veterans for Peace (62 percent; $n = 71$) (www.veteransforpeace.org). Attracting veterans from all wars, this group both advocates against war and provides services for veterans. It attracts members who relate to a Just War position as well as various levels of pacifism. Besides its website, this group promotes its cause through articles, local chapters, and support groups. The annual conferences and local meetings provide education on a range of issues and accelerate networking opportunities among like-minded veterans. Veterans for Peace played a vital role in educating veterans about the antiwar identity as well as providing a collective identity group that served to blend two important identities—veteran and antiwar activist.

Veterans groups are not only educational, but also offer social and emotional support during the veterans' transition to an antiwar identity verification. They used various phrases to describe their affiliation with these groups. One veteran, originally a member of the VFW (Veterans of Foreign Wars) and the American Legion has "now transferred my loyalties to VFP and IVAW."

One Vietnam veteran (Malcomb), shared of his struggles with PTSD, alcoholism, and a suicide attempt when his second marriage was falling apart. His life turned around in 1991 when he attended an antiwar demonstration. "I met members of Veterans for Peace and I found my community. I still get together with these guys and we continue to process Vietnam. There were daily My Lai massacres through bombings and the killing of civilians." Another veteran (Kent) stated that "with my antiwar work, I felt like I was home. Things happen for a reason. God is working in this. It's not easy work; it's frustrating. It's a shame that it takes age and experience to grow wise. I am happy to be a part of this historical movement." Such statements indicate a strong sense of collective identity related to these veterans groups.

It took some veterans decades before they moved to an antiwar activist identity. The veterans often cited the U.S. invasion of Iraq in 2003 as disrupting their thinking about war. After their experiences in Vietnam, they viewed the Iraq War as a similar mistake that the U.S. should avoid at all costs to spare both the soldiers and Iraqis. It was at this point that they found groups such as Veterans for Peace, groups that verified their beliefs and encouraged them to act against the Iraq War.

SIXTH PERIOD – TESTING THE NEW IDENTITIES BY TAKING A PUBLIC STAND WITH ANTIWAR OR LIFESTYLE ACTIVISM

Following the periods of reflection and study, the veterans took a public stand with antiwar or lifestyle activism in order to verify new moral identity standards. The key factor was finding a veterans group or faith community that was compatible with their new beliefs. As veterans consolidated their collective identities as antiwar in various groups, they launched into peace activism for three reasons: faithfulness to the moral identity motivates consistent behavior (Blasi, 1984), the group's identity required the social norm of activism to prove one's membership and activism helped "transform emotions of powerlessness into emotions of resistance" (Leitz, 2014, 26).

Public activism often followed periods of diagnosis and treatment for PTSD or moral injury. These formerly disabled veterans often discovered new energy for activism with a veterans' group. The veterans often felt driven to do this work to protect future generations from experiencing the horrors of war. One veteran confessed that "the weight of the universe is forcing me to do this work." Leitz (2014, 25) also finds that "the construction of a movement collective identity channels anger and converts shame to pride."

The record of the veterans' activism was impressive. They served in several capacities for Veterans for Peace including officers at all levels from national to local, coordinators of annual conferences, and paid staff. Twelve veterans counseled and supported veterans from all wars as a way to make sense of their own struggles with PTSD and other after effects of war.

One example of this period is Tom, who lived on a part-time job so he could be a full- time activist. He protested against U.S. military power even to the extent of becoming a war tax resister. His social justice work included writing letters and going to demonstrations. Another veteran, Steve, called himself a "total activist who is responsible, keeps my word, tells the truth and is well informed." In addition to his peace activism, he worked in a leadership capacity for the Sierra Club, an environmentalist group.

SEVENTH PERIOD – ADJUSTING TO OPPOSITION AND LOSS

Veterans also experienced a period of adjustment to loss, sacrifice, and/or opposition resulting from the new moral identity standards for activism. As the veterans began sharing their new Conscientious Objector status or their opposition to war, they often experienced wrenching losses. A few veterans were disowned by one or both parents. Many became estranged from their siblings because of political disagreements. Old friends and buddies from their military service often left them behind, too. Some veterans lost their jobs if they spoke their consciences in pro-military settings. People cursed at them or assaulted them at protests, while the activists sometimes went to jail on trumped-up charges. "We were physically and emotionally attacked by U.S. politicians. They refused to take responsibility for the problems. At protests, law enforcement would attack you and rough you up" (Max, a leader in the early Vietnam Veterans against the War movement).

It is important to note that active military members face more significant barriers and consequences to their opposition to war than the general population. While the majority of our veterans engaged in antiwar activism post military service, a small portion of our interviewees were on active duty when they spoke with us. First, military regulations of free speech differ from civilian freedoms. Second, pro-war rhetoric suggests the military is united in its support of current wars and third, the negative perception the military holds of protesters. Combine these factors and we find that antiwar activism risks official sanctions such as arrest or loss of benefits that come with an honorable discharge from service. In addition, the soldier risks estrangement from comrades which as we learned from some veterans was the most painful part of the process and finally, there are psychological risks of losing status and security (Leitz, 2014, 33).

Rob took risks to be a truth teller about U.S. foreign policy, including the complicity of the defense industry where he worked as an electrical engineer in exaggerating the threat of the former Soviet Union. As a result of speaking out, Rob was forced into early retirement and lost many of his previous friendships. "I would voice my opinion [at McDonnell Douglas] and would be booed or hissed and taken off the stage. I'm not a yes man. Others who knew [the truth] couldn't come forward. It was strangely silent . . . I felt numb and didn't care. [Once I spoke out], the company began to give me unsatisfactory job evaluations after years of positive ones."

Don gave up his Marine career following his identity disruption in college. He admits that "Today, I don't share my views with my Marine Corps buddies. The changes keep me from the Marine Corps and a happy go lucky life. It's been a burden. It's made life more complicated." One Vietnam veteran (Sam) said that "[Doing this work] is a heavy fuckin' burden. I share this burden with my buddies in VFP."

Despite these significant sacrifices, most of the veterans expressed no regrets. They considered it vital, though, to persist in their work. As Max stated, "I gave up Camelot! I gave up a good time. I wouldn't change it though . . . as it gives me meaning and purpose." In response to these losses, we again discover the important role of a new collective identity group such as Veterans for Peace. Attachment to the new group fosters a positive sense of solidarity and mobilizes individuals to join forces for the cause. Activism "transforms the shame, fear, and guilt to anger at people outside themselves" as well as love for other activists (Leitz, 2014, 26).

EIGHTH PERIOD – SHIFTING OF LOWER LEVEL IDENTITIES

Beyond loss and sacrifice, the veterans experienced a shifting of the lower level identities to become congruent with the new moral identity standards. Identity Change research claims that the moral identity, at the top of the identity hierarchy, creates significant changes in group (Republican to Democrat) and role identities (Career Marine soldier to professor and military peace activist) over time in order to achieve full identity verification. This is called Exchange Bargaining (Burke & Stets, 2009, 179).

Behavioral demands of the moral identity impact actions across a number of situations controlled by lower level identities (Burke & Stets, 2009, 178). Moral identities are usually highest in the identity hierarchy as they are applicable across so many situations from combat to parenting. Thus, they have wide influence to either change the behavior of lower level identities or activate identity standard changes to create verification.

It was common for our veterans to change lower level identities in response to their moral identity change. We saw a striking relationship between adopting an antiwar identity and how the men negotiated masculinity. Another important lower level identity change that is worth exploring further in the future was the adoption of a environmentalist identity by many of our veterans.

One example is Hank, who changed considerably between the ages of 18 and 37. He once identified as a devout Mormon, disciplined athlete, Karate practitioner, and proud Texan. By contrast, now he identified as an active Board Member of Iraq Veterans against the War. He also described himself as a "Gnostic Christian with an affinity toward Buddhism . . . so that every word that you say is prayer." His identity drove him to be "a mad recycler, very politically active against poverty, racism, and ecocide."

Bob also experienced noteworthy changes in his pre-war and post-war identities in areas such as religion and politics. At 18, he was a Catholic, Republican, and a believer that the U.S. "always did good things abroad." Now he identified as a Deist, someone who believes in the existence of a God but not supernatural revelation (www.dictionary.com). As a Liberal/Progressive Democrat, he was a full time antiwar activist who now believed that "we are woefully misled by our government."

Lower level identity change also occurred in Adam, who began his young adult life as a conservative Christian and Republican. When interviewed at age 27, he now saw himself as a changed person who had to make new friends: "I lost my conservative friends." His religious faith also shifted to a progressive Mennonite congregation with an openly gay pastor and active social justice ministry.

The most common political change, then, was a shift toward the left. Democrats now identified as a Socialist or Green Party supporter, while those with anti-gay opinions now accepted the LGBT community and gay marriage. Once consistency was achieved across lower level identities, the person would firmly defend these changes. Veterans with the most dramatic changes in their moral identity were often the most determined activists perhaps to verify their new identities to themselves or others.

There are multiple possible explanations for this consistent shift to the left politically and we believe that all explanations may be operative in our group of veterans. First, perhaps because many of the veterans we interviewed began life as conservative Republicans with fundamentalist Baptist or Catholic backgrounds, if change was going to occur, it could only go left. Second, their new collective identity groups such as Veterans for Peace had clear identifiers and boundaries that included more progressive views on social issues as well as affiliation with the Democrats. Finally, we suggest that the antiwar identity is based on a moral standard of treating all people with equal respect. Achieving mutual verification of all of one's person, role and group identities based on this value criteria required moving to the left as they felt Democrats more clearly prioritized treating all people with equal respect.

PERIOD NINE—FULL IDENTITY VERIFICATION

After all these changes, we find these veterans experienced full identity verification through their antiwar activism. This gave them a sense of freedom and integrity, besides the assurance that they were doing the right thing. When asked how they felt about these identity changes today, they reported similar themes: peace of mind, being true to oneself, and having a clean conscience. These phrases all signify a high level of congruity with their moral identity.

The story of Hank, an Iraq War veteran, exemplifies this period. He still struggled with PTSD and flashbacks because "fear can return too easily." Despite these struggles, he claimed that "I am doing all the things I want to do. I am in charge. I am honest and disciplined." These assertions indicate that he was in a place of identity verification since he could act fully on his moral identity standards or commitments.

Another veteran who had achieved full identity verification is Adam, who responded to his identity changes as being "Great, I love it. I feel happier being who I am. I respect the new people around me. I don't miss anything or anyone. I am doing the things that feel important. I feel important." One benefit from this verification is a "clean conscience" for whistle blowers such as Rob. He paid a high price for reporting on the defense industry, but "I feel good about the class action suit. I have had a good life . . . . I have gained a sense of doing the right thing."

RETURNING TO THE ORIGINAL RESEARCH QUESTION

As described in the Preface, Hart had met Robert Bowman (1934–2013), at a 1986 presentation. His activism had raised the question this book seeks to answer: how do dramatic changes in thinking about the military or war occur? Although Bowman died in 2013 before he could be interviewed, an examination of online interview transcripts indicate some of the nine periods experienced by the veterans in this study.

Bowman began his career in the Air Force, serving for 22 years flying 101 combat missions. He earned a PhD in Aeronautical and Nuclear Engineering from the California Institute of Technology and became involved with U.S. space defense programs. In 1982, Bowman discovered that the Strategic Defense Initiative (SDI, popularly called Star Wars) that the U.S.

Table 9.1. Summary of antiwar identity change rationale ideal types by catalyst group

Initial Rationale for Support of War	Disrupter & Catalyst for Antiwar Identity Change	Behavioral Response to verify new Antiwar identity
Combat Group		
Support of war based on citizen's duty to do good in fight against evil to bring peace.	Experience war as evil that harms everyone and doesn't lead to peace.	Must withdraw support and stop all wars. There are alternatives to war for addressing evil.
Betrayal Group		
Support of war based on U.S. leaders/institutions telling truth based on facts.	Experience a leader or institution lying or omitting the truth about war.	Must withdraw and protest the lies of unjust wars. Only Just wars are permissible.
Religious Conviction Group		
Support of war based on religious beliefs and approval.	Experience new understanding of scripture and/or God in relation to war.	Must withdraw from military due to Conscientious Objection to all wars as contrary to my faith.
Education Group		
Support of war based on basic understanding of history, policy and rationale for war.	Experience new facts and perspectives that teach me critical thinking skills.	Must educate myself, study facts, question everything, and oppose unjust wars.

military was developing "has nothing to do with defense. It is an attempt to deploy offensive weapons disguised as defense." SDI was proposed as a defensive shield against nuclear attacks from the former Soviet Union (www. coldwar.org/articles/80s/SDI-StarWars.asp). He called the project "a smoke-screen for the American people, because they [Reagan Administration] knew that the American people would never approve weapons in space for offensive purposes." SDI, then, symbolized the lie (i.e., betrayal) that disturbed his moral identity standards that required honesty. Because SDI would not protect U.S. allies, this "shield" would not be honoring U.S. defense treaties. Dr. Bowman's unsuccessful attempts to raise concern within the military resulted in the eventual decision to leave the military. By the mid-1980s, he was speaking out against a program that he called "the ultimate military lunacy, easily overwhelmed and vulnerable." Since the catalyst for his identity change was betrayal, we would place him in the Betrayal Catalyst group.

In trying to alter the course of the project, Bowman retired early from the military to establish the Institute for Space and Security Studies. This organization provided accurate information about space security projects. By 1986, he had written a book opposing SDI and spoke publicly about the "truth" about this "shield." After SDI development—and the Cold War—were no longer issues, he continued with his peace activism. He eventually joined Veterans for Peace, opposed the Iraq War, and ran for office for both the Reform and Democratic Parties.

HOW DOES THIS NINE PERIOD MODEL EXPLAIN NON-ACTIVIST VETERANS?

As stated earlier, not all veterans in this study experienced their journeys in this Identity Change Model's nine-period order. However, the Model can explain the difference between the veterans who became antiwar activists and those who did not. In this section we offer suggestions for why some became antiwar activist or pacifist, but others did not by applying our identity change model to the experiences of veterans in our comparison group. However, our comparison is only a small non-representative sample. Thus, future research is need to better understand why some might adopt an antiwar or pacifist identity while others do not.

The first period in the Identity Change Model, Moral Identity Disruption, provides one reason for the comparison group veterans' different responses. Some veteran's moral identities were never disrupted by their military experience or beyond. When and where a soldier served were critical factors, besides whom they were exposed to during and after their military service. Four of the comparison non-activist veterans reported positive service experiences. They either did not serve during a time of war or did not serve in combat. Not confronted by combat that challenged their moral standards for war, these veterans were not asked to behave in a way that disturbed their moral standards during their military service. Identity disruption did occur years later for some of these veterans but with changes to group identity (e.g., Christian or Republican or patriotic American) rather than moral identity.

Besides moral identity disruption, another difference between the activist and non- activist veterans is that the non-activists were able to change their behaviors in a way that would allow them to verify their moral identity. For example, some could refuse to participate in future behaviors that they deemed immoral. These veterans might have removed themselves from combat situations or avoided comrades who were behaving in ways they perceived as immoral. Thus, these veterans could verify their high moral standards with a new behavior. By contrast, the activist veterans realized that their own behavior changes could not verify their moral identity. The activist veterans, then, moved to the third period of reflection and self-appraisal.

The third period, Deep Reflection and Movement toward Healing, was not automatic for all veterans. The activist veterans discussed how reflection had resulted in error messages about their moral identity. By contrast, the non-activist veterans did not report taking time for introspection about their military experience after leaving the military. They also did not report incongruence within their own moral identity or share feelings such as guilt, shame, anger or confusion. This lack of reflection could have resulted from PTSD-related symptoms of psychological numbing, avoidance, and denial. This may explain the one vet with PTSD in the comparison group. Another possible cause may be the quick transition from the military to the demands of career, marriage, family, and daily life. We suggest that without time to inventory one's feelings and memories from their military experience, identity change will not occur.

The fourth period, a period of study, usually followed the period of deep reflection and healing if the veteran experienced a disruption in the moral identity. The activist veterans not only took time to reflect on their identity disruption and painful emotions, they also educated themselves about U.S. policy and history. These activists were searching for a coherent alternative to war. Veterans who couldn't live with a belief in war (or a particular war) being a necessary evil, sought a new coherent moral identity related to war. When found in either Just War Theory or pacifism, they sought ways to act on their new moral stance.

The non-activists, though, did not report a period of study about the Just War philosophy and related issues. Instead, these veterans indicated an acceptance of the violence of war as a necessary evil to counter violence and injustice. For them, war was sometimes the only effective option in today's world. Most of them also, not having felt betrayed, trusted U.S. leaders to make those decisions.

After the activist veterans experienced a period of study, many moved on to the fifth stage of seeking a new collective identity to replace their military one. They found groups who affirmed their perspectives about war and justice. As a result, many veterans became protest activists and/or lifestyle activists as they continued to confirm their new identities in their chosen groups. Non-activist veterans, by contrast, often joined churches that supported or even encouraged Christians' participation in wars.

Sixth, the differences in levels and types of activism are explained by the type of group the veteran chooses for his or her Collective Identity. This varied from a pro-war church or pro-war veterans group for the non-activist veterans to an antiwar church or antiwar veterans group for the activist veterans.

Once the antiwar veterans took a firm stand and acted on their new moral identity, they experienced various forms of opposition from old friends, bosses, and affiliations that no longer fit with the new collective identity group. This required major adjustments in career and friendships. The non-activist veterans faced little opposition to their more passive non-support for the Iraq War and thus we find very little evidence of the need for adjustment in the seventh period.

Eighth, all activist veterans in the study experienced a series of changes over time in their lower level group and role identities. These included political affiliations, masculine role ideals, career changes, reduction in prejudice against minorities and understandings of faith among other things. For the non-activist veterans we find few changes in lower level political, career or masculine identities. When they began life as Democrats or Christian Baptists, they remained with these groups today.

Ninth and last, we find strong evidence of full moral identity verification in the ways the antiwar activist veterans describe how they feel about their lives today. The non-activist veterans who may still have become Just War Theorists respond differently to the question, how do you feel today about these changes in your thinking. They more often feel "good" about their lives today but it is in relation to their faith commitments, their educational achievements or their career success rather than adopting statements related to moral identity such as today "I have a clean conscience," "I am at peace" or I am "doing the right thing."

Thus we conclude that although all veterans have changed their views on the appropriate use of war since serving, they are responding to different motivations. The non-activist vets often describe their changes as part of "a natural progression" or maturation process while the activist antiwar veterans are responding to a significant moral identity disruption often involving moral injury. This disruption has resulted in a prolonged search for new ideas, collective identity groups, and behaviors that together allow them to live at peace. Moral identity, high in the identity hierarchy, whose disruption impacts many lower level identities, plays a key role in the veterans pathways to pacifism and antiwar activism. When the moral identity is not disrupted, there is less motivation to search for new understandings or identity groups, to change one's identity standards or to act on one's commitments. In the final chapter, we will outline some conclusions and implications for faith communities and the military as a result of these findings.

Conclusions and Implications

We have examined the stories of 114 veterans who served in U.S. conflicts from World War II to the Iraq War. Their journeys to Just War Theory, pacifism and/or antiwar activism were difficult in many different ways. They experienced traumatic combat, disillusionment with once-trusted leaders, a new narrative of U.S. history or policy or a new understanding of their religious faith.

Post military, many of the veterans had difficult adjustments to civilian life: work, marriage, parenting, and faith communities. Veteran's stories included painful periods of reflection on their military service. Some veterans sought to escape their memories by turning to alcohol, drugs, or work. Some lost their jobs, marriages, families, and even their dignity as PTSD and/or moral injury cast a shadow over their lives. Veterans had to cope with depression, suicidal ideation, and alienation. They often searched for years to find inner healing and peace. Fortunately, most of these veterans did find inner peace as they journeyed to a place of integrity and moral identity verification.

The loss, trauma and pain experienced by the veterans in our study are not, unfortunately, unique or rare. There are many human costs beyond war causalities that are incurred by soldiers, veterans, and their families. Suicide among soldiers and veterans has reached epidemic proportions. In 2010, the Veterans Administration claimed "veterans account for approximately 20 percent of the estimated thirty thousand suicides committed in the U.S. each year. This amounts to 18 veterans on average per day" (Laich, 2013, 98; Nakashima Brock & Lettini, 2012, xii). In 2012, the Department of Defense reported that 482 service members committed suicide compared to 310 who died in combat during the year (Laich, 2013, 98; Leitz, 2014, 233).

Although it is estimated that 20–30 percent of Iraq/Afghanistan veterans have PTSD, only 50 percent of them will get the necessary treatment. Because of the strong correlation between PTSD and suicide, violence, drug abuse and depression, the lifetime cost to treat each soldier with PTSD was estimated in 2012 to be $1.5 million in disability compensation (Laich, 2013, 100).

According to the National Coalition for the Homeless, veterans are only 10 percent of the general adult population but represent approximately 25 percent of the homeless population in the U.S. Veterans' homelessness is related to PTSD, traumatic brain injury, prescription and illegal drug abuse, alcohol abuse, crime, depression, and difficult family relationships (Laich, 2013, 101). Laich demonstrates that drug abuse problems leading to homelessness are correlated with the military's need to deploy combat troops before they had sufficient rest. The military changed its drug policy to allow for greater use of psychotropic drugs to deal with stress, anxiety, depression, sleep disorders, anger, paranoia and suicide and troops became addicted (Laich, 2013, 105).

Military families also suffer from frequent deployments. Domestic violence, for example, occurs when a veteran returns home with unresolved issues. One study found that a male soldier with PTSD is two to three times more likely to use aggression toward his female partner than a soldier without PTSD. Child abuse is another risk for military families. From 2001 to 2011, the Army reported that substantiated crimes of domestic violence increased 85 percent and child abuse increased 44 percent (U.S. Army 2012 Report Generating Health and Fitness in the Force).

To add to this dilemma, the Veterans Administration has been dealing with a significant backlog of cases. Veterans need help to restore and maintain their physical and psychological health. According to a December 2012 report of the General Accounting Office of the U.S. Government, the average length of time it took to complete a V.A. claim rose from 161 days in 2009 to 260 days in 2012. Meanwhile, the U.S. military budget continues to grow. In 2015, it reached nearly $600 billion dollars annually with few reductions in sight due to the continuing war on terrorism (www.nationalpriorities.org/campaigns/military-spending-united-states).

In this final chapter we will highlight the need for continued research on the identity change process, antiwar veterans, and collective identity. Our study raised many questions that we were simply unable to answer. We present these to the reader and offer ideas for future research. We also suggest a number of recommendations for the U.S. military and faith communities to better serve soldiers/veterans in their quest to make sense of their experiences and achieve moral identity verification.

DIRECTIONS FOR FUTURE RESEARCH

So where does the research go from here? Our study provides ample fuel for future research. To begin, our study has several limitations which future research might consider addressing. One key limitation is our sample. We obtained our participants through purposive and snowball sampling techniques. The nature of these techniques resulted in a sample that over-emphasized connections to the Mennonite Church USA and veterans against war groups. Future research should attend to this limitation by employing a sample that captures veterans outside of these groups.

Furthermore, our research is limited to the U.S. experience. It would be valuable to consider how this identity change process might look in a different setting. For example, one could study veterans from other countries that participated in the Iraq War.

Similarly, our "comparison group"—that is, individuals that did not adopt an activist antiwar or pacifist identity—was relatively small. We solicited the narratives of seven veterans that we termed non-activist. We compared this group to the 107 veterans who did adopt an antiwar or pacifist identity in an attempt to better understand why some veterans had such a significant identity change and some did not. However, given the small size and scope of our non-activist group, our conclusions are limited. There is a need for further research that compares individuals or veterans with an antiwar and/or pacifist identity to a more representative group of veterans that have not experienced this type of identity change. There remains a need to understand why some individuals experience such profound and holistic changes in their identity and some, even when experiencing similar moral identity disruptions, do not undergo such identity change.

Some additional areas for study include a more detailed reflection on the identity change process itself. It is unclear from our research what the impact of repeated error messages versus one profound error message might have on seeking new understandings of peace and war. The four catalyst groups that we identified suggest different patterns in error messages. For example, it appears that for some vets, one profoundly traumatic combat experience can so disrupt pro-war identity verification that there is motivation to search for new ways to verify the moral identity right away. This would also be true for the betrayal group as they often point to one deeply disturbing incident that disrupted their moral identity verification regarding war. By contrast, it appears that for the religious conversion and education catalyst groups, that there were a series of disruptions over months or even years that accumulated and eventually led the veteran to seek new ways of viewing the world and themselves. So, examining patterns for responding to various types of disruptions would be informative.

We proposed an expanded model of identity change in relation to moral identity. This nine-period model needs further empirical verification. Such verification might entail a quantitative study that involves a larger representative sample. Future researchers will need to grapple with how each period is measured. A longitudinal study that follows a cohort of individuals from the time they join the military to their exit would also be illuminating. Such a study would address a significant limitation of our study, namely that our view of the identity change process is based solely on the memory of our respondents. Such recollections may not adequately capture the change process.

Furthermore, we postulate in our change model that full antiwar identity verification is preceded by the successful testing of their opposition to war among family and friends. Veterans must find a strategy to cope with opposition to their new identity before a change in lower level identities (political party or religion) can occur. What is unclear is how the strength of opposition to the new identity might abort the process of full change to an antiwar identity. In addition, what is the role of holding a collective identity with a group such as Veterans for Peace that have successfully maneuvered individual and societal opposition to war.

Yet another question arose with the 25 veterans who claimed a diagnosis of PTSD. It is unclear how symptoms of PTSD, especially post combat, might keep the veteran emotionally numb to hearing the error messages from non-verification or to reflect on the resulting negative emotions and seek healing. Some type of healing, from medication to counseling to Alcoholics Anonymous groups preceded a period of studying alternatives or testing out new antiwar groups in our population. Understanding this might help to explain why some veterans who share a traumatic combat experience become active antiwar activists and others continue with a pro-war identity.

Finally, there is a need for research that continues to explore the role of collective identity and antiwar social movements in the identity change process. During some periods of U.S. history, antiwar groups and literature have been more available than others. Access to both groups and literature that represent a coherent antiwar or pacifist belief system are a necessary part of the identity change process in our group of veterans. What happens to veterans whose identity is disrupted by combat, betrayal, education or religious conviction but are unable to find a coherent alternative? In addition, what is the role of chance in connecting with a particular social movement group such as Veterans for Peace versus Veterans of Foreign Wars in becoming antiwar?

Recommendations for the U.S. Military

Beyond directions for future research, we believe this research has implications for helping soldiers, veterans and their families while serving and post military to make sense of their experience and better facilitate their transition to a civilian role identity. While most of the veterans in our study were able to find identity verification and ultimately some type of internal peace, this process was often decades long and difficult enough to require assistance. We suggest several specific recommendations for two social institutions, the U.S. military and faith communities within the U.S.

The antiwar veterans in our study hold strong positions about how the U.S. government should avoid unjustifiable wars, wars that harm both U.S. soldiers and countless civilians in the affected areas. Some of the study's veterans regarded this mission, saving future soldiers from the wounds of war, as their life's work. The following recommendations are both our own recommendations as we consider the implications of our findings, as well as recommendations that were directly articulated by the veterans in our study. The first six recommendations apply to the U.S. military, while the last four are for faith communities of worship.

Recommendation One: Approve Selective Conscientious Objection to Some Wars and Develop More Alternative National Service Opportunities for Young Adults

The U.S. military regulations determine that Conscientious Objectors (CO) are individuals whose moral, religious, or ethical belief systems cause them to refuse to participate in any and all wars. Regulations allow a soldier to shift to these beliefs after joining the military but they do not allow for selective objection to a particular war based on Just War Theory or other criteria (Leitz, 2014, 52–53). Even when successful, soldiers who achieved the CO status maneuvered a lengthy and burdensome process that alienated them from their comrades and friends. Among veterans in our study, CO applicants often reported harassment or threats when their process was made public. For example, Gary, a career Air Force pilot who became a Conscientious Objector, concludes that:

> Continued emphasis on approving selective conscientious objection—objection to foreign military engagements and support for defending against armed domestic threats—is an important conversation for the church to engage. Presently Conscientious Objector status is granted only to persons who renounce any form of violent behavior while being subjected to a grueling, often intimidating interrogation.

The military both teaches soldiers to kill and "principles of Just War and ethical conduct in war. This includes the protection of noncombatants and to refrain from torturing prisoners" (Nakashima Brock & Lettini, 2012, xvii). However, current military regulations require all soldiers to fight all wars regardless of their evaluation of the morality of a particular war. This requirement can lead to deep inner conflict, moral identity disruption and at times moral injury caused by participation in acts that transgress deeply held moral beliefs. In addition, the effectiveness of getting soldiers to shoot reflexively that has improved kill rates since World War II, has also caused anguish when civilians are shot reflexively prior to evaluating a situation (Nakashima Brock & Lettini, 2012, xvii).

Despite the instability that would be created by offering selective Conscientious Objection to particular wars, the military must consider options such as transferring a selective CO to an alternative theater or role. Otherwise, moral injury may cause distress in unsupportive veterans for years to come. We believe veterans, their families and soldier's morale would all benefit from removing unsupportive service men and women from certain combat theaters.

Gary, also spoke for multiple veterans in 2016, when he discussed the need for alternative national service options for young adults. These options would provide alternatives to college and also offer the benefits of military service such as job training, heroic service, and college funding for young adults who are not comfortable with the ultimate mission of the military, to protect the U.S. using force:

> I believe the introduction of a youth service program would be a tremendous support to and nurturing experience for our youth. Patterned after the management/organization of the military institution, this program would offer all capable youth the opportunity after high school to serve a two year ministry with their choice of either entering into military service or electing to serve in a constructive social-community service program. Each of these programs would provide the same benefits for participants.
>
> Congress has been consulted about this idea in the distant past, but a youth service program of this nature has not been popular enough to receive serious discussion. However a youth service program might be something you would find helpful for the church to promote. I believe some faith communities have sought to provide alternatives to their youth, yet without broad community support—national/federal support—it does not compare to the attractions of military service for [some] youth who have few options for establishing themselves in a sustaining career.
>
> I expect many/most persons enter the military not wanting to fight and kill but as a way to survive and to be trained for an occupation they hope to pursue outside military service. Thus having to perform combat traumatically disconnects the emerging person from the innate human spirit. I believe this idea has the potential to move international relations into a more balanced, less confrontational dimension.

Recommendation Two: Increase Funding for Veterans Benefits to Support Healing from the Consequences of Their Military Service

One way to increase funding is to evaluate the current system for allocating funds. The budgets for the U.S. Department of Defense (DOD) and the Veterans Administration (VA) are totally separate. In 2015, the Pentagon budget was $598.5 billion dollars. This accounted for 54 percent of all federal discretionary spending (not included in discretionary spending are Medicare and Social Security). Veterans benefits, including the Veterans Administration that serves the health care needs of veterans, their families and survivors post military are separate and accounted for six percent of discretionary spending or $65.3 billion dollars in 2015 (www.national priorities.org/campaigns/military-spending-united-states). The VA also receives approximately $86 billion in mandatory funding that covers education and other benefits. This separation between the DOD and VA budgets protects the Pentagon from facing the consequences of its decisions regarding military interventions around the world. Whenever organizations or businesses remain unaccountable for their actions, they are less likely to change course. Todd, a Navy sailor, believes that this lack of accountability could lead to more unnecessary wars and more harm to soldiers and their families in the future:

> I believe it is too easy for the military to just pass off any veterans with injuries to the Veterans Administration. If the disability system were preserved as it is but came out of the Department of Defense budget (DOD), that would significantly affect the DOD's bottom line and maybe give them pause to commit to so many actions and also to take better care of military members while they are on active duty.

In addition, the backlogs veterans hospitals and clinics report in serving veterans are problematic in many ways. Veterans requiring immediate care to avoid life-threatening mental and physical problems may die from preventable causes. When veterans needs are not met promptly, not only does their health suffer unnecessarily but their families suffer, their work performance suffers and the U.S. psyche suffers due to our failure to live up to our commitment to care for those who have served the security needs of the U.S. With more V.A. funding for health and other benefits, we strengthen our workforce, our veteran's families and our overall well-being by addressing the root causes of veterans high rates of drug use, depression and other mental illnesses, domestic violence, homelessness, and suicide.

Recommendation Three: Promote Alternative Veterans' Organizations to Support Formation of Diverse Collective Identities

We found through our interviews that replacing the military identity with a new collective identity was integral to the reintegration process. Many of our veterans discuss the role that antiwar groups, such as Veterans for Peace, played in solidifying their new civilian identity. Within these groups, the veterans found like-minded individuals to share their military experiences with and find empathy, validation, healing and ongoing support. Through a shared definition of morality, history, and politics, veterans were able to verify their new post service identity in part through organized public activism in support of veterans as well as in opposition to a particular war. These activities helped them find meaning to their suffering and move on with their lives.

Soldiers leaving the military should be made aware of a variety of veterans groups beyond the VFW. Furthermore, the military should help to promote and legitimize groups that offer support to veterans even if the ideals of those groups do not necessarily align with those of the military.

We applaud the work of the veterans' organizations (VFP, IVAW and VVAW) whose members contributed to this study. These organizations' services helped veterans to tell their stories and feel heard. The veterans could then forgive themselves and others, seek treatment, and heal the invisible wounds of moral injury and PTSD. They were then able to reconstruct new moral and collective identities. These veterans groups provided comrades who bridged the gap between the military experience and their yearning for peace. Such groups are necessary to the healing and re-entry process (Leitz, 2014). The veterans found wholeness by working with these groups in various functions: leading, protesting, organizing, networking, blogging, attending vigils, counseling, advocating for legislative change, returning to the sites of their trauma or moral injuries or simply by developing friendships.

These veterans' movements also provided a new cohesive collective identity that connected their previous Army, Navy, Air Force or Marine identity with their seemingly contradictory identity as antiwar activists (Leitz, 2014). Veterans were only then able to face their guilt and anger with support. Their negative emotions were often channeled into meaningful protests and advocacy that would save future soldiers from harm. Now the veterans could exchange their moral injury shame (e.g., for killing innocents or torturing their prisoners) for pride in the group's work (Leitz, 2014). They framed their protest in moral terms as "doing the right thing" (Leitz, 2014). Thus they were able to verify their moral identity standards that had been disrupted by combat, betrayal, religious conviction or education.

Finally, the antiwar veterans in these veteran's groups were able to describe their opposition to war as pro-troop, a claim which would be less credible from a civilian antiwar protester (Leitz, 2014). The veterans in our study often sought to end U.S. involvement in Iraq and Afghanistan and to bring the troops home. The veterans' emotional testimonials, besides the attention-getting combination of being veterans and antiwar activists, mobilized public opinion to end the Iraq War more quickly (Leitz, 2014).

Recommendation Four: Improve the Military's Identification and Treatment of Moral Injury as Distinct from PTSD

As discussed in the Identity Theory chapter, military service confronts many soldiers with moral dilemmas. Fortunately, resolution of these moral dilemmas can often occur through dialogue, leadership, and training. Sometimes, though, combat and operational experiences violate the deeply held moral standards of a soldier. These violations (or disruptions) may occur due to acts of commission or omission, others' actions, witnessing intense human suffering, and/or the aftermath of a battle.

"Moral injury results when soldiers violate their core moral beliefs, and in evaluating their behavior negatively, they feel they no longer live in a reliable, meaningful world and can no longer be regarded as decent human beings" (Nakashima Brock & Lettini, 2012, xv.). Thus moral injury is similar to non-verification of one's moral identity but involves a personal behavioral transgression that makes it difficult to forgive one's self (Litz et al., 2009). Moral injury is a newly defined issue that requires a different type of treatment.

Treatment strategies must be multidisciplinary. Interventions may be spiritual, social, and/or individual. Treating moral injury, then, means involving religious or spiritual leaders, peers or trusted social group members as well as counseling psychologists (Nakashima Brock & Lettini, 2012, 97). These multidisciplinary strategies are necessary to address the self-oriented negative moral emotions of guilt and shame that often result from moral injury. Some of the veteran's group members interviewed in this study discussed moral injury and their work with fellow veterans recovering from moral injury.

As apparent in the veterans' stories, the shame associated with moral injury is caused by the expectation that others will evaluate one's "self" negatively. Thus, moral injury compels some veterans to hide or withdraw from social contacts. Research has found that forgiveness by others for our transgressions aids recovery from causing social harms. In addition, self-forgiveness including acknowledging events, accepting responsibility for them, experiencing the negative emotions from the event, devoting sufficient energy to healing and committing to living differently in the future are necessary for recovery (Fisher & Exline, 2006).

Without this recognition of moral injury, many veterans may suffer from depression, suicidal ideation, and homelessness. This moral injury healing process clarifies why some veterans gravitate toward antiwar identities, groups and activism. They are seeking and finding sense of inner peace through forgiveness and identity verification.

Recommendation Five: Increase Exposure to Alternative Perspectives on War in Basic Training

While new recruits are exposed to Just War Theory and pacifism in their basic training, it appears that it does not always register internally. Perhaps the presentation is quick or unconvincing. Perhaps it is difficult to overcome the simplistic black and white, good and evil thinking of 18 year old development. Regardless, our group of veterans often describe hearing about these alternative perspectives on war for the first time either during their military service or after, only once they are experiencing moral identity disruption. In addition, when they raise concerns, they often report feeling silenced, marginalized or afraid for their wellbeing. At best, they are sent to a Chaplain or a psychologist to explore their options.

We believe that by allotting additional time in basic and ongoing military training using an Integrative Approach to moral decision making (Narvaez, 2008) service men and women could avoid some of the injury of moral identity disruption. The Integrative Approach to Moral Education encompasses both the reflective moral thinking and commitment to justice advanced by Lawrence Kohlberg as well as the development of specific moral traits and skills already incorporated into basic training (interpreting situations accurately, communicating effectively, respecting others, acting responsibly, reasoning ethically, understanding consequences, resolving conflicts, asserting respectfully, implementing decisions, working hard and persevering through difficulties).

This combination of methods allows the young adult recruits to discuss moral dilemmas they will face, encourages empathy and perspective taking, and encourages them to reflect on their moral behaviors in relation to values of obedience, fairness and social unit responsibility. Research demonstrates that this method leads to an improvement in team/unit sense of community, an increase in prosocial behavior, better interpersonal understanding and an increased ability to problem solve in real time (Battistich, 2008) This teaching methodology would better prepare recruits to respond in a constructive manner to difficult and ambivalent situations, a manner that is able to verify their deepest moral identity standards.

Recommendation Six: Reinstate the Military Draft

Developing realistic alternatives to the all-voluntary military service in the U.S. today to create "skin in the Game" for all U.S. citizens would mean reinstating the draft. Major General Retired Dennis Laich, author of *Skin in the Game: Poor Kids and Patriots* (2013), posits that the current all-volunteer force (AVF) no longer works in a world defined by terrorism, U.S. debt, and widening social class differences. Laich is a 35-year Army veteran, a graduate of the U.S. Army War College and a graduate of Harvard's National and International Security Program. Since moving to the all-volunteer military in 1973, less than one percent of U.S. citizens serve in the military. Most of these volunteers come from poor and middle class families while few come from the top twenty percent of the population.

Other writers have called the AVF the "poverty draft"—a sign of social injustice described by some of our veterans. The consequences of war (physical, mental, and emotional) as found in our interviews thus disproportionately impact poor and middle class families for decades to come. Since so few legislators or citizens have "skin in the game," engaging in wars requires little sacrifice from them making the choice of war over nonviolent options easier. A new draft based on a lottery system could close the civil-military gap, provide the necessary personnel for our future national defense needs and reduce the number of deployments currently demanded from our AVF. Multiple deployments with insufficient rest are associated with more PTSD and moral injury.

A lottery draft for all 18 year olds that includes conscientious objector and non-combatant options would address these concerns in many ways. Clearly, politicians would have to justify military actions to the public more clearly because more Americans would be affected. Theoretically every individual in America could have a relative or close friend drafted, wounded, or killed. Hopefully, this political reality would lead policymakers to seek nonviolent alternatives (e.g., economic sanctions, diplomacy, treaties, International Court of Justice). This could result in war being the truly last resort based on Just War criteria. It is possible that fewer soldiers would experience physical and moral injury from fighting what they believe to be an unjust war.

Recommendations for Faith-Based Communities of Worship

During difficult times in life, some people turn to their faith for assurance, hope and meaning. Faith-based communities of worship are one of the few, yet important, places to voluntarily adopt new identities. Similarly, identity change is at least part of the mission of most if not all faith-based places of worship.

Many of the study's veterans claimed to have lost their faith due to their experience in war. Once they oppose war, they often face rejection by their old faith communities. Faith leaders and faith communities can and should provide needed support to veterans and their families both during and after periods of war. Many of our recommendations are specific to Christianity but may also be applied to other faith traditions.

Recommendation Seven: Expose All Members of the Faith Community, but Especially Youth, to Multiple Perspectives on War, and Explicit Teaching on Violence and Treatment of Enemies

Twenty-one percent of the study's veterans had a moral identity disruption caused by religious conviction. Many of them urged Christian churches to carefully study Jesus' ministry, especially in relation to Just War Theory and pacifism with their youth more carefully. These veterans claimed that if they had known what they learned post military about their faith, most of them would have considered other service options.

As churches seek to form their youth, their education should include the realities of war, various perspectives on violence and war, and alternatives to military service. In the peace churches, youth Sunday school classes and youth groups actively engage with Just War Theory and traditions of Christian pacifism. The youth also discuss the viability of alternatives to the use of violence such as nonviolent direct action, diplomacy and mediation as well as advancing norms of democracy and human rights. These concepts are tied to scripture related to love of neighbor and enemy, forgiveness and the ministry of reconciliation.

For some faith-based communities this might involve counter-recruiting. The counter-recruiting, in which many of the study's veterans were involved, included leafleting outside high schools and military recruiting centers. These leaflets described the veterans' perspectives on war and alternatives to the military such as SOY (Sustainable Options for Youth). Counter-recruiters prepare young persons to respond to military recruiters and government documents required for applying for college loans. These official documents help track youth for military recruitment offers. Tom reflected:

> I dream of a day when any Christian who thinks of enlisting sits down with church members, elders, a pastor perhaps, and discusses how Christ and church teachings impact their decisions about enlisting, participating in war and in wars in which they would participate. Imagine young Christians of enlistment age making covenant or other agreements in which they state what conditions must be met for them to participate in war and what behaviors they would and would not engage in- even during war. Such discussions and statements would be a huge step in preventing and ending war.

Faith communities should also provide education on and service options that offer a viable alternative to the military. For example, Brad, a veteran from the 1970s and now a Mennonite Pastor discussed the following:

> For lower income families, the military provides an economic boost, which it did for me. I would not have gone to college if I did not go into the military. It would be nice if churches, especially mainline denominations, had programs for young people who were not planning to attend college. The Mennonite Church has programs, like Radical Journey, Service and Learning Together [SALT] and various voluntary service programs.

Recommendation Eight: Faith-Based Communities of Worship Need to Educate Themselves about Veterans' Issues, Especially Combat-Related PTSD and Moral Injury in Order to Provide Support

Brad, an Air Force veteran from the 1970s who is now a Mennonite pastor serving a Methodist congregation insisted that the church become more involved with troubled veterans:

> The church must become aware of veterans in distress. The church is too entrenched in the culture, including the culture of militarism, to realize that veterans in distress are any more than the costs of protecting the freedom that Americans enjoy, especially the freedom to worship. For many churches in American culture, the military plays a major role in our society by protecting our freedoms, including the freedom to worship. Veterans in distress have paid the price of that freedom, and it, evidently, is a cost worth bearing.

Faith communities could play a significant role in the healing of veterans who are experiencing identity conflict or strain. The combat veterans with PTSD and moral injury deserve extra attention. Churches must study the issue before offering support to veterans in distress regarding their previous pro-war identity. This support may include veteran-focused websites, support groups near military bases, and films that feature veterans on a healing journey. Also, faith communities should educate their congregations with texts that offer a coherent Just War and pacifist perspectives without demonizing veterans. A discussion on new scriptural interpretations on violence and war could also be beneficial (Wink, 2000).

Recommendation Nine: Provide a Non-Judgmental and Compassionate Outreach to Veterans, Families, and Friends

Regardless of a veteran's position on war, churches should reach out to them. Many veterans are in turmoil due to PTSD, drug addiction, homelessness, and depression. Church, mosque, synagogue and other members of religious communities should reach out to returning veterans as neighbors, college students, and co-workers. Church members can walk with the veterans on their journey to making peace with their wartime experiences. Listening to veterans' stories is another way to serve those who have served this country. Pastoral counseling is an often free and less stigmatized form of seeking help.

A veteran from the Religious Conviction group said he would like to see churches take Jesus' words in the New Testament more seriously. As a theology graduate student, Tom challenged the church to teach members about the connections between Christianity (which is often misunderstood or not taken seriously) and social psychology (as a social and behavioral science which is taken seriously):

> Make strong connections between scripture and Jesus and what the vets are experiencing. In [the New Testament book of] Mark, the verb repent is "metanoia" in Greek which means to have a change of heart and mind—a change in the way we see, feel and understand things. Also, the Gospels have Jesus talking about being "born again" as a way of describing a significant transformation. So since transformation is important to all of us, what can we learn about the conditions that brought about metanoia and rebirth in veterans? In other words, bridge the gap between social psychology and Christianity by comparing changing identities, negotiating identities and creating congruence with "dying to the world and being born again" with wholeness/holiness, redemption or sanctification. Also, I'd suggest that the churches become sanctuaries in which troops and veterans with conflicted consciences can come, read, discuss, learn and pray in order to form their consciences. Churches should be places where Christians and non-Christian troops can come to be reborn, to experience metanoia and/or to drop old identities, and adopt new ones to create congruence.

Besides emotional and social support, financial support is also critical. One Christian group providing financial support to veterans who have fallen through the cracks is Centurions Guild (www.centurionsguild.org). It provides funding for medical and emotional support when the Veterans Administration is not able to help a veteran due to their strict guidelines for services.

Recommendation Ten: Partner with Antiwar Veterans Groups

For some faith communities, especially those in the peace tradition, it would be beneficial to partner with groups such as Veterans for Peace and Iraq Veterans against the War to promote alternatives to war and military spending. Combining the resources of both faith communities and antiwar veterans groups would result in a powerful movement. Veterans groups hold tremendous credibility with the public that Christian Pacifists lack in discussions of war and peace. Passionate about preventing war, the veterans sponsor public events, advocate for legislative change, hold veteran support groups and educational conferences. Faith communities can learn much from these veterans. By giving financial support and sharing their faith, many (but not all) faith communities would be natural allies with the antiwar veterans groups.

FINAL WORDS

No matter the origin of these conclusions and recommendations, they all point to a desire to save lives from the carnage of unnecessary wars. Antiwar veterans and other peace activists also want to avoid the injuries to the human spirit caused by wars. Building on this common ground, we want to end on a positive note with the work of psychologist Steven Pinker in *The Better Angels of Our Nature* (2011). Based on extensive historical data on all forms of violence over the past five thousand years, he concludes that war and other forms of violence are declining and humanity is becoming less violent, racist and sexist.

Pinker traces this decline from the rise of civilization when the power of larger kingdoms and later the nation/state system could override the spirals of revenge violence. The Age of Reason and the printing press also diminished the level of violence as these exogenous factors enabled people to spread good ideas more easily and to challenge bad ideas. Societies were better able to learn from mistakes of the past. These good ideas led to more equality for women and other minorities. Minority groups eventually gained power. The combination of commerce and trade has further supported peaceful relations, especially between democratic nations.

Finally, the growing acceptance of universal human rights have discouraged small scale aggression against various minority groups. Pinker's conclusions are supported by the political scientist Joshua Goldstein, author of *Winning the War on War: The Decline of Armed Conflict Worldwide* (2011). He argues that despite the recent wars and terrorist attacks, killing has declined significantly since the 1400s on a worldwide basis. He also states that if you want peace, you must work for peace. Like Pinker, Goldstein believes that humans have the capacity to do great violence against others but also the capacity for empathy, cooperation, and self-control. When societal conditions limit our drive for justice through revenge, our peaceful inclinations, reason and empathy can dominate our behavior.

In their pathways to inner peace through moral identity verification, the study's veterans devoted their time and energy to protect future soldiers and civilians from the scourge of war. We are grateful for their willingness to share their journeys in our quest to better understand the role of identity change in making the world a more peaceful place. We acknowledge that we follow in the footsteps of sociologists, psychologists, political scientists and others who seek to understand pathways to a more peaceful and just world.

Hopefully, this book has given readers a deeper understanding of veterans who oppose some or all wars, their pathways to pacifism and antiwar activism, and the powerful role of the moral identity in transforming behavior for building a more peaceful world.

Appendix A

Interview Questions from Phase 1 of Study

Name
Contact Info
Date & Location Interview
Birthdate
Age
Race
Primary Occupations
Religious Background early & now
Higher Education: where, when, what
Marriage/Family
Military Service Branch, Years, locations

1. What type of change in thinking about war have you had? Following response, ask to identify the point or points that best described their view on the appropriate use of war at age 18 when they joined military and where they are on the continuum today.

The Militarist/Pacifist Continuum Scale: What did you believe about the appropriate use of war when you were 18 and what do you believe today? More than one response or a different response than those listed is fine.

1. It is appropriate for a nation to respond to an injustice anywhere in the world in any way it sees fit.
2. War is appropriate only to defend one's national self-interest.
3. War is appropriate if it meets the criteria of being a "Just Cause" to redress a wrong. (this is a loose application of Just War Theory).

4. War is only appropriate if it meets all eight Just War criteria. These include:

- A just cause such as self-defense or to redress a wrong
- Waged by an authority determined to be legitimate, i.e., a government
- Must be formally declared rather than covert
- Must be fought with intention to establish peace versus for resources
- Must be a last resort; all other options must be exhausted first
- There must be a reasonable hope of success to redress the wrong
- Violence and suffering of the people must be proportional to the outcome that is possible
- The weapons used in war must discriminate between combatants and non-combatants

5. Christians or persons of conscience should never be involved in war but the use of war by the nation/state is sometimes necessary.
6. Neither the Christian or person of conscience or the nation/state should engage in war under any circumstances because it is contrary to the life and teaching of Jesus or another leader the person follows.
7. Neither the Christian or person of conscience or the nation/state should engage in war because all human life is sacred.
8. I believe there are nonviolent means to resolve conflict peacefully without recourse to war or violence.

2. Tell me a little about your family background. Include grandparents, parents and siblings religion, occupation, politics, social and economic status, education and family patterns.

3. Now back to the change in your thinking on war, when did the change occur? Over what time period? How old were you? What happened?

4. What important events surrounded the attitude change on war, i.e., social, cultural or political events, change in job, trauma, move, behavior, spiritual change?

5. How did you understand the change and deal with it while it was happening? Were you aware of it while it was happening? Was it hard or easy? Did it seem like a natural evolution or what?

6. Is there anyone like a professor, friend, author, event who encouraged you in this change or acted as a role model?

7. Did you experience resistance to the change? How did your family & friends respond? How did you deal with the resistance?

8. What important events followed the change? How did the time immediately following the change feel?

9. Did you share the change with others? Did you join any organizations? How have you acted on your new attitude, i.e., talked to people, wrote letters, demonstrations, got out of military?

10. How do you currently feel about the change? Has it been a burden, a joy, freeing, difficult?

11. How have you come to understand what triggered the change?

12. What did you have to give up or let go of to move in this new direction in your thinking (i.e., conformity to social expectations, a role identity, a career, a relationship)?

13. Is there a key memory from childhood or young adulthood that has driven you in the direction you have chosen in your life- sometimes called a defining moment?

14. How would your parents have characterized you as a child, i.e., curious, sweet, challenging, smart? How do you describe or characterize yourself today?

15. What other attitude changes occurred with the war/pacifist change, i.e., understanding of God/faith/bible, lifestyle issues, career/calling/vocation, political affiliation, social group/friends, etc.?

16. Is there anything that we haven't touched on that is important to understanding your story? Do you have any questions for me?

17. General Impressions:

Appendix B

Significant Identity Change Interview Questions Phase 2–2013

Name
Contact Info
Date/Location Interview
Birthdate
Age
Race
Primary Occupations
Religious Background early & now
Higher Education: where, when, what Marriage/Family
Military Service Branch, Years, locations Category Catalyst etc. Met with this interviewee

I. Masculinities Questions

1. Think back to when you were 18 and try to identify 5–10 of your most important identities/roles, personal characteristics, or group affiliations at that time (i.e., son, friend, student, athlete, soldier, Christian, Republican, caring, worker).

Characteristic
What did this require of you at 18?

2. Now try to do the same, identifying 5–10 characteristics or identities that best describe you today and what each of them includes or requires of you (i.e., what is a good son?).

Characteristic

What does this require of you or mean today?

3. If you did not name male or female initially, please try to identity what it meant to you at age 18 and what it means or requires of you today.

Characteristic

Meaning or characteristics of a good male/female

4. How did becoming a solider impact your understanding of what it meant to be a man?

    a. How was manliness portrayed in the military?
    b. How did that impact you?

5. How did becoming "antiwar" change the way you interacted with other men?

    a. Men in general?
    b. Other veterans?
    c. Significant male figures in your life?

6. How was your understanding of "manliness" changed after you became antiwar?

7. How did you respond to this change?

8. Was your manhood ever challenged? Tell me about it.

    a. Prior to joining the military
    b. While in the military
    c. After becoming "antiwar"

II. Stigma Management Questions

9. How have you dealt with being different from your former veterans, friends or family members in the way you feel about war?

    a. Do you avoid talking about your views with certain groups and if so, can you give an example?
    b. Did you or do you seek out like minded individuals and if so, can you give an example?
    c. How has this experience of being antiwar sensitized you to other individuals who are different from the norm, i.e., homosexuals, racial minorities, immigrants?

    d. How do you understand or make sense of veterans or other U.S. citizens who remain very supportive of war in general or the Iraq or Vietnam wars in particular?

    e. Do you ever wish that you hadn't gone through the changes in attitude or identity related to issues of war and peace? How might life be different?

    f. Other

III. Religion Questions

10. What different roles or identities did you experiment with in adolescents/young adulthood? For example, were your parents Democrats and you experimented with Republican thought? How firm were each of the following at 18 years old and how have these changed today?

    —Parents' aspirations for you?
    —Tested in Adolescence? Tested later?
    —Commit. Today?
    —Career/work goal
    —Political Affiliation
    —Spiritual/religious
    —Marital hopes
    —Intellectual: smart?
    —Sexual: hetero?
    —Geographic/ethnic
    —Special interests
    —Personality: introvert?
    —Body image: attractive, fit?

10a. What significant events occurred in your adolescence or young adulthood that raised questions/concerns for you or caused you to change directions?

11. Have you ever had an experience of religious conversion or transformation? Can you tell me about your experience? When, where, how, and in what context did it occur? Was it . . .

    a. Sudden or gradual

    b. Active or passive

    c. Intellectual or social or moral or emotional

    d. Identification more with spirit/God, a religious group, whole of humanity

    e. Did you change within your religious tradition (Catholic to Methodist), between religious traditions (Catholic to Buddhist), or did the intensity of belief or actions change within the same group you were raised in?

    f. How did the experience change you in the first year?

    g. How has it changed you since that first year?

    h. How dramatically did it change things for you? Examples?

    i. What needs did the conversion or religious affiliation fill for you (safety/security, belonging/social/connection, esteem, sense purpose, self-actualization, intellectual stimulation, change, fun, justice/fairness, control/order, acceptance, peace, clarity, authenticity, competence)?

    j. Are there any specific experiences that have "defined" or intensified your faith?

12. How important was religion to your parents (for the majority of your youth)? Was it . . .

- Mom: Very important? Moderately important? Not so important?
- Dad: Very important? Moderately important? Not so important?
- Other: Very important? Moderately important? Not so important?

13. How often did your mom, dad and/or significant other adult attend worship services (during the majority of your youth)

- Mom: At least once a week? At least once a month? Less than 12 X yr.? Never?
- Dad: At least once a week? At least once a month? Less than 12 X yr.? Never?
- Other: At least once a week? At least once a month? Less than 12 X yr.? Never?

14. What did your primary faith tradition teach or expect regarding killing, participation in war, compassion for enemies? How has that changed over time? (religious belief system variable)

15. Think back to when you were 18, when your thinking about war was in transition, and now.

- How many and what type of friends were you spending regular time with?
- What types of religious beliefs did they hold and how committed were they?
- Did you participate or discuss religion on a regular basis (once daily? Weekly? Monthly? Yearly? Never?)

How many religious friends or %?	Type of friends?	Frequency discussions?
a. Age 18?		
b. During transition?		

How many religious friends or %?	Type of friends?	Frequency discussions?
c. Now?		

- How much of a role did religion play in the community you grew up in? Were there many church functions or gatherings? Were there many churches in the area? Would you describe it as a "church based" community or more of an independent community?

16. How would you characterize your relationship with your parents during the majority of your childhood? Explain.

- Mom? Dad? Other Significant Adult Loving relationship? Supportive?
- Dependent one-way relationship? Distant relationship?
- Relationship full of distrust and tension? Hostile relationship?

17. During your transition in thinking about war, what percentage of time did you spend each week in an environment that was supportive of your emerging views on war?

- What was that environment and how would you describe it?
- How much time do you spend in a supportive environment today? Describe this current environment.
- Describe this current environment.

General Impressions:

Appendix C

The Militarist/Pacifist Continuum Scale

What did you believe about the appropriate use of war when you were 18 and what do you believe today? More than one response or a different response than those listed is fine.

1. It is appropriate for a nation to respond to an injustice anywhere in the world in any way it sees fit.
2. War is appropriate only to defend one's national self-interest.
3. War is appropriate if it meets the criteria of being a "Just Cause" to redress a wrong. (This is a loose application of Just War Theory.)
4. War is only appropriate if it meets all eight Just War criteria. These include:

   • A just cause such as self-defense or to redress a wrong
   • Waged by an authority determined to be legitimate (i.e., a government)
   • Must be formally declared rather than covert
   • Must be fought with intention to establish peace versus for resources
   • Must be a last resort: all other options must be exhausted first
   • There must be a reasonable hope of success to redress the wrong
   • Violence and suffering of the people must be proportional to the outcome that is possible
   • The weapons used in war must discriminate between combatants and non-combatants

5. Christians or persons of conscience should never be involved in war but the use of war by the nation/state is sometimes necessary.
6. Neither the Christian or person of conscience or the nation/state should engage in war under any circumstances because it is contrary to the life and teaching of Jesus or another leader the person follows.
7. Neither the Christian or person of conscience or the nation/state should engage in war because all human life is sacred.
8. I believe there are nonviolent means to resolve conflict peacefully without recourse to war or violence.

Glossary

Key Concepts Important to Understanding the Text

antiwar activism: Taking specific actions such as protest, political advocacy, counter recruiting or speaking out in opposition to a particular war or preparation for war.

catalysts of change: These are the key factors or experiences that cause a moral identity disruption regarding the appropriate use of war. We identified four catalysts of identity change: combat, betrayal, religious conviction, and education.

Comparator: Component of the identity control or feedback system that compares the input perceptions of meanings relevant to an identity with the memory meanings of the identity standard. It then produces an error signal about the difference between the input and the identity standard (Burke & Stets, 2009, 66).

gender identity: A self-meaning of being masculine or feminine.

group or social identity: Includes important groups one identifies with such as Christian, U.S. Marine, and Republican (Burke & Stets, 2009, 118).

hegemonic masculinity: The privileged masculinity that is set in opposition to "lesser" forms of masculinity and femininity within a particular time and place.

Just War Theory: The belief that war can be justified morally if and when it meets several stated criteria such as: the war must be waged by a legitimate authority; it can only be waged for a just cause such as the protection of innocents; only the proper means must be used (that protect noncombatants); there must be a right intention in the objective sense such as bringing about a peaceful world; there must be a right intention in the subjective sense of not being motivated by hatred or pride and war must be a last resort (Yoder, 2009, 30–33).

identity: Parts of one's self composed of the meanings that persons attach to multiple roles (Stryker & Burke, 2000). A person holds many identities. Identity is an agent that acts out different roles or parts. "The self originates in the mind of persons and is that which characterizes an individual's consciousness" of his or her own being or identity (Burke & Stets, 2009, 7–9).

identity change: The condition by which one either no longer accepts an identity or modifies the meanings of an identity. Identity change often occurs because individuals hold multiple identities that are arranged in a hierarchical system and the identity standard requirements of a higher identity (such as the moral identity), alter the identity standards for lower level role or group identities (such as soldier or Christian) (Burke & Stets, 2009, 175, 188).

identity disruption: "A situation or event that causes non-verification of one's current identity standards." Disruption (i.e., disturbance or incongruence) is caused by the comparator's evaluation that one's identity performance is unsupported by one's self or others' expectations (Burke & Stets, 2009, 43–50, 62–69). In this study, the veterans' identity disruptions were caused by four catalysts—combat, betrayal, religious conviction, and education.

identity hierarchy: One's identities are ordered in an identity hierarchy from most to least important. The position of a particular identity in the hierarchy is determined by its prominence and salience. Prominence refers to the importance of an identity and salience is determined by commitment to an identity. This "commitment is measured by what a person might lose, in terms of relationships and access to resources if they fail to maintain an identity" (Burke & Stets, 2009). The most important identities are relevant in many different situations and have the most control over the actions of the identities lower in the hierarchy (Burke & Stets, 2009, 40–41).

identity standards: "The set of meanings and criteria an individual associates with each of his or her identities." The meanings are stored in the memory and available to the comparator that evaluates input from the environment about how one measures up to one's expectation (Burke & Stets, 2009 63–66).

Identity Theory: A theory rooted in Structural Symbolic Interactionism that explains the formation of one's self via a continuous self-regulating cycle of identity verification. According to identity theory, one's identity is formed, maintained and changed via "a self-regulating feedback loop" through which one receives input about his or her identity, compares this to his or her identity standards and verifies or disrupts one's identity. This theory emphasizes the importance of social interaction in the formation of one's self (Burke and Stets, 2009).

identity verification: A state when there is agreement between the input one receives about his or her identity and the meanings one holds as the identity standard. Individuals seek identity verification. When they do not receive verification, the comparator sends out an error signal that the individual can choose to react to in various ways (Stets & Carter, 2012).

masculinity: Is achieved as men and women perform gender in a variety of contexts. Masculinity is both a macro-level social position and a micro-level identity (Stets & Burke, 1996). There are multiple masculinities that are rank ordered within society and set in opposition to an inferior femininity (Connell & Messerschmitt, 2005; West & Zimmerman, 1987).

militarism: The opinions or actions of people who believe that a country should use military methods, forces, etc. to gain power and to achieve its goals (Merriam-Webster Dictionary online). The tendency to regard military efficiency as the supreme ideal of the state and to subordinate all other interests to those of the military (dictionary.com). "Advocacy for the use of the military by the rulers of a state without restraint" (Yoder, 2009, 28–29).

military masculinity: Defined as "a set of beliefs, practices and attributes that can enable individuals, men and women, to claim authority on the basis of affirmative relationships with the military or with military ideas" (Belkin, 2012, 3).

moral authenticity or congruence: A state in which one's moral identity is verified. Moral authenticity occurs when one's behavior and reflected appraisal aligns with his or her identity standard. This verification results in positive emotions (Stets & Carter, 2012, 125).

moral identity: A type of person identity that includes one's meaning of justice and care (Gilligan, 1982; Haidt and Kesebir, 2010; Kohlberg, 1981). Others have identified the meaning dimensions of harm/care, fairness/reciprocity, in-group/loyalty, authority/respect and purity/sanctity as moral foundations (Stets & Carter, 2012, 124). One's moral identity is high in the identity hierarchy and thus holds influence over a number of lower level identities. "Faithfulness to one's moral identity provides the motivation to act" (Blasi, 1984). Moral behavior is "conduct instilled with the expectation to do what is right or good based on social consensus," such as behaving in a just and caring manner (Stets & Carter, 2012, 124)

moral injury: Defined as "perpetrating, failing to prevent, bearing witness to, or learning about acts that transgress deeply held moral beliefs and expectations" (Litz et al., 2009). Thus moral injury is another way of talking about the non-verification of one's moral identity from Identity Theory but from a clinical psychologist's perspective. Moral injury or non-verification results in guilt and shame (Stets & Carter, 2012, 125).

pacifism: The belief, either due to a specific law or revelation, that there can never be a warrant to destroy human life (Yoder, 2009, 29). While there are various forms or levels of pacifism as well as rationale, the common denominator is that there is no rationale for ever taking a life.

person identities: The unique attributes an individual holds of him or herself such as being intelligent, organized, and caring. These attributes are highest in the identity hierarchy (Burke & Stets 2009, 124).

Reflected Appraisals: "Inputs to the identity control or feedback system" that include self-perception and how a person thinks others see them in a situation in relation to their identity standards (Burke and Stets, 2009, 62, 64–66, 192).

role identities: Include the expectations tied to a social position one holds such as being a male, a parent, a teacher, or a soldier (Burke & Stets, 2009, 114).

References

Arendell, Terry. 1997. "Reflections on the researcher–researched relationship: A woman interviewing men." *Qualitative sociology, 20*(3): 341–368.

Barrett, F. (1996). The organizational construction of hegemonic masculinity: The case of the US Navy. *Gender, Work & Organization, 3*(3), 129–142.

Belkin, A. (2012). *Bring me men: military masculinity and the benign façade of the American Empire 1898 to 2001*. New York, NY: Columbia University Press.

Blasi, A. (1984). Moral Identity: Its role in moral functioning. In Kurtines, W.M. & Gerwitz, J.L., eds., *Morality, moral behavior, and moral development* (pp. 128–139). New York, NY: Wiley.

Brock, R. N., & Lettini, G. (2012). *Soul repair: Recovering from moral injury after war*. Boston, MA: Beacon Press.

Broom, A., Hand, K., & Tovey, P. (2009). The role of gender, environment and individual biography in shaping qualitative interview data. *International Journal of Social Research Methodology, 12*(1), 51–65.

Brown, M. T. (2012). *Enlisting masculinity: The construction of gender in U.S. military recruiting advertising during the All-Volunteer Force*. New York, NY: Oxford University Press.

Burke, P. J. (1991). Identity processes and social stress. *American Sociological Review, 56*, 836–884.

Burke, P. J. (2004). Identities and social structure: The 2003 Cooley–Mead Award address. *Social Psychology Quarterly, 67*, 5–15.

Burke, P. J. (2006). Identity change. *Social Psychology Quarterly, 69*(1), 81–96.

Burke, P. J., & Stets, J. E. (2009). *Identity Theory*. New York, NY: Oxford University Press.

Charmez, K. (2006). *Constructing Grounded Theory*. London: Sage.

Christensen, A. D., & Jensen, S. Q. (2014). Combining hegemonic masculinity and intersectionality. *NORMA: International Journal for Masculinity Studies, 9*(1), 60–75.

Cockerham, W. C. (1973). Selective socialization: Airborne training as a status passage. *Journal of Political and Military Sociology, 1*, 215–229.

Cockerham, W. C. (1978a). Attitudes toward combat among U.S. Army paratroopers. *Journal of Political and Military Sociology, 6*, 1–15.

Cockerham, W. C. (1978b). Self–selection and career orientation among enlisted U.S. Army paratroopers. *Journal of Political and Military Sociology, 6*, 249–259.

Cockerham, W. C. (1979). Green Berets and the symbolic meaning of heroism. *Urban Life, 8*, 94–113.

Collins, J. J., & Holsti, O. R. (1999). Civil–military relations: How wide is the gap? *International Security, 24*(2), 199–207.

181

Connell, R. W., & Messerschmidt, J. W. (2005). Hegemonic masculinity: Rethinking the concept. *Gender & Society, 19*(6), 829–859.

Cooley, C. H. (1992). *Human nature and the social order.* New York, NY: Transaction Publishers.

Coston, B., & Kimmel, M. (2012). Seeing privilege where it isn't: Marginalized masculinities and the intersectionality of privilege. *Journal of Social Issues, 68*(1), 97–111.

De Andrade, L. L. (2000). Negotiating from the inside: Constructing racial and ethnic identity in qualitative research. *Journal of Contemporary Ethnography, 29*(3), 268–290.

Demers, A. (2011). When veterans return: The role of community in reintegration. *Journal of Loss and Trauma, 16*, 160–179.

Dowd, J. J. (2000). Hard jobs and good ambition: U.S. Army generals and the rhetoric of modesty. *Symbolic Interaction, 23*, 183–206.

Duncanson, C. (2009). Forces for good? Narratives of military masculinity in peacekeeping operations. *International Feminist Journal of Politics, 11*(1), 63–80.

Duncanson, C. (2013). *Forces for good? Military masculinities and peacebuilding in Afghanistan and Iraq.* London: Palgrave Macmillan.

Duncanson, C. (2015). Hegemonic masculinity and the possibility of change in gender relations. *Men and Masculinities, 18*(2), 231–248.

Faris, E. (1932). The primary group: Essence and accident. *American Journal of Sociology, 28*, 41–50.

Faris, J. H. (1975). The impact of basic training in the volunteer army. *Armed Forces and Society, 2*, 115–127.

Faris, J. H. (1995). The looking–glass army: Patriotism in the Post–Cold War Era." *Armed Forces and Society, 21*, 411–434.

Feaver, P. D., & Kohn, R. H., eds. (2001). *Soldiers and civilians: The civil-military gap and American national security.* Cambridge, MA: The Belfer Center for Science and International Affairs at Harvard University.

Filteau, M. (2015). A localized masculine crisis: Local men's subordination within the Marcellus Shale Region's masculine structure. *Rural Sociology, 80*(4), 431–455.

Foley, D. E. (2002). Critical ethnography: The reflexive turn. *International Journal of Qualitative Studies in Education, 15*(4), 469–490.

Flesher Fominaya, C. (2010). Collective identity in social movements: Central concepts and debates. *Sociology Compass, 4*(6), 393–404.

Gilligan, C. (1982). *In a different voice: Psychological theory and women's development.* Cambridge, MA: Harvard University Press.

Goffman, E. (1959). *The presentation of self in everyday life.* Garden City, NY: Doubleday.

Goffman, E. (1963). *Notes on the management of spoiled identity.* New York, NY: Simon and Schuster.

Goffman, E. (1976). *Gender advertisements.* New York, NY: Harper and Row.

Goffman, E. (1982). *Interaction ritual: Essays on face to face behavior.* New York, NY: Pantheon.

Goldstein, J. (2001). *War and gender: How gender shapes the war system and vice versa.* Cambridge, England: Cambridge University Press.

Haidt, J., & Kesebir, S. (2010). Morality. In S. T. Fiske, D. T. Bilbert, & G. Lindzey (Eds.), *Handbook of Social Psychology* (pp. 797–832). New York, NY: John Wiley and Sons.

Hedges, C. (2003). *War is a force that gives us meaning.* New York, NY: Anchor Books.

Hendin, H., & Haas, A. P. (1991). Suicide and guilt as manifestations of PTSD. *American Journal of Psychiatry, 148*(5), 586–591.

Hinojosa, R. (2010). Doing hegemony: Military, men, and constructing a hegemonic masculinity. *The Journal of Men's Studies, 18*(2): 179–194.

Jackson, J. J., Thoemnes, F., Jonkmann, K., Ludtke, O., & Trautwein, U. (2012). Military training and personality trait development: Does the military make the man, or does the man make the military? *Psychological Science, 23*(3), 270–277.

Just, W. (1970). *Military men.* New York, NY: Knopf.

Kanuha, V. K. (2000). "Being" native versus "going native": Conducting social work research as an insider. *Social Work, 45*(5), 439–447.

Kellett, A. (1982). *Combat motivation.* Boston, MA: Kluwer.

Kilshaw, S. (2009). *Impotent warriors: Perspectives on Gulf War syndrome, vulnerability and masculinity.* New York, NY: Berghahn Books.

Kirkby, R. J. (2015). Dramatic protests, Creative communities: VVAW and the expressive politics of the Sixties counter culture. *Peace & Change, 40*(1), 33–62.

Kohlberg, L. (1981). *The philosophy of moral development.* San Francisco, CA: Harper and Row.

Labaree, R. V. (2002). The risk of "going observationalist": Negotiating the hidden dilemmas of being an insider participant observer. *Qualitative Research, 2*(1), 97–122.

Laich, D. (2013). *Skin in the game: Poor kids and patriots.* Bloomington, IN: Universe.

Langton, K. P. (1984). The influence of military service on social consciousness and protest behavior: A study of Peruvian mine workers. *Comparative Political Studies, 16*(4), 479–504.

Leitz, L. (2014). *Fighting for peace: Veterans and military families in the anti– Iraq War movement.* Minneapolis, MN: University of Minnesota Press.

Lienenberg, I. (2013). Evolving experiences: Auto–ethnography and military sociology: A South African immersion. In H. Carreiras & C. Castro (Eds.), *Qualitative Methods in Military Sociology: Research Experiences and Challenges* (pp. 50–60). New York, NY: Routledge.

Litz, B. T., Stein, N., Delaney, E., Lebowitz, L., Nash, W. P., Silva, C., & Maguen, S. (2009). Moral injury and moral repair in war veterans: A preliminary model and intervention strategy. *Clinical Psychology Review, 29*(8), 695–706.

Lusher, D., & Robins, G. (2009). Hegemonic and other masculinities in local social contexts. *Men and Masculinities, 11*(4), 387–423.

Maguen, S., & Litz, B. (2017). Moral Injury in the Context of War from the U.S. Department of Veterans Affairs; Health Care; PTSD: National Center for PTSD. www.ptsd.va.gov/ professional/co-occurring/moral.

Mead, G. H. (1934). *Mind, self and society; From the standpoint of a social behaviorist.* Chicago: University of Chicago Press.

Meagher, R. E. (2014). *Killing from the inside out: Moral injury and Just War.* Eugene, OR: Cascade Books.

Messerschmidt, J. W. (2012). Engendering gendered knowledge: Assessing academic appropriation of hegemonic masculinity. *Men and Masculinities, 15*, 56–76.

Moskos, C. C. (1970). *The American Enlisted man.* New York, NY: Russell Sage Foundation.

National Conference of Catholic Bishops. (1983). The Challenge of Peace: God's Promise and Our Response: A Pastoral Letter on War & Peace. Retrieved from www.usccb.org/ issues–and–action/human–life–and–dignity/war–and–peace/nuclear– weapons/upload/statement–the–challenge–of–peace–1983–05–03.pdf.

Niva, S. (1998). Tough and tender: New world order masculinity and the Gulf War. In M. Zalewski & J. M. Parpart (Eds.), *The Man Question in International Relations* (pp. 109–128). Boulder, CO: Westview Press.

Padavic, I. (2005). Laboring under uncertainty: Identity renegotiation among contingent workers. *Symbolic Interaction, 28*, 111–134.

Passy, F., & Giugni, M. (2001). Social networks and individual perceptions: Explaining differential participation in social movements. *Sociological Forum, 16*(1), 123–153.

Pini, B. (2005). Interviewing men: Gender and the collection and interpretation of qualitative data. *Journal of Sociology, 41*(2), 201–216.

Santrock, J. W. (2008). *Adolescence,* 13th Edition. New York: McGraw Hill.

Schwalbe, M. L., & Mason–Schrock, D. P. (1996). Identity work and group process. *Advances in Group Processes. 13*, 113–147.

Smith, T. R. & True, G. (2014). Warring identities: Identity conflict and the mental distress of American veterans of the wars in Iraq and Afghanistan. *Society and Mental Health, 4*(2), 147–161.

Stets, J. E., & Burke, P. J. (1996). Gender, control, and interaction. *Social Psychology Quarterly, 59*(3), 193–220.

References

Stets, J. E., & Carter, M. J. (2011). The moral self: Applying Identity Theory. *Social Psychology Quarterly, 74*(2), 192–215.

Stets, J. E., & Carter, M. J. (2012). A theory of the self for the sociology of morality. *American Sociological Review, 77*(1), 120–140.

Stiehm, J. H. (2012). *The US Military*. New York, NY: Routledge.

Stryker, S. (1968). Identity salience and role performance. *Journal of Marriage and the Family, 4*, 558–64.

Stryker, S. [1980] (2002). *Symbolic interactionism: A social structural version*. Caldwell, NJ: Blackburn Press.

Stryker, S., & Burke, P.J. (2000). The past, present and future of an Identity Theory. *Social Psychology Quarterly, 63*(4), 284–297.

Stryker, S., & Serpe R. T. (1994). Identity salience and psychological centrality: Equivalent, overlapping or complementary concepts? *Sociological Quarterly, 57*(1), 16–34.

Wamsley, G. L. (1972). Contrasting institutions of Air Force socialization: Happenstance or bellwether?" *American Journal of Sociology, 78*, 399–417.

West, C., & Zimmerman, D. H. (1987). Doing gender. *Gender & society, 1*(2), 125–151.

Weston, C., Gandell, T., Beauchamp, J. , McAlpine, L., Wiesmen, C., & Beuchamp, C. (2001). Analyzing interview data: The development and evolution of a coding system. *Qualitative Sociology, 24*, 381–400.

Williams, J. E. (2002). Linking beliefs to collective action: Politicized religious beliefs and the Civil Rights movement. *Sociological Forum, 17*(2), 203–222.

Wink, W., Ed. (2000). *Peace is the way: Writings on nonviolence from the Fellowship of Reconciliation*. Maryknoll, NY: Orbis Press.

Woodward, R. (2000). Warrior heroes and little green men: Soldiers, military training, and the construction of rural masculinities. *Rural Sociology, 65*(4), 640–657.

Yoder, J. H. (1992). *Nevertheless: Varieties of religious pacifism*. Scottdale, PA: Herald Press.

Yoder, J. H., Koontz, T. J., & Alexis–Baker, A. (2009). *Christian attitudes to war, peace, and revolution*. Grand Rapids, MI: Brazos Press.

Zurcher, L. A. (1965). The sailor aboard ship. *Social Forces, 43*, 389–400.

Zurcher, L. A. & Wilson, K. (1981). Role stratification, situational assessment, and scapegoating. *Social Psychology Quarterly, 44*, 264–271.

Index

About the Authors

Julie Putnam Hart is an associate professor of sociology at Ohio Dominican University in Columbus, Ohio. She received her MA in International Peace Studies in 1992 and PhD in Sociology in 1995, both from the University of Notre Dame. Hart specializes in: causes of collective violence, nonviolent social change, ethnic relations and conflict resolution. Her research has focused on dynamics of social change in political and educational organizations. Currently, her research examines dynamics of significant identity change among antiwar U.S. veterans. Hart has volunteered with Christian Peacemaker Teams each summer from 1997 to 2015 doing human rights work in Israel/Palestine and Colombia. She also lived and worked in Guatemala for two years doing peace & justice education with the Mennonite Church USA. Hart enjoys gardening, reading, walking and biking.

Anjel Stough-Hunter is an assistant professor in the Department of Sociology at Ohio Dominican University, where she teaches sociology courses on research methods, sociological theory, sociology of health and illness, women's issues and deviance. She earned a PhD in Rural Sociology at The Ohio State University. Her research interests include community and place, gender, health, and the environment.